# Working With Superior Students:

## THEORIES AND PRACTICES

A collection of selected papers presented at conferences conducted by the NCA Project on Superior and Talented Students

### EDITED BY BRUCE SHERTZER

North Central Association of Colleges and Secondary Schools
Project on Guidance and Motivation of Superior and Talented Students

 SCIENCE RESEARCH ASSOCIATES•CHICAGO

The views expressed in this publication are those of
the individual contributors. They do not necessarily
constitute official policy of the North Central Association of Colleges and Secondary Schools or the
Carnegie Corporation of New York, supporters of
the Project on Guidance and Motivation of Superior
and Talented Students.

North Central Association of Colleges and Secondary Schools
Project on Guidance and Motivation of Superior and Talented Students
259 East Erie Street, Chicago 11, Illinois

A project designed to identify superior and talented high school students, to provide guidance services for them, and to motivate them to make appropriate educational and occupational choices

**Project Staff**

> J Ned Bryan, Director
>
> Bruce Shertzer, Associate Director

**NCA Committee**

> Clyde Vroman, Chairman; University of Michigan
> Ann Arbor, Michigan
>
> Frank Endicott, Northwestern University
> Evanston, Illinois
>
> J. Fred Murphy, Broad Ripple High School
> Indianapolis, Indiana

**Consultants**

> Lyle Spencer, President, Science Research Associates
>
> Jack Kough, Vice President, Science Research
> Associates

*This project is supported by a grant from the Carnegie Corporation of New York*

41193

# Preface

Identification, guidance, and motivation of secondary school boys and girls whose ability or performance or both place them in the upper quarter of the population are concerns of critical importance in today's competitive world. Numerous studies have documented the fact that many of these students—capable of pursuing education beyond the high school—fail to do so. The unnecessary misuse of such ability and the discouraging of efforts to attain excellence—caused by inadequate attention to the problems of finding, providing for, and encouraging superior and talented students—are tragedies for both the individual and society. This book is designed to prevent these tragedies by carefully examining many of the problems related to the education of the gifted child.

Recent political and economic developments have caused educators to think with renewed vigor about the education of the talented youth in our society. Education of talented youth is at the crossroads. Modern thinking, particularly in the fields of educational psychology and sociology, has generated an intellectual revolution. Educators find that they cannot avoid the questions related to the education of talented youth.

This book will have special appeal to counselors, teachers, school and college administrators, and all who are interested in or responsible for superior student programs in secondary schools. It is intended for a wide range of readers: for students preparing either to teach or to administer, for leaders of youth groups, for teachers and others actively engaged in superior student work, for parents and citizens; in other words, for all who are, or should be, consciously concerned with intelligent and effective education for superior and talented students.

The preparation of this book was the work of many persons. The papers included were selected from a number of excellent presentations made to ten conferences held during the summers of 1958 and 1959. The papers present points of view, relevant research, and practices currently operating in the field of work with superior and talented students. The statements were presented as complete topics at different conferences, so that some duplication occurs, particularly in introductory observations.

The conferences involved teams composed of an administrator and a counselor from each of one hundred schools participating in the North Central Association of Colleges and Secondary Schools Project on the Guidance and Motivation of Superior and Talented Students. They were held during the summers of 1958 and 1959 at the following universities: Michigan, Northwestern, Oklahoma, Minnesota, Colorado, Ohio State, Chicago, Omaha, Missouri, and Wyoming.

The North Central Association of Colleges and Secondary Schools (NCA) Project on the Guidance and Motivation of Superior and Talented Students (STS) was initiated by a grant from the Carnegie Corporation of New York, in March 1958, to conduct a research and action program. Superior and talented students were defined operationally as those who were in the top quarter nationally on the basis of scores on tests of mental ability and other selected criteria, or both.

Three major hypotheses to be tested were established:

1. The faculties in project schools are capable of organizing action programs designed to develop and improve provisions and practices to identify, guide, and motivate superior and talented students.

2. The improvement of provisions for identifying, guiding, and motivating superior and talented students will be greater in project schools than in control schools.

3. Superior and talented students in project schools will be more motivated and better guided to make and carry out appropriate educational and occupational plans than will comparable students in control schools.

Each of the pilot programs in the various project schools includes the following common elements: careful identification of superior and talented students through use of mental ability tests, achievement tests, past performance data, and teacher observations; intensive counseling of these students; adjustment of the curriculum to challenge them; appropriate motivation of these students through counseling, special classes, and special recognition of them in the community; and encouragement of home-school co-operation and mutual support. These programs are expected to have two effects: the levels of achievement and aspirations of the identified students will be more nearly commensurate with their abilities; and more of them will seek education beyond the high school.

The organization of this book reflects the evolution of a talent development program in a school: the rationale for a talent development program; a review of current research; basic essentials of a program; and summaries of four such programs in action. The terms superior and talented, bright, able, talented, and superior and gifted are used interchangeably throughout the book by the authors and the editor. These terms are equally valid, and since different authors have different preferences, we have considered them synonymous.

This book can have true value only if it stimulates educators to examine, define, and extend their provisions for able students. During the past three years schools have made great progress in locating and providing for able students. Now it is necessary to build upon the foundations of previous experience and to broaden the provisions so that no able student will be neglected.

The project staff and the NCA committee on the STS Project are extremely grateful to the distinguished contributors for their professional assistance in the ten conferences and for their permission to publish the reports that follow. These contributors have all been eager to share with others their insight into the topics they discuss. The great demands made upon them as teachers, writers, and lecturers in the field make their contributions especially significant.

Bruce Shertzer

# ACKNOWLEDGMENTS

We acknowledge our gratitude to the following for permission to quote from their publications:

    Carnegie Foundation for the Advancement of Teaching
    Columbia University Press
    D. C. Heath and Co.
    Harcourt, Brace, and Co.
    Harper & Brothers
    McGraw-Hill Book Co.
    National Association of Secondary-School Principals
    National Education Association
    National Society for the Study of Education
    Office of Education, U. S. Department of Health,
       Education, and Welfare
    The Ohio State University
    University of Chicago Press

# CONTENTS

# SECTION I

## THE SEARCH FOR TALENT
## IN OUR SCHOOLS

A primary goal of American education has always been to develop in each individual the desire to achieve up to his maximum potential. One of the most important functions of public education in the United States has been to discover the interests, aptitudes, and achievements of students and then to develop educational programs appropriate for the student population under consideration. Today, promoting the full development of the individual is more important than ever because of the pressing national demand for high-ability manpower. Aside from the national need for talent, the neglect of our talented is unfair to the students themselves. Providing school programs designed to salvage and develop talent is consistent with our belief that every individual should be helped toward self-realization.

One has only to read the employment advertisements in current newspapers to become aware of the demand for highly trained persons in almost every field of endeavor. If this demand is to be met, careful consideration must be given to the superior student while he is in high school. When schools prepare to offer this consideration, however, issues and questions always arise: Should talent development programs be undertaken to satisfy national needs or for the sake of the individual involved? Can schools undertaking such programs develop the superior student and at the same time maintain a concern for the full personal development of all students?

In the past, teachers, counselors, and administrators have not always taken full advantage of their opportunities to develop challenging programs for superior students. Some of the reasons advanced for this situation have been: (1) a preconceived notion that students' social development will be seriously impaired if their intellectual development greatly exceeds that of their average classmates; (2) a belief that students, if they are bright, need no intellectual challenge or stimulation; and (3) a failure to understand and modify the desire, operative in our society, to be as much like the "average" as possible.

Recently, however, there have been conscious and organized efforts to develop superior student programs as well-planned, integrated parts of the total school program. There is no longer a question as to whether or not schools should search for superior students and provide programs that will challenge their intelligence. Now the question is that of how such programs can be most effective in the expanding framework of existing school organizations. Organizing a superior student program is a challenge to all administrators, counselors, and teachers. No school system is too small or too large to offer a co-ordinated and well-planned superior student program. The degree of success of such a program depends to a great extent on the leadership of the school's administration and the support of parents and the community.

Specifically, why do schools organize programs for superior students? Some of the reasons offered are: (1) differences exist in students' abilities and needs and such programs can provide for these differences; (2) such programs provide flexibility in a school's program for superior students; (3) such programs can be structured to challenge and stimulate bright students toward high academic achievement; (4) such programs help bright students to understand their own abilities, opportunities, and responsibilities; and (5) such programs co-ordinate a school's personnel, resources, and facilities.

To make these programs as efficient and worth while as possible, research efforts have been made to analyze the loss of talent that results from the following three conditions: (1) *underachievement* (differences between ability level and achievement level), being studied by the Horace Mann-Lincoln Institute of School Experimentation (New York City), the Quincy (Illinois) Youth Development Project, and the Portland (Oregon) Public Schools; (2) *under-developed capacities* (capacities that have atrophied because of poor early environment, retarded language development, cultural disadvantages, or emotional problems), being studied by the National Scholarship Service and Fund for Negro Students and the Division of Special Education, Arizona State University; and (3) *low level of goal setting* (aspirations not commensurate with level of abilities), being studied by the North Central Association's Superior Student Project and the Demonstration Guidance Project of the New York City Schools.

Our schools are now engaging in an unprecedented search for talent. More than ever before, educators are anxious to find and develop all the academically talented youth who are (or should be) in school. James B. Conant summarizes the situation when he says:

> First of all, talents should be developed before leaving high school. . . . If they are not, it is too late in terms of the national interest.
>
> Second, it is quite out of the question to do what a few laymen would suggest, namely, to develop the academic talents through a required curriculum. One of the unfortunate by-products of Sputnik is the contention that everybody should be required to study mathematics or foreign language for four years. . . . this is utter nonsense. Furthermore, these talents cannot be developed by a required curriculum even for the able, academically talented students. . . .
>
> . . . I do believe . . . . that because of the national interest, which is quite different from what it was in the 1930's, nationwide, those who have academic talents should be urged to develop them to the full while they are in school, and then go on to college.
>
> As for mathematics and languages, I believe that those who have the potentialities for both should study them in high school; otherwise, many doors will later be closed—and I am not referring to college or university admission, which is quite a separate matter. I submit that there is a great deal of evidence that in every school there is a certain fraction who can do both, and many others who have the talent to do one or the other.
>
> I have visited widely comprehensive high schools where a good share of the academically talented students in four years elected eighteen or twenty courses with homework; and a good deal of homework certainly is required by the program I am recommending.
>
> In addition to studying four years of one foreign language and four years of mathematics I think they should study three years of science, four years of English (which ought to be required of all), and three or four years of social studies, too (42).*

---

*Index numbers throughout the book refer to references in the general bibliography at the end of the book.

In Chapter 1 of this section, Lyle Spencer discusses the need for talent development programs in our schools. He compares current estimates of the educational loss of talent with previous estimates, and deduces that major progress has been made in the identification of talent over the past five years. He notes a shift from the large general problem of identification of talent to the specific problems of identifying talent among groups with cultural disadvantages.

J Ned Bryan, in Chapter 2, describes a rationale for superior student programs. He cites expanding school enrollments as evidence of the increased importance of providing for individual differences. He lists five principles upon which superior student programs in the comprehensive school may be based.

In Chapter 3, Paul Witty discusses current concepts in programing for superior students. Witty believes that the many different terms used to designate superior students have caused some confusion in the field of superior student work. He explains some common conceptions of superior students and urges a broader, more inclusive definition of giftedness. According to Witty, creative ability in music, painting, drawing, and other fields should be identified and developed in today's schools.

# 1 NEW DIRECTIONS IN ACADEMIC TALENT HUNTING

*LYLE M. SPENCER*
*President, Science Research Associates*

Progress toward the American dream of equal educational opportunity for every young person has been measurable during the last decade. Spurred by its critics, this progress of our educational institutions has been fastest in the area where public faultfinding has been most severe: the need for identifying more of our bright youngsters and encouraging them to obtain the advanced education that would enable them to employ their talents at the highest achievable levels.

Futhermore, the stirrings of constructive discontent with things as they are in thousands of schools across our country lead to the encouraging hope that further progress toward educational programs of higher quality will be even faster during the 1960's. The plain fact seems to be that the attitude of an influential segment of the American public toward the importance of academic achievement has changed considerably in the last few years and is moving rapidly toward the recognition that *outstanding intellectual ability in our youth is both a national resource and a national responsibility.*

## A HISTORICAL PERSPECTIVE

The influence of changes in public attitudes has been demonstrated repeatedly in American history. In Teddy Roosevelt's day the powerful movement to conserve our soil and natural resources—previously considered mainly a matter of individual responsibility—produced new laws and government policies to preserve both public and privately owned lands. Conservation of natural resources has continued to be a matter of national concern and vigilance ever since.

In the 1930's continuing mass unemployment led gradually to

public recognition that if a diligent man could not find a job, and neither local nor state resources could solve his problem, its solution ultimately became a federal responsibility.

National concern is now focused squarely on human talent—the least tangible but most important of our national resources. Trends indicate unmistakably that during the 1960's the uncovering and nurturing of this talent will be recognized both by law and by public attitude as a national responsibility. The consequences of this changing public opinion will be vast.

The evolution of this changing attitude during the last fifteen or twenty years is interesting. Two shocking incidents that occurred during World War II produced an impetus that, although little recognized at the time, may have had considerable influence on present trends.

During the war years, draft boards paid almost no attention to the deferment of outstanding youngsters who could be the scientists and the intellectual and professional leaders of their generation. This unwise national policy resulted in a deficit of trained brain power that can never be made up—probably about twelve thousand people at the Ph.D. level alone. Although the manpower shortages of the other major participants in the war—notably England, the U.S.S.R., and Germany—were even more acute than our own, none of them committed a similar policy error.

Even more startling was the story of the Army Specialized Training Program, formed early in the war to provide a continuing supply of highly trained technicians and specialists. The induction centers skimmed the intellectual cream of young army draftees for this elite corps. Late in 1944, when the shortage of combat military manpower became intense, the program was abruptly disbanded and the students were unceremoniously transferred to the infantry.

Unhappily, such incidents accurately reflected public estimates of the national value of intellectual achievement during these years. Nevertheless these incidents left an indelible impression upon thoughtful students of American manpower problems and the emerging national needs that they foresaw for greatly increased numbers of highly trained personnel.

Severe shortages of engineers, scientists, teachers, and other professional and skilled workers greatly hampered America's postwar transition to its curiously melded peaceful-but-prepared economy during the late 1940's. Widespread publicity was given to these hamstringing shortages in *specific* occupations; but oddly enough, few researches during this period drew the general inference about the national need to conserve and develop *all* forms of intellectual talent.

Nevertheless, when the Korean War in 1950 shocked Americans into a renewed realization of the responsibilities of international leadership, enough lessons had been learned to impel the Selective Service Administration to overhaul its draft policies drastically. College students who earned above-average grades or made reasonable scores on the new *Selective Service Qualifying Test* could be automatically deferred from military service until their college education was completed, without regard to the occupation for which they were preparing. Freshmen in the upper half of their class could be deferred through their sophomore year; sophomores in the upper two-thirds of their class could be deferred through their junior year; and juniors in the upper three-fourths of their class were permitted to complete the senior year. These deferments were also granted to students who scored 70 or better on the *Selective Service College Qualification Test*.

## GROWING AWARENESS OF THE PROBLEM

Progress in defining and describing the importance of intellectual ability as a national resource has been relatively rapid since that time. In 1951 the Commission on Human Resources and Advanced Training pointed out that only about 10 per cent of our country's young people who possessed an IQ of 110 or above actually went to college. (An IQ of about 110 was defined by the commission as the lower limit of the intellectual ability required for success in college.)

During the years 1950-54 a number of sociologists and social psychologists estimated that colleges were educating only about two-fifths of the top quarter of students who actually graduated from high school, and they commented pointedly on the economic and social consequences that resulted from this talent waste. (Psychologists estimate that about one-fourth of all students have an IQ of 110 or above.)

A widely read book was the important study of Dael Wolfle,

*America's Resources of Specialized Talent* (267), which appeared in 1954. Wolfle estimated that America's best high school graduates (which he defined as being the top 20 per cent according to rank in class) had only about a 50-50 chance of going to college. This estimate stuck in the American consciousness and has been endlessly quoted and misquoted by both the critics and the defenders of our educational system. It has proved to be an important catch phrase in helping to get programs for superior students started. Literally thousands of new scholarship and financial aid programs for superior students have sprung into existence since that time. Possibly the most important of these—and the one that best expresses the changing temper of the times—has been the National Merit Scholarship Program, which was organized in 1955 to engage —according to NMSC's fourth annual report (218)—"in the discovery, recognition and encouragement of exceptionally talented young people. Upon such unusual boys and girls—provided adequate education and training is given them—depends the future leadership and destiny of America."

By the spring of 1960 the National Merit program had achieved almost a census-type coverage of high schools in the United States in its annual search for the current year's new crop of academic talent. Some 580,000 juniors in more than 15,100 high schools participated in that year's competitive examination. Though the evidence is not yet conclusive, it is estimated that these high schools enrolled something over 85 per cent of all the juniors attending school. The widespread coverage of this voluntary, co-operative program is unprecedented in American education annals and undoubtedly reflects the keen national concern about the identification and utilization of intellectual ability.

## THE ROLES OF INCOME AND SOCIAL STATUS

Throughout the 1950's two other important factors operated to assist able youth to obtain a college education. First was the rise of the average American family income, which chalked up a gain of approximately 15 per cent in constant dollars during the first eight years of the decade. Even the U.S. Internal Revenue Service came through with a modest financial assist by declaring that students still in school when they reached the age of twenty-one could still be counted as dependents for federal income tax purposes, if their parents are contributing at least half of their support.

Second was the growing social status attached to persons who had attended college. Increasing numbers of young people coming into the labor market found ruefully that scores of occupational doors that were formerly open to high school graduates were now closed to all applicants except those who had at least passed through college portals.

Together these factors account for a large share of the steadily increasing college enrollments, which have been creeping upward at the rate of about one per cent per year of the college-going age group. Today more than 36 per cent of this group at least starts college, and the growth rate seems to be accelerating.

## OTHER DEVELOPMENTS

And in 1958 came the National Defense Education Act, which has poured unprecedented sums into educational channels to increase the numbers and improve the training of guidance counselors, to improve school testing programs, and to provide low-interest loan funds for needy college students.

The cumulative effects of these and numerous other factors (among which the sputter of the Soviet sputnik in October 1957 deserves prominent attention) cannot yet be assessed fully, but they are unquestionably tremendous. Preliminary indications are that we may be well on our way toward solving the talent identification problem in the sense in which this problem was defined ten years ago.

For example, a recent study conducted by Donald S. Bridgman (29) for the National Science Foundation estimated on the basis of a nationwide school sample made in 1958 that, of the brightest 10 per cent of high school seniors selected through a standard college admissions test, about 95 per cent of the boys and 60 per cent of the girls later went to college. Or, taking a talent cut as large as the top 30 per cent of high school graduates, 90 per cent of the boys and between 55 and 60 per cent of the girls were later college matriculants.

An additional finding of interest in the Bridgman study was that among the brightest 10 per cent who started to college, some 80 per cent later earned a college degree. And of the top 30 per cent, a surprising three-quarters did so. There was not much difference between men and women in terms of college completion.

Follow-up studies made by the National Merit Scholarship Corporation tend to confirm these findings. Of the 10,000 semifinalists selected in its annual competition, about 96 per cent later went on to college, even though they did not win NMSC scholarships.

Indeed, the talent loss among the very best students may have been less for many years than has been commonly assumed. As far back as 1946, Leo Phearman found in a study (141) of Iowa high school seniors that among those who scored in the top 2 per cent on the Iowa Tests of Educational Development, about 92 per cent enrolled in college the following fall. It should be noted, however, that Iowa had a statewide testing program to identify talented youngsters many years before most other states did.

In any case, the conclusion now seems inescapable that great strides are being made toward reducing the talent loss problem in the United States. Indeed, the day may not be far distant when almost any bright student who does well in school can look forward to the opportunity of obtaining a college education, no matter what his financial circumstances. Keeping the occupational mobility channels of our society open by this means may be as important a guarantee as we have that our democratic form of government will continue. And the benefits, both economically and culturally, should be large.

Every new educational movement has unexpected consequences, and the growing national concern about the intellectually talented is no exception. Grass-root school programs for the gifted are proliferating almost beyond the capacity of bibliographers to keep track of them. This book represents a mine of information about proven programs already in operation that could be adapted to the needs of almost any high school.

Possibly the most stimulating feature of these school programs for the gifted is the leavening effect they are having on curriculums for *all* students. Exciting progress is being made toward better tailoring of classroom activities to fit the individual differences among students. The specialized attention devoted to the talented has also resulted in a fresh look at the problems of students at the other end of the intellectual spectrum: the handicapped of all kinds, particularly the culturally deprived. The fourteen largest cities in the country, for example, have just launched an ambitious co-operative project to find new ways of coping with the academic problems of students who come from underprivileged homes.

Spearheaded by the Conant studies (41), searching re-examinations of great promise are being made of the high school curriculum. Nurtured both by federal money and private foundation grants, large studies are being made of all the sciences taught in high school, and of mathematics, English, and foreign languages. All these studies have essentially the same objective: to improve the quality of instruction in depth, incisiveness, and variety. With human knowledge growing so rapidly—geometrically in many technological areas—new and better ways must constantly be devised to help us all learn better and faster.

A refreshing willingness to experiment is also beginning to permeate many of our secondary schools. Programs that would have received little recognition only a few years ago, such as advanced placement programs and even early admissions plans, are being tried out in hundreds of schools. Some of these educational inventions may not prove practical, but the ones that do will usually be beneficial not only to talented students but to those at other intellectual levels as well.

## NEW DIRECTIONS

Finally, a word should be said about the new directions toward which current research and development programs concerning the talented seem to point. Most research projects raise two new questions for every old one they answer, although the new questions typically are more sophisticated. Research in the field of the gifted is no exception.

With most of the tools and techniques now at hand for identifying superior students at the high school level, and encouraging progress being made in devising financial and motivational means of helping get them to college, what should the next steps be?

An immense amount of high-quality work still remains to be done, of course, upon important talent problems that have been clearly pinpointed by recent research studies. High on the priority list is finding better ways to utilize the intellectual talent of women, where the greatest wastage now occurs. The Russians are far ahead of us in this respect. More than half of all professional workers in the Soviet Union are women, as compared with 39 per cent in the United States. The disparity would be much greater except for the large preponderance of women teachers in the United States. It is estimated, for example, that about three-quarters of all the physicians in the U.S.S.R. are women, as are half the economists and one-third of the engineers.

Of considerable importance also are the special problems of students growing up in rural areas and of those coming from foreign parental homes and from families where academic achievements are not highly valued. Puzzling problems remain to be solved in helping underachievers and students with highly specialized intellectual and artistic gifts. The list of such problems is long.

Research studies on the distribution of talented youth in our society also raise several disquieting questions at a more fundamental level, for which no early answers are in sight. Several of these questions are discussed in more detail in later sections of this book. Here are a few of these questions:

1. Why do students from high schools with enrollments of less than one hundred so rarely win in the national scholarship contests?

2. Why do students from suburban high schools within commuting distance of the big cities typically do so much better on college admissions tests, and later in college, than do students from city high schools? Does young talent grow better in suburbs than in cities?

3. Why do students whose fathers are professional, managerial, or technical people do so much better on the average than those whose fathers are unskilled workers or farm laborers?

4. Why is it that, although Negroes represent about 10 per cent of the American population, fewer than 2 per cent of college students are Negroes? Or that only 1 per cent of medical school enrollees are Negroes? Or that when an occasional Negro does win in a national scholarship contest, his home is usually in the North rather than the South?

The partial answers to these questions that are now available are not very palatable. But they illustrate why large-scale ongoing research and development work to help talented youth and to improve our schools will continue to be so important.

Many researchers have found that a significant correlation exists between social class and what we call scholastic ability, with relationships being generally higher among older children than among younger ones. The suspicion arises that our present talent identification methods may be almost as much measures of the educational quality of the schools that students attend and the cultural environment in which the students were reared as of the innate abilities of the students themselves.

It should not be inferred, however, that students who score well on tests and earn good marks in their later high school years may very well fail to do good work in college or in their adult careers. The evidence is overwhelming that by the junior and senior years in high school the die is already largely cast.

The question should still be raised, however, of whether the students who are judged brightest when they graduate from high school were also a select intellectual group at birth, or even in kindergarten and first grade. Fragmentary evidence suggests that the superior students at the twelfth-grade level are to a considerable degree those who remain after huge numbers of additional youngsters with great potential have either stopped trying in school or have dropped out altogether—their minds permanently smothered by a decade of education that was mediocre or worse, and their background usually one in which family and community either were indifferent to intellectual ability or unwittingly punished rather than rewarded academic attainment.

The new frontiers in educational talent hunting clearly lie in research among youngsters during their early school years. Already the experts say that talent discoveries made at the ninth-grade level are generally too late to have maximum constructive effect. The beginning of junior high school is becoming a new focus of interest. Preliminary explorations are already being made in the primary grades, where basic attitudes toward education and even toward life aspirations are often formed. Another decade of hard work, indeed, may produce even more impressive results at this level than are now being achieved with high school students.

# 2

# A RATIONALE FOR SUPERIOR STUDENT PROGRAMS

J NED BRYAN
*Director, NCA Superior Student Project*

Planning and executing programs for the development of potentially superior and talented students are not easy tasks. Such programs are planned by educators and laymen who recognize that we must provide differential treatment for the various levels of ability. In the second half of the twentieth century, programs which challenge each student to high achievement and which provide the opportunity for such achievement become a critical need, particularly if, as Guilford (82) has suggested, knowledge of new mental factors causes "training of the mind" to become again one of the highest objectives of education.

Although great strides have been made in recent years toward providing more adequate education for academically able students, many of these youths still are not challenged in secondary schools and do not continue their education beyond high school. Too many schools continue to avoid the difficult task of providing programs which stimulate able students to perform to the best of their ability. Neither society nor the individual can afford the loss in human resources which results.

## HISTORICAL PERSPECTIVE

A brief glance at the history of American education indicates that, as a rule, schools have reflected the values and needs of the society in which they exist. For example, Broome points out that the Latin grammar schools met specific needs in colonial America. He says,

> The aim of the grammar school of the seventeenth century was to prepare for college; the aim of the college was to supply the people with

14

an enlightened clergy; the course of study was doubtless regarded a most efficient one for the purpose, a thorough grounding in the classics . . . (30).

In the first half of the eighteenth century, the development of trade and industry and the emergence of a new middle class built up public pressure for a school that differed from the Latin grammar school. These demands were met, in part, by small proprietary schools and, on a more systematic basis, by private or semiprivate academies. The academies—designed to provide a practical and general education in addition to preparation for college—broadened the concept of liberal education, provided secondary education for girls, and provided a supply of teachers for the elementary schools.

By the turn of the twentieth century, a different secondary school, the public high school, had become an important part of the educational system in the United States. As noted by Cremin (47), the extension of the franchise and the concept of universal eligibility for public office, the growth of a labor class and the endeavor to maintain social equality, a liberal Christianity and a democracy which produced new concepts of man's role in society, and a growing national spirit had by this time given rise to the American conviction that every youth has the right to a secondary education at public expense.

Significantly, enrollments in public secondary schools in the United States doubled five times during the first half of the twentieth century. The population in the United States aged fourteen through seventeen, however, increased little more than 80 per cent during the same period (203). This great increase in school enrollments was accompanied by a significant increase in the range of academic abilities to be served. Because they believed that equal educational opportunities should be provided for all youth, many educators felt that the same techniques and the same materials should be applied to all students. Even at mid-century, school practices based on this philosophy of "equalitarianism" served as serious blocks to efforts to provide educational programs capable of meeting individual needs.

In the second half of the twentieth century, America must build educational programs that are appropriate to an era in which science, technology, the arts, and social conflict call for the maximum use of intellectual potential. Just as their national progenitors found ways to provide educational programs to meet the needs of their times, so Americans today must examine anew the values and needs of society and adapt their educational system to the demands of the present and the future.

## INDIVIDUAL DIFFERENCES

The writer bases his ideas about superior and talented student programs on the following assumptions: individuals do differ; individual differences are observable and significant; and effective educational programs must take these differences into consideration. The writer does *not* believe that unlimited educational opportunities, strong motivations, and perseverance will make it possible for any given individual to achieve *any* goal. Individual achievement is partly a function of individual ability. Even though differences do exist among individuals, however, we should attach neither social status nor social stigma to an individual because he happened to be born with more or less ability than another individual.

Most human characteristics can be distributed along a continuum. In populations of adequate size, for example, academic abilities and specialized talents are usually distributed according to the normal probability curve. Further, the range of such abilities and talents in most comprehensive high schools is such that the extremes are readily identifiable. The differences between students at either extreme and those at the center are so marked that instruction and services designed to fulfill the needs and interests of students at the center of the distribution are likely to harm the individuals at the extremes. These differences are clearly demonstrated in cases of extreme physical variance and of extreme or severe mental retardation. The differences, however, are more difficult to observe in superior and talented boys and girls, particularly when their achievement does not measure up to their ability. The possibility of underachievement makes it doubly important that such young persons be located, motivated, educated, and evaluated in terms of their specialized abilities.

## SOME GENERAL PRINCIPLES

The policies upon which a superior and talented student program is based will, of course, be determined by the atmosphere of the community in which the program exists. The school practices which are followed will, in turn, be determined by the governing policies. Regardless of what these policies and practices may be, however, the following are some of the general principles which ought to be considered by those responsible for drafting program provisions.

*The success of a program for superior and talented students is directly related to the amount and kind of active support, effective involvement, and pertinent knowledge of members of the community, the board of education, the administrative directors of the educational system, and the local school faculty.*

The spark that kindles interest in special provisions for superior and talented students in a given community or school may come from almost any source. It may be the result of a national concern, such as the anxiety caused by Sputnik. It may stem from the realization that increased enrollments in the schools of a given community have resulted in teaching practices that have regressed toward the mean. It may evolve from a consideration of the needs of the handicapped and the observation that some of them may be academically talented. It may arise from the realization that many potentially superior students have low aspirations and are not motivated to high academic achievement. Whatever the source of the spark, however, the tinder must be available before the flame can come alive.

If the value systems of a community are negative or neutral with respect to high academic achievement, if the board of education is more concerned with keeping taxes down than with keeping performance up, or if the school administration encourages the status quo and the faculty is complacent, the spark of interest may not be strong enough or last long enough to get a program under way. The existence of such conditions indicates not that we should avoid the issues involved, but rather that careful preliminary planning is necessary before a program may be initiated.

The means used to prepare a community to accept and support a program for the talented, and the time required for this preparation, depend on local conditions and goals. In communities where academic achievement is not prized, where talent is not valued, and where the desire for immediate rewards takes precedence over long-term goals, it may be necessary to emphasize that one of the primary goals of education is to help one learn how he may adjust to various environments. Such a community must be brought to the realization that, as her people become more mobile, there can be "no such thing as local education in America in mid-twentieth century" (203).

Whether the task of eliciting support and involvement is difficult or relatively simple, key figures in the school and community must be fully and continuously informed concerning the program. The time required to develop and implement a program may be shortened if the school becomes involved in a co-operative effort such as the North Central Association Superior and Talented Student Project (175). Or up to five years may be required to develop a program fully and to make it an integral part of the educational environment (88).

In the final analysis, not only must the community know about and support the program, but also (1) the board of education or the trustees of the school must be willing and able to spend money for the program; (2) the superintendent and principals must be willing and able to provide a democratic administration within which the program can function; (3) the school system must have a co-operative and knowledgeable counseling service dedicated to the program and its purposes (88); and (4) the faculty must recognize, be involved in, and support the program as an integral part of the educational endeavor.

*The success of a program for superior and talented students is directly related to a careful delimitation of the population to be served, effective operational definitions of that population, early and continuing identification of all individuals included in the population, the listing of these individuals by name, and the availability and professional use of the list.*

Within wide limits, the range of academic abilities and talents to be served in a given program for superior students may be arbitrarily established. Although this establishment of a range allows a school system certain freedom, it also imposes a strict responsibility for defining both the limits and the population. If clear definitions are not arrived at, the result will be misunderstandings, a breakdown of communications, and eventual failure of the program.

Definitions of the bright and gifted, the academically talented, the superior and talented, the able and ambitious, or groups with other such titles, vary widely. The gifted group studied by Lewis

M. Terman comprised the upper 1 per cent of the population in terms of general intelligence. The academically talented were defined for a National Educational Association conference as those whose ability placed them 1 standard deviation or more above the mean of the total secondary school population. The NCA STS project defined superior and talented students as those in the upper quarter of the ability spectrum on the basis of specified criteria. In defining the population for a given program, criteria may be based on psychometric measures such as the intelligence quotient, psychological measures such as drives, sociological measures such as aspiration levels, or measures of achievement. Usually a combination of measures is preferable. In any case, the criteria should be specific, observable, and subject to critical measurement.

These characteristics of the selected population which set it apart from the total population must be specifically delineated. There are many accounts which describe such characteristics. Sidney L. Pressey has provided some interesting insights into genius (193). Early studies and reports by Terman (233), Cox (46), and Hollingworth (111), and a later report by Terman and Oden (234) describe many characteristics of superior students.

There are many techniques and procedures for identifying individuals who belong in a given program for superior students. Testing programs of various types, systematic observations based on specific check lists, the recording and evaluation of anecdotal materials, and the organized involvement of administrators, guidance personnel, and teachers in the selection process all play an important part in identifying the population for the program. It is especially important that the potentially superior students be discovered early and that the identification process be continuous. The progress of those selected previously should be evaluated and a systematic search should be made for those boys and girls who might have been missed during an earlier screening and who obviously belong in the group.

Unless individuals who are identified as belonging in the group —particularly those whose talents are latent—are known by name to the entire professional staff of the school, the program will fail to operate at maximum efficiency. Listing such students does not in itself guarantee effective action, but without a list of the gifted boys and girls no program at all is possible.

*The success of a program for superior and talented students is directly related to the degree to which planning is long-range, educational discontinuities are avoided, and motivation toward high achievement is systematic and continuous.*

In a comparative study of achieving boys (A's) and underachieving boys (U's) of equally high intelligence, Frankel (69) found certain significant differences in the occupational and educational backgrounds of their families. While the two groups of equally able boys did not differ with respect to (a) the number of rooms in the home, (b) the number of people living at home, (c) the size of the family, (d) the number of disrupted family patterns, or (e) the birth order of the subjects, there was a difference in the education and occupations of the families. More fathers of the A's than of the U's, for example, were professionals, semiprofessionals, proprietors, managers, and officials. While the fathers of the A's had significantly more formal education than the mothers, the fathers and mothers of the U's had about the same amount of formal education. Further, significantly more of the mothers of the U's worked (and they worked in lower occupational groups) than did the mothers of the A's. This study seems to suggest that family backgrounds and expectations do influence achievement.

Superior student programs that fail to provide for able youths until the final years of their secondary schooling, that lack a firm emphasis upon planning for the future, and that neglect opportunities for effective articulation at all levels of education may have little positive influence on bright underachievers who lack outside encouragement. In situations where the out-of-school environment is not conducive to high expectations, an effective program must be designed to raise the aspirational level of the individual and to demonstrate how new goals can be achieved. Education must be shown to be a continuous process, one in which tomorrow's success depends upon today's practice.

*The success of a program for superior and talented students is directly related to the degree to which specific individuals are held responsible for specified elements in the program and are given the authority and support to implement that responsibility.*

If one or two individuals attempt to develop and "run" the program or if individual faculty members feel no personal responsibility for its success, the effectiveness of the program is reduced and real opposition to it may develop. The principal, for example, cannot be solely responsible for a program. Dan C. Shannon suggests that "the principal must speed up the reactions of the student-teacher relationship, but not enter directly into this contact. He must realize—and act in conjunction with the realization—that the teacher plays the major role in pupil adjustment" (212). As an educational leader, however, the principal can do much to provide the setting for effective involvement in a program.

The principal, through his actions, can help establish a climate in a school that not only encourages students and teachers to be creative, but actually expects it. The principal can further this cause by placing gifted students in classes taught by teachers especially fitted for the education of superior students (212). The principal should be responsible for implementing policy, for administering the program for superior students, and for delegating authority and responsibility to individual staff members.

Counselors should have a definite responsibility for advising individual students and for helping them choose goals and educational programs. Such guidance should be based upon full and complete information about the individual, his background, his potential, and his aspirations. Counselors should be responsible for obtaining this information, for evaluating it, and for making pertinent facts and judgments available to students, parents, and faculty members.

The major responsibility of the high school teacher lies in the area of instruction. He has been described in a National Education Association brochure as follows:

> He is creative, imaginative, informed. He is a scholar and continues to maintain a scholar's interest in his field of specialization. He is passionately committed to the subject he teaches and yet is aware of its proper place in relation to other subjects. He is the product of a good liberal education—often with an M.A. or its equivalent in the subject area he teaches. The teacher of the academically talented is probably himself academically talented.
>
> He has the enthusiasm and the knowledge that will lead the student to move continuously to concepts of an increasingly higher order of complexity.
>
> He is aware that good teaching demands fresh ideas and an ever increasing body of knowledge. He is willing to work hard for this in summer study, special institutes, and through in-service training. He continues eagerly to explore the subject matter in independent study and research.
>
> He must be willing and able to respond fully to the challenge of the academically talented student, seeking always to deepen the student's interest and perceptions and his own (43).

An effective program must be clearly drawn in terms of responsibilities and authority. Of course, co-operation is important and desirable, but a task that is the responsibility of all can, and frequently does, become the responsibility of none.

*The success of a program for superior and talented students is directly related to the degree to which an evaluation of the program in terms of stated operational objectives provides an effective feedback, which in turn modifies and refreshes practice.*

Initiating a superior student program may, in the first flush of excited interest, prove to be relatively simple. Keeping such a program at an effective level of operation, however, may, over a period of years, become most trying. To be most effective, a program must have a built-in conscience. Critical assessments of the outcome of the program must be systematically provided for in its structure, and evaluative techniques must be based upon established criteria, measurable objectives, and determined needs. The conscience must also have a voice. The results of the evaluations must be made known to all those who are interested in the program or affected by it. The conscience must cause action. Only when needed changes result from the critical insights that evaluations have produced can a program retain its vitality.

## CONCLUSION

New elements in our society call for new educational endeavors. In this age of science and technology, intelligence is a "premium product." To meet the need for "trained brains," we must reassess our present educational practices and develop new programs wherever they are necessary.

In the past, Americans have changed their educational systems to meet the requirements of their day. Now, both the character of American society and the population of American schools require that modifications be made in today's schools.

The development of programs designed to serve the needs of superior students is a part of this educational task. The success of these programs depends upon firm commitment to the following principles: key personnel must be involved; the task and the population must be defined; the program must avoid educational and motivational discontinuities; responsibility for action must be fixed; and an assessment of outcomes must be made.

Only if we work hard to design and carry out programs based on the foregoing principles can we expect to meet the educational demands of our day.

# 3 CURRENT CONCEPTS CONCERNING THE SUPERIOR STUDENT

PAUL WITTY

*Professor of Education and Director of the*
*Psycho-Educational Clinic, Northwestern University*

Since the launching of Sputnik I, there has been widespread interest in the education of gifted, "academically talented," and superior students. This emphasis is relatively new in American education; only a little more than a decade ago Catherine Cox Miles commented, "The gifted, the potential leaders, discoverers, and creators . . . are usually left to develop their own skills, in their own way, and in terms of personal initiative alone" (162).

Current interest in the superior student is partly due to the recent spread of knowledge about gifted children and youth. The American Association for Gifted Children prepared a book entitled *The Gifted Child*, which was published in 1951 (4). This widely read book helped to rekindle interest in the education of the gifted. Chapters in the book presented data from genetic studies and portrayed the nature and needs of gifted children and youth. The book also gave an overview of educational offerings available at that time for the superior student. It pointed out that in the future the United States might not produce enough leaders if home and school did not co-operate more effectively to foster full development of capable and promising students.

During the years following 1951, the situation scarcely changed.

This article is adapted from the following writings by Paul Witty:
*Creativity of Gifted and Talented Children* (New York: Bureau of Publications, Teachers College, Columbia University, for the American Association for Gifted Children, 1959).
"Educating the Gifted Child," *The Packet* (Boston: D. C. Heath & Co., Fall 1957).
*The Gifted Child* (Boston: D. C. Heath & Co., 1951).
"Who Are the Gifted?" Chapter III in *Education for the Gifted* (Fifty-Seventh Yearbook of the National Society for the Study of Education, Part II. University of Chicago Press, 1958).

In what is probably his last written comment on this problem, L. M. Terman stated:

> Failure to make the most of our intellectual resources has been thoroughly documented by several recent researches, especially by those of Wolfle and the National Manpower Council. Wolfle estimates that 41 per cent of our youths who rate in the top 1 per cent for tested ability either do not enter college, or, if they enter, do not remain to graduate. He further estimates that of those who have the intelligence to earn a Ph.D., less than 2 per cent do so. Of my large group of gifted children with IQ's of 140 or higher who were located in California thirty-five years ago, 15 per cent did not enter college and 30 per cent did not graduate. Though all of these presumably had the ability to earn a Ph.D., M.D., or their equivalent, only 15 per cent of the men and 5 per cent of the women did so (100).

In a similar vein, President David D. Henry of the University of Illinois recently made this statement: "Of 2,250,000 young people who reach the age of eighteen each year, 152,000 . . . 7 per cent . . . have a rating of ability higher than that of the average college graduate. . . . Only a little more than half of them enter college, and fewer than half finish. Two per cent receive Doctor's Degrees" (65).

The foregoing statements point up a concern for the neglect of verbally gifted students. Americans are also becoming increasingly concerned about the neglect of other types of gifted pupils. Terman stressed the importance of perspective in dealing with various types of gifted students. Even before the appearance of Sputnik I, he cited the danger of giving too much attention to the development of scientists while neglecting potential leaders in other areas.

> The current Zeitgeist, under the influence of the cold war, is pointing up the need for many more scientists and engineers than we have, with the result that a desperate effort is being made to increase their number. Granted the great need for such increase, that fact should not lead to the neglect of other kinds of talent. What I propose is that education of the gifted should be planned not merely to satisfy the felt needs of a given time but also to prepare the way for future appreciation of needs not yet recognized. By encouraging the development of all kinds of special talent and of aptitude for every kind of leadership and scholarly achievement, the Zeitgeist itself would, in time, be molded along more liberal lines and to the appreciation of whatever enlarges the spirit of men (100).

## TERMS USED TO DESIGNATE SUPERIOR PUPILS

Until recently, a high score on an intelligence test was the single criterion used to identify a gifted child. In the last few years, however, new criteria have been introduced and new descriptive terms for the children identified have evolved. Some of these terms refer to students having high potential as indicated by scores on aptitude or intelligence tests (the students in a special class or school for the gifted); others refer to students demonstrating very high educational attainment (the scholarship winners); others refer to the "academically talented" students (the upper 15 or 20 per cent scholastically among secondary school students); and others refer to students having aptitude in a special area such as music or art (the talented students in the Portland, Oregon, experiment).

The following statement illustrates the broad concept underlying the selection of superior students in a project co-operatively undertaken by the Reed College faculty and the Portland (Oregon) school officials. The project includes not only:

the intellectually gifted and academically skillful but also those with high capacity in art, music, dramatics, dancing, creative writing, mechanical skill and comprehension, and social leadership. Moreover, the Reed faculty advisers to the project and the co-operating public school teachers have concentrated attention on personality characteristics such as drive, self-direction, creativity, curiosity, and some sixteen more. Students who rate high on these are identified as gifted, even though their scores on intelligence tests are ordinary. When identified and grouped by fields, these high school students are given seminars, many of them participated in by Reed instructors (100).

This article will discuss the various classifications of gifted and superior pupils and will examine the nature and needs of each group. Despite the increased tendency to recognize various types of giftedness, the type most frequently studied and provided for in American schools is the verbally gifted group—those with high IQ's as indicated by their scores on standardized tests.

## IDENTIFYING THE VERBALLY GIFTED PUPIL

With the advent of the intelligence test and its widespread use, gifted children were defined and selected according to their IQ scores. L. M. Terman in his early work considered as gifted those children who had scored an IQ of 130 or higher on the *Revised Stanford-Binet Scale*. His investigations showed that about 1 per cent of elementary school pupils were in this category.*

*Recent studies show that the IQ delimiting the upper 1 per cent is nearer 135. Children whose IQ's are 135 or above are more accurately referred to as potentially gifted.

The intelligence test became the generally accepted means of identifying gifted children. A high IQ is a determining factor in the selection of children for special classes such as the Major Work Classes in Cleveland or for special schools such as the Hunter College Elementary School (4). For example, an IQ of 125 or above is required of candidates for Major Work classes. In more recently initiated programs in cities such as Indianapolis and St. Louis, the minimum IQ has been set at 130, as it was in the pioneer work in Allentown (Pennsylvania), Los Angeles, and other cities.

Factors in addition to IQ, however, are usually considered. In selecting gifted high school students, a lower delimiting IQ sometimes has been used. It has been proposed that two groups of superior high school students be designated: the moderately gifted (IQ 120 to 137) and the highly gifted (IQ 137 or above).

Relatively few schools and classes for the gifted have been organized in the United States. Moreover, most of the facilities that do exist are in large cities, despite the fact that perhaps half the gifted children of our nation live in the smaller cities, towns, and rural districts. Therefore, in many localities the responsibility for identifying and encouraging gifted children rests upon regular classroom teachers. To accomplish the task of identification, teachers should utilize the results of standardized tests as well as their own discriminating observation of their pupils.

## THE NATURE AND NEEDS OF THE VERBALLY GIFTED PUPIL

The gifted child is not the physical weakling and social misfit sometimes pictured. Genetic studies have revealed that he is generally physically superior, attractive, and well-rounded. The verbally gifted child usually excels in his school work. By the time he has reached the upper elementary grades, he has acquired knowledge and skills which surpass those of children in classes two or three grades above his own.

Studies also show that the typical verbally gifted student continues to display outstanding academic ability throughout his high school career. Among other significant findings are those of L. M. Terman and M. H. Oden, who noted the following:

> Nearly 90 per cent of the (verbally gifted) group had had some schooling above the secondary level, and about 70 per cent have graduated from college. Two-thirds of the men and three-fifths of the women

who graduated from college had had one or more years of graduate work (4).

Although the above-cited group as a whole did superior academic work, there were some students who failed to achieve in accordance with their ability as indicated by mental test results. In analyzing the many factors contributing to the failure of such students, Terman and Oden stress the "absence of educational procedures adapted to children of exceptional ability" (4). This group generally was outstanding in adult adjustment and in vocational success. Terman and Oden concluded that "the prognostic significance of superior childhood IQ has been established beyond question" (4).

## THE IMPORTANCE OF MENTAL HEALTH

Like all other students, gifted students from time to time need individual help with personal problems. Although instability is less common among the gifted than it is among students generally, some rather conspicuous problems are frequently found in this group. These problems include feelings of inferiority, disappointments traceable to lack of agreeable companionship, insecurities resulting from conflicts with home and parental values, and various other forms of frustration and anxiety.

Feelings of inferiority are sometimes due to physical factors. For example, the gifted student who is very quick in performing certain mental feats may be relatively much slower in learning exercises of physical skill. In one study, highly gifted adolescents were found to be below average in participation in extracurricular activities (4). Moreover, their efforts to relate themselves to the activities of adults were often thought by their teachers to be inadequate or futile.

Another problem in which the gifted adolescent frequently needs help is that of finding satisfactory outlets for his talents. Although some gifted youth do find numerous opportunities for expression of their talents, many others fail to do so.

As is inevitable, another source of difficulty for the highly gifted person is working out an appropriate set of values and aspirations. It is especially difficult for some to reconcile their values and aspirations with the pressures and demands of their parents and families.

These families, predominantly upper middle class, exhibit all the drives for advancement of their social status and for competitive success that [Lloyd] Warner has found characteristic of the upper middle class as a whole. Of superior intelligence, they hold high standards for themselves, and high expectations for their children. At the same time they reveal more awareness of the disparity between what life might be and what it is, more frustration in themselves, and more apprehension for their children.

The need to work through and resolve these inconsistencies and conflicts is one of the major sources of adolescent stress in America.

The higher the adolescent's intelligence the more insistent is this need. At the same time, the higher the intelligence the more difficult the problem (4).

The gifted student needs skillful guidance if his talents are to be detected, directed, and encouraged. Moreover, he needs expert help from time to time in meeting problems of adjustment and in developing an appropriate ideal of self. Greatly expanded guidance services will be required in the comprehensive high school if these goals are to be achieved.

## THE "ACADEMICALLY TALENTED" STUDENT

Currently, the needs of the potentially gifted scientist are being explored and emphasized. *The Gifted Child* (4), published in 1951, was one of many publications that cited the neglect of promising students in the field of science. This neglect was also stressed in numerous articles that appeared during the decade before Sputnik I. These articles reported that secondary school courses in science were inadequate, in both number and content, to challenge the superior student. They also observed that the high school curriculum did not seem to be challenging superior and gifted youth in other areas.

Extension and enrichment of the curriculum have been proposed as methods of providing for superior and gifted secondary school students. A conference to discuss this problem was called in Washington, D. C. in February 1958. James B. Conant, the chairman, made the following statement:

. . . Throughout the conference, we used the phrase, "academically talented" to refer to that 15 to 20 per cent of an age group who have the ability to study—effectively and rewardingly—advanced mathematics, foreign language, physics and chemistry. Obviously, the gifted would be included in this broader definition (43).

The "academically talented" student was described as follows:
. . . He is in the upper 15 to 20 per cent of the secondary students in

the United States. In your school he and his academically talented fellow students may constitute 90 per cent of their class or 5 per cent (43).

The conference recommended that a comprehensive program for academically talented students be initiated in the high school. Requirements suggested for these students were: (a) four years of English; (b) four years of one modern language; (c) one year of a physical science and one year of a biological science; (d) one year of American history, one year of history other than American, and in addition one year of some other aspect of social science; and (e) three years of mathematics.

## BRIDGING THE GAP BETWEEN HIGH SCHOOL AND COLLEGE

Programs designed to help students bridge the gap between high school and college have been sponsored by the Ford Foundation. Acceleration is an important part of these programs. For example, the Fund for the Advancement of Education (established by the Ford Foundation) in 1951 sponsored an experiment (68) involving superior high school students. Four hundred twenty boys and girls, most of them aged sixteen and under, who had completed at least the tenth grade and seemed "ready, both academically and in terms of personal maturity, to enter college" were given Ford scholarships to any one of eleven colleges under the Early Admission Program. A twelfth college joined the program in 1952, and 440 scholarships were awarded that year. In 1953 and 1954, additional grants brought the total of Ford scholars to 1350.

Another plan sponsored by the Ford Foundation and the College Entrance Examination Board provides for college-level work in high school, leading to advanced standing in college. The College Entrance Examination Board, through the Advanced Placement Program, provides high schools with descriptions of college courses in twelve fields, and prepares examinations for these courses. Students who pass the examinations and are admitted to colleges that are members of the Advanced Placement Program can either complete college in less time, take more advanced work, or venture into fields they otherwise might not have had time to explore. In 1953-54, the first year of the program, eighteen secondary schools and 532 students participated. In the years since 1954, the number of students and colleges participating has increased (68).

Reports on these Ford Foundation programs indicate that they have been successful. According to Elbert Fretwell, the accelerated students have been successful in college courses and also rather well adjusted and socially effective. Administrators say these students assume leadership in school activities and stimulate college instructors to raise scholastic standards (73).

S. L. Pressey, after studying the relationship of acceleration to success in college, concluded: "The evidence was practically unanimous that younger entrants were more likely to graduate, had the best academic records, won the most honors, and presented the lowest disciplinary difficulties" (195).

## NATIONAL MERIT SCHOLARSHIPS

Awarding scholarships is another method of stimulating and challenging gifted students. Several programs, such as the Westinghouse Science Talent Search, have offered substantial help to qualified students. In 1956 the National Merit Scholarship Corporation conducted its first qualifying test with the objective of granting 556 four-year scholarships to talented high school students.

> As a first step, 58,158 high school seniors ranking in the top 5 per cent of their class were nominated as participants by high school principals throughout the United States, including Alaska, Hawaii, and Puerto Rico. This sample was given a preliminary screening test measuring verbal and mathematical aptitudes. Next, a sample of 5078 students or finalists was secured from participant sample by selecting the highest-scoring students on this test from each state in proportion to the size of the high school senior population for that state. . .
>
> Last, a selection committee composed of eight educators made the selection of 556 students from the sample of 5078 (109).

Recent studies have shown that in many ways these "scholars" resemble the "gifted" adolescents of earlier studies. The number of four-year scholarships granted has been greatly increased in the subsequent years of the program, with 737 being granted in 1959.

## THE STUDENT GIFTED IN SCIENCE

When mentally gifted young people drop out of high school and college in large numbers, serious shortages in superior personnel may be anticipated. Accordingly, many persons in the United States are concerned that in the future there may be too few outstanding scientists for our country to keep up technologically with other countries. Increasing efforts are being made to identify promising scientists and encourage their education.

Students potentially gifted in science are typically characterized by high verbal ability, high mathematical ability, and superiority in the scientific abilities that can be measured by tests. Such students are also characterized by drive or determination to use their abilities, as well as by a searching, inquiring attitude. Of course, they are also interested in various aspects of science.

There is a great need to provide more adequate science offerings in high schools throughout the United States. There is a shortage not only of good science teachers, but also of the materials and laboratories necessary to offer an effective high school program in science. Undoubtedly, the comprehensive high school is best suited to deal with this problem.

## A BROADER DEFINITION OF THE GIFTED

The foregoing discussion is concerned with students of high academic attainment, scholastic aptitude, and scientific promise. There are also students whose rare abilities in art, music, or writing can be recognized largely through performance rather than intelligence tests.

It may be desirable, as was suggested earlier, to broaden our definition and consider as gifted any child whose performance in a valuable line of human activity is consistently or repeatedly remarkable. Abundant opportunities should be offered in both home and school for the release and expression of such abilities.

There is a noteworthy tendency to think of the gifted according to this broader definition. In the Portland experiment mentioned earlier, teachers' judgments and the results of standardized mental and achievement tests are used for screening children of high ability, with a view to enrichment of their school programs. "Children are also screened for exceptional talent in the areas of art, music, mechanical comprehension, creative writing, creative dance, creative drama, and social leadership" (96).

The authors of *A Survey of the Education of Gifted Children* state:

There is a three-fold importance in looking for a variety of talent in children. First, such discovery points out to teachers that there are other bases besides intelligence for talent in children. Second, it calls attention to more children than a single-talent criterion does. Third, it encourages the teacher to use a variety of avenues of approach to children, whereas a single measure of giftedness narrows her approach (96).

This broader concern for the gifted is also expressed in *Education for the Gifted,* the Fifty-Seventh Yearbook of the National Society for the Study of Education.

> . . . The talented or gifted child is one who shows consistently remarkable performance in any worthwhile line of endeavor. Thus we shall include not only the intellectually gifted but also those who show promise in music, the graphic arts, creative writing, dramatics, mechanical skills, and social leadership. Although most of the attention of educators has been directed toward the intellectually gifted . . . we think of such special attention to the intellectually gifted as a weakness or shortcoming in the kind of program for gifted children that we should like to see in existence (100).†

This broader definition of giftedness does not minimize the significance of attempts to provide more adequately for children who are gifted in abstract intelligence. These children constitute one important type of gifted children. They often have other special gifts. However, there are some students whose gifts cannot be identified by intelligence tests, since the relationship between high IQ and ability in such areas as art, creative writing, and music is not necessarily close. The same is true in the areas of mechanical skill and social leadership.

## IDENTIFYING TALENTED STUDENTS IN ART, MUSIC, AND WRITING

There are few reliable measures of ability and appreciation in the fields of art, music, and writing. Consequently we must depend to a considerable degree on subjective judgment to identify artistically talented youth.

> Judgment of talent, of course, cannot be made lightly or hastily. The teacher who believes a pupil possesses unusual artistic talent might be wise to enlist from time to time the opinions of some others, including artists and art teachers. Opinions of these well-informed people, furthermore, might well be sought over a relatively long period of time. What at first appears to be talent may later prove to be merely a remarkable but temporary, development of skill. What might be artistic talent in

† Copyright 1955 by the University of Chicago.

early years may disappear as the child develops divergent interests which channel his energies and abilities into other directions (100).

Several interesting and seemingly effective techniques are being used to detect remarkable performance in the arts. In one experiment, the symbolic and imaginative film by the distinguished cameraman, Arne Sycksdorff, *The Hunter in the Forest,* was shown in seventy-nine classrooms in forty schools located in thirty-four cities (261). This eight-minute motion picture subtitled "A Story Without Words," has neither narration nor dialogue. It has a musical score, with sound effects accompanying the appearance of birds and animals.

After viewing the film, pupils are invited to write their own stories about it. A film guide, developed for teachers, suggests related language experiences and some steps to be followed in seeking genuine expression from children.

Over two thousand compositions written by children about the film were judged according to the degree the writing reflected (a) genuine feeling; (b) sensitivity to the value of particular words, phrases, and larger units in expressing their reactions; (c) recognition of the film maker's intent and the significance of symbolic presentations; and (d) correct and appropriate use of English.

Study of the compositions showed that about 60 per cent of the pupils had written effective prose or poetry. Two hundred three, or about 10 per cent of the total number, were judged to be outstanding and to suggest potential ability on the part of the writers. Two illustrations of these remarkable compositions are given here. The following highly imaginative poem was judged indicative of promise.‡

> The hunter steps silently from his door
>    Out into the woodland.
> The trees grow tall, the grass grows high
>    On the forest floor.
> The time is spring.
>
> The fawns have come
> And soon a shot will ring
>    Only to make them lie silently
> On the forest floor.

---

‡ Fifth-grade composition, Hazel Valley, Washington.

CURRENT CONCEPTS CONCERNING THE SUPERIOR STUDENT 35

The following composition represents the highest quality of prose.§

## The Hunter and the Forest, or World Perfect

Once upon a time there was a beautiful forest. In it were the graceful deer, the comical grouse, and the beauty of flowers and trees. Near this forest lived a hunter, oblivious to these things. He was out for sport. He walked through the beautiful forest, crushing the tender blossoms, and breaking boughs of the lovely trees. He saw a grouse, done up in feather finery, and killed it. He then put one of its tail feathers in his hat. Then he went home satisfied with the day's kill. Then a rain came. The flowers, sprinkled with shining diamonds did their exotic rain ballet. The trees swayed, too, with the gentle beat of the rain. The next day, the hunter again went into the forest. He set up a net for some unwary animal. Then something caught his eye. It was a deer family, grazing peacefully by the water. His hand touched the trigger. Just then something wonderful happened. As a flower opens, slowly, slowly, so the hunter's heart and eyes opened, slowly, slowly. The hunter, the destroyer of nature, awoke. Why, this wasn't something to destroy. It was something beautiful, sacred, it was the unspoiled, perfect beauty of God and nature. The hunter took down his net, lowered his gun, and started home. Instead of a stalk, his steps were light and springy. The birds chirped. The squirrels chattered. Why hadn't he seen this before? He threw down the grouse feather, the symbol of his slaughter, and put in its place a delicate flower. He walked along whistling.

It was thus that the hunter found what so many long to find, a new world, a heaven on earth, a paradise. It's everywhere. It's beauty, purity, exotic grace. It is beauty of Venus, the kingdom of Pan, the haunts of Diana. Here, there is no past, no future, just now. Beautiful, happy now!

Creative ability may also be displayed in music, painting and drawing, and other fields. To identify children gifted in these other areas, the teacher must observe closely their creative work, produced under various stimulating conditions. The teacher may observe that a girl enjoys drawing and painting, is original in her expression, and shows an unusual appreciation of form and color in her compositions. Her frequent superior performance may cause the teacher to regard the girl as potentially gifted in art.

The child who has a potential gift in dancing and appreciation of rhythm may very early demonstrate ability in reproducing rhythm,

§ Fifth-grade composition, Elizabeth, New Jersey.

rapid learning of dance skills, and enjoyment of some particular form of the dance. Creativity in dramatics may be revealed by performance that is consistently and repeatedly superior. Potential physical skills and mechanical abilities and aptitudes may be similarly revealed (131).

In all of these areas, potentially gifted children may score high on standardized tests of creativity in a particular field. Although such tests are often undependable and experimental in nature, they may yield supplemental information which is valuable in the identification of potentially gifted pupils.

In the area of social leadership, relatively few techniques for the identification of promising pupils have been developed. Studies of verbally gifted students suggest that there is a positive relationship between intelligence test results and potential in this area. However, little is known about the intelligence of various types of social leaders. Some writers believe that the group leader must not be too far removed in intelligence from the people he leads (110). This hypothesis and others should be examined experimentally.

Although very little has been accomplished in the identification and study of the child potentially gifted in different areas of social leadership, in several projects—such as those in Quincy, Illinois, and Portland, Oregon—criteria are being sought for identifying such children. In the work of school student councils, too, there have been some promising results. Much remains to be accomplished in this field, however.

## CONCLUSION

Although much of the experimental work with gifted children has dealt with the verbally or academically gifted student, a beginning has been made in other areas. This is heartening since we need in the United States men and women of outstanding ability in business, art, education, journalism, labor, scientific research, and government.

To realize their youthful promise, potentially gifted students of various types must have appropriate and challenging educational experiences. They also need patient guidance and encouragement in the development of desirable character traits and in the appreciation of social responsibility.

Studies suggest that in this country we are failing to foster the full development of many gifted and talented students. Hopefully, the future will bring more widespread recognition of the problems of gifted child education, as well as more determined efforts to deal with these problems effectively—including the promotion of creativity in various areas. These efforts must be integrated into a framework of education within which the optimum development of every boy and girl can take place according to his unique nature and needs. In this way, some of the dangers referred to in the following passage by John Hersey may be avoided:

> It is time to restore perspective to our views on help for the gifted. Educational practice is a set of slow pendulums. Just now the gifted child is in fashion—and in a little danger, too. School systems all over the country, sensitive to fierce pressure from our society for technicians and experts of every kind, are rushing headlong into the programs to produce highly efficient, useful, skilled, dependable, ready-made cogs for a scientific economy. . .
>
> But the job of freeing talent does not lend itself to this kind of attack. Talent is elusive, fragile, manifold, fast-moving, luminous, tantalizing, and incredibly beautiful, like aurora borealis on a cool September night. Who would give a weatherman a bag of money and tell him to go out and catch some northern lights?
>
> The perspective that is needed is this: Our uncertainty about exactly how to develop talent is only one part of the greatest unsolved problem in American education—the problem of how to help every child realize his maximum potential. . . the problem of individual differences (100).

# SECTION II

## A REVIEW OF CURRENT RESEARCH

Educators have long been aware of the diverse needs, abilities, and interests of the superior students in American schools. Many studies and projects have sought to discover the appropriate curriculums, materials, and methods for educating superior students. For the worker in the field of superior students, what guidelines and directions are indicated by the studies that have been completed? What tentative philosophies have evolved from such studies? What ideas have been corroborated? What does the literature tell us about the achievement, aspirations, self-concepts, aptitudes, attitudes, and social adjustments of able students? What methods are most successful in identifying the superior student? What administrative devices or provisions best stimulate achievement of talented students? What does recent research reveal about the mental growth of these students and the effects of social class and life adjustment on their aspirations, achievement, and occupational choices?

It is said that implications of theory and of research findings are always at least fifty years ahead of day-to-day school practices. The special aim of this section is to consider critically and constructively the results and implications of current educational studies of superior students. The importance of presenting such a review of research seems great because of the unprecedented activity in talent development programs and studies. Never before in the history of programs for superior students has so much been written and published.

Too often school officials initiate programs that are based on habit or on preconceived notions of the best means and practices for gifted students, instead of using data provided by current research. An examination of the recent research can give a school worker a perspective that will help him to initiate, organize, and extend his program for superior students.

The knowledge, conclusions, and facts of research studies of schools' efforts to provide for gifted youth are seldom final truths. New experiences, additional data, and new insights constantly change the picture. The contributions of recent studies and projects, however, do provide a base line of knowledge about certain approaches for dealing with superior students and the effects and results of these approaches. Such knowledge of actual research activities can be invaluable toward achieving success in carrying through programs.

The questions raised above, and many others, are discussed in the following section. The three authors are interpreters of research in the field; they have the training, insight, and desire to think their way through studies and translate the results into useful knowledge for the worker in the superior student field.

In the first chapter in this section, Chapter 4, Miriam Goldberg reviews current studies and projects. She compares recent findings with past outcomes and analyzes the trend of such studies. Her review of the literature helps to answer not only the question, "What are the results of current studies of superior students?" but also such questions as, "How do these results compare with previous findings?" and "What trends are indicated by these studies?"

In Chapter 5, Elizabeth Drews analyzes the results of recent studies dealing with the growth of intelligence. She reveals how recent changes in our society have affected social classes and personality development. She documents the need for a reconsideration of intelligence, social class, and life adjustment.

Collins Burnett, in Chapter 6, reviews eight research studies of the superior student in college. The significant implications of these studies provide considerable guidance to secondary school teachers, administrators, and counselors in organizing and implementing programs for their gifted students.

# 4 RESEARCH ON THE GIFTED

MIRIAM L. GOLDBERG
*Assistant professor of education, Teachers College,
Columbia University, and research associate, Horace
Mann-Lincoln Institute of School Experimentation*

Recent concern with the education of superior students has resulted in a sizable crop of research studies. To report them all comprehensively, or even briefly, would be a task beyond the scope of this paper. Rather, this report has three aims: to compare some recent findings with others from past research; to examine the extent to which current projects are seeking solutions to perennial problems that have remained unsolved; and to discuss efforts to study uncharted ground.

## SOCIAL AND PERSONAL CHARACTERISTICS OF THE GIFTED

What is the superior youngster like? What are his personality traits, interests, and aptitudes? What are his social background and school behavior? Such questions have bothered students of the gifted since Lewis M. Terman began his monumental studies in the 1920's. And now, to what extent are the personal and social characteristics attributed to gifted youngsters of the past descriptive of the gifted youngsters of today? Current research answers this question partly. Compared with average children, both at the elementary and secondary school levels, gifted youngsters secure higher grades (60), have more positive attitudes toward schools (2), and excel in their ability to read (2 and 223). They participate in more extracurricular activities (60 and 134), and have more hobbies and out-of-school interests (2). Like their counterparts of the twenties and thirties, they are more concerned than average children with abstract ideas such as religion and morality, and they are especially troubled by problems of world peace (223).

41

Today, as in the past, research points repeatedly to the adequate social and personal adjustment of gifted youngsters. They are successful in sports (2), better satisfied with their relations with their peers than are average youngsters (223), more confident, and aware of their above-average ability (60). High school boys with high IQ's were also found to rate higher on behavioral control and to be less apt to show lability of mood, social delinquency, carelessness, and impatience, especially in matters requiring long-term personal investment of an intellectual nature (231).

Some current analyses of socioeconomic status and ethnic group membership of gifted students support earlier findings that there is a disproportionate distribution of those identified as gifted among the various subcultural groups (8). A follow-up of graduates of the Major Work Classes of the Cleveland (Ohio) Public Schools (8) found more gifted students from German, English, or Jewish backgrounds, and fewer from Polish, Italian, or Negro backgrounds than would be expected on the basis of census figures. More than half of these gifted students came from middle class homes: 40 per cent from professional or managerial homes, and 30 per cent from homes of semiprofessional or clerical status. Less than one-third of the group came from laboring class homes. Similarly, the National Merit Scholarship Corporation (171) report indicates that whereas scholars come from hovels and mansions alike, more than half of them come from homes in the upper business or the professional group.

Drews's (60) study in Lansing, Michigan, however, suggests somewhat of a departure from previous findings. Of the 150 gifted high school students selected through initial city-wide group intelligence testing and then through individual *Stanford-Binet Scale* testing, 75 per cent came from homes of skilled, unskilled, and lower-level white-collar workers. Although the small number of upper middle class, professional, and high-level managerial families (about 10 per cent of the Lansing population) still accounted for more than their share of gifted children, the average and below-average families were more equitably represented.

It is possible to hypothesize that intellectual ability, as measured by intelligence tests, tends to be found somewhat more proportionately throughout the population today than in the past, but that the high achievement which results in winning a National Merit

Scholarship award is more often associated with higher socioeconomic status. In view of Drews's results, which report broader socioeconomic representation in the ranks of the gifted, other time-honored findings relative to the physical, social, and emotional superiority of the gifted may no longer stand up. For some time, questions have been raised regarding the effects of socioeconomic status on the findings that gifted children are superior in nonintellective as well as intellective areas of development and behavior. Bonsall (20) found that temperamental differences between gifted and average students were more a function of socioeconomic level than of IQ. When socioeconomic background was held constant, the few significant differences remaining either were in cognitive functions, such as greater thoughtfulness or objectivity, or were related to behavioral control. Differences in ascendance, emotional stability, sociability, friendliness, or co-operation were related to social class rather than to intelligence. A similar analysis of physical characteristics of gifted children as well as of the values they hold may find differences previously attributed to intelligence to be more significantly related to home background.

Another challenging area of difference between past and present findings is in the analysis of similarities between average and gifted boys and girls. For example, several studies have found that although gifted youngsters read better and more, especially at the elementary and junior high school levels, their reading tastes are "limited, trite or poor" (2). Unlike Terman's subjects, they do not voluntarily go beyond the books read by the average children of their age. Nor does their intellectual behavior necessarily reflect outstanding ability to conceptualize, see subtle relationships, or probe in depth ideas of which they seem capable. In a study of gifted junior high school students, Kirshner (126) found that these youngsters were very articulate—in fact glib—when left to their own devices, but that their thinking was superficial at best. They liked to read, but would not voluntarily tackle more difficult books than those read by average students. His experimentation led him to conclude that the expected abilities are there, in latent form, but that they emerge only when the school sets learning tasks that require gifted students to perform in accordance with their intellectual capacities.

What accounts for disuse of potential ability and failure to attain excellence? Are these children following the path of least resistance —making just enough intellectual effort to get by? Or are some of them afraid to appear too brainy? In the latter connection Strang (223) found that the voluntary reading of gifted students decreased as they progressed from junior to senior high school, and suggests that this decrease may be partly due to fear of being considered bookworms by friends, as well as to increased homework demands. Further support for this theory comes from interviews with gifted high school students (83). When asked whether they thought outstanding grades jeopardized a student's social standing, the response was generally in the affirmative. One boy said, "Well, some kids study all the time, and maybe they don't know, but the class usually doesn't like them. . . . If I really wanted to I could get one of the highest marks in the class, but if I did that I wouldn't have very many friends. . ." It is possible that some abilities may atrophy with disuse, and in the absence of challenge youthful promise may never be fulfilled.

One additional insight into the characteristics of the gifted emerges from Drews's (60) study, not as a departure from previous findings, but rather as a provocative notion which merits further exploration. She found that instead of the approximate one-third which would be expected by chance, over half of her gifted students were first-born (or only) children. Terman (234) and Barbe (8) reported similar findings, as did Roe (202) in her study of eminent American scientists. Do these findings suggest that there is some quality in the relationships between parents and their first-born which is particularly conducive to the development of intellectual ability? Or are we dealing with a sociobiological phenomenon related, perhaps, to the younger age of parents when the first child is born? It would be well to understand this phenomenon more fully in order to learn if the family and school can develop compensations for children who are not first-born.

## IDENTIFICATION OF THE GIFTED

Information on the characteristics of the intellectually able child is fairly abundant, but our methods of identifying him still lack precision. No available measuring instrument is a certain predictor of academic success. In fact, the use of multiple criteria for identifying gifted children is becoming more widespread. Hill *et al.* (105) report the use of teacher judgment, cumulative grade averages, and IQ scores for identifying gifted students. Of the twenty-four students included in their final selection, 90 per cent would have been identified by teacher judgment alone. These findings suggest a higher degree of relationship between teacher judgments and objective test scores than had been reported previously. Further research on the use of multiple criteria is necessary in order to discover what identification devices prove to be the best predictors of success in specific talent areas and in what combinations these predictors are most effective.

Although we can measure some kinds of intellectual ability fairly accurately by means of intelligence, aptitude, and achievement tests, we have, until recently, been unable to explore dimensions of giftedness not amenable to study through conventional measures. Nor do we know enough about the nonintellective factors that may be crucial in predicting high level achievement.

## Creativity

Exploration of creativity as a dimension of giftedness in cognitive areas was reported by Getzels and Jackson (79). Through the use of specially designed measures of creativity and conventional intelligence tests it was possible to identify—out of five hundred students, grades 6 through 12—a group in the top 20 per cent of the total sample on IQ measures, but not in the top 20 per cent on measures of creativity; and another group that ranked in the top quintile on creativity, but not on IQ. There was a mean difference of 23 IQ points between the two groups. Although both groups were *equally* superior to the general population on standardized verbal and mathematical achievement tests, teachers showed a clear preference for having the high IQ child as a class member, rather than the highly creative child. The groups differed in preferred characteristics; the high IQ group favored high marks, pep, character, and goal-directedness, and desired to possess *now* those qualities which would lead to success in adult life. The creative group favored wide range of interests, emotional stability, and above all, sense of humor; they were less apt to select present aspirations in terms of remote success goals. While self-ideals of the high IQ students agreed with what they perceived to be the expectations of teachers, the creative children showed a slightly negative correlation between their own ideal image and what they perceived to be the teacher's image of an ideal student. Getzels and Jackson suggest that unless conventional identification procedures are supplemented by measures of creativity, a group of truly gifted people able to effect novelty in the learning process as well as remembrance of course content will be overlooked.

## Nonintellective Factors

A series of studies of nonintellective factors, sponsored by the Social Science Research Council (215) investigated such components of intellectual achievement as socioeconomic status, ethnic or religious group membership, family patterns, and child-rearing practices, as well as self-concept. In studies of family interaction patterns among Jewish and Italian residents in an eastern city, Strodtbeck (225) found a positive relationship between egalitarian relations in the home and the son's ability to move to new loyalties in larger systems outside without rupturing family controls. Family democracy (a relatively powerful mother) was found to be positively related to achievement values. And the extent to which the family not only voiced a belief in man's ability to control his destiny, but actually allowed the son to act in accordance with this belief, affected the development of ideas of success and achievement in the son. A son is not likely to accept his father's expressed belief in man's ability to control his destiny if, in practice, he is "pushed around" by the father. Strodtbeck suggests that a value system which endorses the concept of the perfectibility of man, and consequently the improvement of society, is more conducive to the development of strong achievement motivation than a value system which is more concerned with establishing dominance in face-to-face relationships.

Similar motivational patterns were reported by Kahl (121), who studied the aspirations to attend college among lower middle class boys of high intellectual ability. He found that where the father was satisfied with "getting by" the son was less apt to consider going to college than was true in families where there was a striving to "get ahead." Students from families satisfied with their low status generally were bored with school, aspired to jobs like their fathers', and preferred to "have fun" with their friends. The boys whose families believed in "getting ahead" took school much more seriously and aspired to better jobs than their fathers'. The study suggests that a family's attitudes toward its occupational status have a greater influence on the achievement expectations of the sons than does actual social class status.

## Differentiation of Abilities

Despite the importance of certain nonintellective factors in fulfilling intellectual promise, a test of general intelligence, preferably an individual one, has been considered the best single predictor of academic success, especially at the elementary school level. At this stage, it is believed, no marked differentiation of abilities has yet developed. At the high school level, tests of educational development appear to be most effective in discovering both general and specific strengths and weaknesses. For the prediction of college success, the psychological examination is giving way to measures more closely related to achievement, which have been found to predict academic performance more accurately.

In view of the generally accepted belief that there is little differentiation of intellectual abilities in young children (6), the recently initiated study at Hunter College Elementary School (56) should prove illuminating. The study hypothesizes that as early as first grade, children can be identified who are outstanding in one or two, but not necessarily in all, such special abilities as word meaning, numerical facility, spatial orientation, logical reasoning, and social leadership. It further hypothesizes that school programs can be developed that are peculiarly suited to educating children with these diverse strengths within a single class.

Certainly, more systematic research on identification is needed. We must recognize the multifaceted nature of giftedness or talent and explore the best means of assessing the various facets, as well as their interaction. If standardized tests of mental ability are administered to the total student body of the school, it is easy to identify the "able and ambitious" student when ability is defined in terms of intelligence tests; then, he almost identifies himself. But it is not easy to locate the highly creative student. We do not know the proportions of ability, creativity, and ambition necessary to produce high-level achievement, nor do we understand the workings of the various components of ambition as they motivate toward success in academic or creative areas.

## ADMINISTRATIVE PROVISIONS

Administrative procedures—especially ability grouping and acceleration—for taking care of exceptionally able students have long been a source of concern to teachers and administrators. Both these practices arouse heated arguments, and research findings seem powerless against the vested emotionality of educators and laymen alike.

### Ability Grouping

What does recent research tell us about grouping? It generally confirms past research: although the academic achievement of able students tends to be somewhat greater in narrow-range ability groups than in broad-range classes, these findings are neither conclusive nor consistent (162). The lack of definite differences may be partly due to the use of standardized achievement tests, which generally measure accelerated coverage but do not measure the development of greater depth of understanding, critical thinking, and self-directed learning activities. Since most gifted children, especially at the elementary level, score near the ceiling of the generally used tests, any differential growth due to grouping may be masked by ceiling effects. The lack of consistent differences in achievement may also be due to the fact that little is done in special classes for the gifted that is different from what is done for them in broad-range groups. Thus, grouping—though possibly a facilitator of better learning experiences for bright children—does not *per se* result in greater achievement in the basic skills or general content (230).

There is some evidence, however, that grouping results in the development of more realistic self-concepts among gifted students. Recent studies by the Talented Youth Project (230) found that when bright students were moved from broad- to narrow-range groups, their self-estimates tended to go down, and the gap between their perception of their present status and of their wished-for status increased, thus leaving more psychological space for improvement. Instead of fostering snobbery and conceit, membership in the special class tended to take the students down a peg.

In an effort to retain the possible achievement benefits of narrow-range grouping while fostering broad social relationships, several schools have instituted partial grouping, whereby gifted children are assigned to special classes for part of the day and to regular classes for the rest of the day. An evaluation of one such program in a Dade County (Florida) elementary school (53) found that the youngsters so grouped showed better academic achievement than a comparable group in regular classes. An assessment of ratings by their peers in the ungrouped situation indicated that the gifted children placed in neither the most-liked nor the least-liked group. The gifted youngsters themselves stated that they felt more at home in the special class than in the regular class.

Further evidence comes from a study by Mann (154), who analyzed the acceptance and rejection patterns of elementary school children in the Colfax School (Pittsburgh, Pa.), where partial grouping had long been standard procedure. He found that even though gifted children had frequent social and academic contacts with typical children, gifted children chose and rejected other gifted children much more frequently than they chose and rejected typical children. Typical children also seemed to prefer and reject their own. In all instances, both the acceptance and the rejection seemed to be stronger within ability groups than between them. Gifted children generally preferred to have other gifted children criticize their work and react to their products. Mann also found the same patterns in the out-of-school friendships of the gifted. In general, the results of the study indicated that the belief that "because we group children together we have trained them to accept each other for what they are" (154) is by no means supported.

Until now, most studies on grouping have dealt with the effect of ability grouping on the superior student. Some studies, however, have dealt with special classes for retarded or slow-learning students. A broader statement of the issue might be: What are the effects of ability grouping on the intellectual, social, and personal development of all youngsters? In tackling this problem, the Horace Mann-Lincoln Institute (230), in co-operation with the New York

City Public Schools, involved forty elementary schools in organizing some eighty fifth-grade classes on the basis of specific grouping patterns. These classes were maintained for two years. Some included only youngsters of IQ 130 and above (based on a third-grade nonreading group intelligence test); others included those of highest and next highest ability; some included the total ability spectrum. Some classes had no gifted youngsters in them; others were limited to average-ability students; some included only the slow. Thus it was possible to see whether average youngsters, for example, fared differently when there were bright youngsters in their classes than when there were none; or whether they fared differently when there were slower youngsters in their classes than when there were none. Similarly, the bright and near-gifted were studied in various classroom situations. Before and after the experiment, these students were tested in all achievement areas: in self-attitudes, school interests, and acceptance and rejection of brighter and less able students; in creative writing ability; in friendship and leadership ratings; and in teacher ratings. It was hypothesized that children at all ability levels would, in general, fare better when the class range was narrow than when it was broad. Analyses of the achievement data showed no significant differences due to grouping at any of the ability levels. The analyses, however, have revealed some very interesting phenomena. A group that was designated as narrow-range on the basis of third-grade IQ scores became broad-range in character by the end of the sixth grade, when a more verbal intelligence test was administered. In addition, groups that were considered narrow on the basis of IQ showed, in many instances, a six-year reading range at the fifth-grade level. Therefore, narrowing the range on one variable does not necessarily narrow the range on other variables, even where there is a fairly high correlation between them.

While ability grouping on the basis of IQ scores does not seem to result in significant achievement differences for average and below-average students, it does seem to be related to differences in their levels of aspiration. When gifted children are taken out of broad-range groups, the wished-for status of the remaining students goes up, a phenomenon not observed where the gifted remain in the regular classroom. It would appear that removing the most able students lifts the aspirational ceiling for the rest, enabling them to aspire to a level of excellence that seemed unattainable before. Thus, taking the bright children out of regular classes seems to have a potentially uplifting, rather than a depressing, effect on the remaining students.

In summary we may say with some assurance that grouping able youngsters together may be a useful administrative device, since it enables teachers to work with a narrower range of abilities, to devote more time to the gifted than is possible when there are slow children who need help, and to enrich the curricular offerings. Furthermore, desirable changes in self-attitudes may occur for both the gifted and the nongifted; and there is no evidence to support the notion that grouping has adverse effects on the social or personal attitudes or behavior of children. Nor, on the other hand, does broad-range grouping foster greater mutual acceptance among children of various ability levels.

Ability grouping, however, is by no means a *sufficient* condition for insuring greater academic achievement at any ability level (71). At best, it provides a framework within which enhanced learning can be more effectively planned and executed. The crux of the problem of providing more meaningful learning experiences lies not so much in the grouping patterns used as in what goes on in the classroom. Here there is much speculation as well as strong conviction, but there is little concrete knowledge of what a truly challenging program should be like.

## Acceleration

Acceleration is second only to ability grouping in arousing emotional response. There is hardly a person who cannot conjure up at least one example of how acceleration ruined a child's life, or at any rate caused serious unhappiness. Yet it is difficult to find a single research study that shows acceleration to be harmful to any group of students (170). This is one area in which research results are clear and consistent. From the early studies of the 1930's until the recent report by the Fund for the Advancement of Education on its Early Admission Program (236), acceleration has proved to be a very satisfactory method of challenging able students.

Certainly, caution needs to be exercised in selecting candidates for accelerated programs. It would be foolhardy to disregard a child's physical and emotional development in moving him to a grade beyond his years. Where possible, it is probably better to move whole groups of youngsters through at an accelerated pace than it is to move a single child (119). In the small school, where there are few exceptionally able children and curricular adjustments within broad-range classes are difficult to achieve (which, of course, is true not only in small schools), acceleration can raise the level of challenge and stimulation for the superior child.

To the extent that getting youngsters out of school earlier is *per se* a worthwhile end, acceleration is certainly both desirable and practical. There is some evidence to support the contention that gifted youngsters should complete their formal schooling at an earlier age than they now do. Lehman (136) has shown that for some fields of endeavor, particularly the physical sciences and mathematics, greatest productivity is achieved during the twenties. Such findings stress the importance of freeing the potential producer from the apprenticeship of schooling at a sufficiently early age to make possible maximum freedom for original work and experimentation during the third decade of life.

Available research does not, however, support the contention that acceleration is the best method of providing greater challenge for able students. Studies dealing with acceleration of one kind or another compare their accelerants with youngsters who are carefully matched in ability, but the comparison is inevitably made with a group whose curriculum is rarely different from the standard fare in the school. There is no proof that an accelerated group would do better than an equally able group that had had an additional year or two of stimulating advanced work. For example, how would students who take Advanced Placement Program courses in high school—for which they may receive college credit and thus have time to take a richer program in college—compare with students in the Early Admissions Program, who are admitted to college a year or two before graduating from high school?

Where finances are a problem, students may be able to save a year or more in their high school-college career by acceleration in high school, early admission to college, or advanced standing in college through the Advanced Placement Program. This shortened time span may make it possible for students with financial problems not only to go to college, but also to go on to postgraduate work.

And for *all* students who go on to postgraduate work, the shortened time span will make it possible to enter into independent adult life at a more normal time.

In the light of all the factors that have been considered here, a combination of acceleration and more stimulating curriculums may be the most desirable approach to the problem.

Acceptance of acceleration as a desirable procedure does not, however, answer the question of when to accelerate. The optimum time for acceleration is not known. Gifted accelerants have been generally successful whether they were early admittees to kindergarten, grade skippers in elementary school, members of special progress classes in junior high school, or early admittees to college. But is one time better than another for acceleration? Are there developmental factors that mean that at certain ages there may be more dangers or, at least, more discomfort for the child? Hobson (107) suggests that early admission to kindergarten is the ideal method of acceleration. In a follow-up study of children admitted to kindergarten early on the basis of physical and psychological tests, he found that this group was scholastically superior through the elementary and high school grades, engaged in more extracurricular activities, won more honors and awards than did older students, and were more often admitted to accredited four-year colleges of superior standing. However, there are as many proponents of early admission to college as there are of early admission to kindergarten, and again as many for each of the stages in between.

We must conclude that although we do not have all the answers to this problem, there is certainly nothing in research today that would gainsay Terman's recommendation (232) that acceleration of no less than one year and probably no more than two is the most satisfactory procedure for bright youngsters, no matter what other plans may be used.

## Other Administrative Procedures

Schools are experimenting with administrative arrangements other than grouping and acceleration to provide for superior students. Three kinds of programs are worth noting.

*Seminars for Rural Youth.* A seminar for able rural youth was instituted in 1956 in Lewis County, New York (230). In this rural county, where schools are small and spread over a large area, twenty-five eleventh- and twelfth-graders from six high schools were brought together for one afternoon a week. The central theme of the seminar was communication, and students were exposed to classical and modern literature, music, art, and drama. A special trip to New York City, with visits to the opera, concerts, United Nations headquarters, art museums, and other points of interest, was part of the seminar's activity. Evaluation thus far shows that the seminar members have grown in self-expression and in critical thinking. As compared with students in past years, an increased number went on to higher education.

Similar work is being done by the Catskill Area Project in Small School Design, which brings able students from many small high schools in the Catskill area to Oneonta State Teachers College (Oneonta, N. Y.) for special seminars in mathematics, science, and the humanities.

Whether such seminars can be successfully developed in other rural areas depends upon availability of suitable personnel, either within the local school system or through the co-operation of a neighboring college, industrial plant, or government station. The personnel would largely determine the content of the seminar.

*Evening Science Seminar.* Another plan that is spreading rapidly is the evening science seminar (94), in which outstanding scientists from the community or nearby places work with selected students, both in groups and individually. Such an arrangement should provide potential young scientists with opportunities for original research and experimentation, often lacking within the school program. A modification of this plan, which was started two years ago in Dade County, Florida, allowed selected students to complete their regular daily program two hours early and spend their afternoons working in local community laboratories. Several colleges have organized special all-year (Saturday) or summer-session programs for gifted students, especially in mathematics and science.

*Guidance Provisions.* Although everyone recognizes the importance of guidance for the maximum development of superior students, little has been done to discover whether the problems faced by the superior group are sufficiently different from those faced by average students to warrant special attention or new approaches, or to discover just what these special problems are.

An attempt to identify some of these problems and to experiment with group guidance for a section of superior students under a specially trained person is now under way at a Denver, Colorado, high school (230). Follow-up studies comparing the special group with equally able students spread throughout regular guidance sections should shed some light on whether grouping gifted youngsters for guidance and organizing the content around their special needs have important effects on their success in high school, college, and adult life. Further evidence regarding the unique problems of the academically talented should emerge from the various guidance workshops being sponsored under the National Defense Education Act.

Another attempt at guiding more able students is the Project on the Guidance and Motivation of Superior and Talented Students, which is co-operating with one hundred schools in nineteen member states of the North Central Association (175). Selected schools are developing various procedures for stimulating more able students to achieve greater academic success in high school and to plan post-high school education. This program will also evaluate special guidance efforts for able students.

## COURSE CONTENT AND METHODS

Regardless of how adequately a school handles the problems of grouping, grade placement, and guidance, the major question in educating talented youngsters still remains unanswered: How should the actual course content and teaching method be differentiated for these students? The easy answer is: Enrich the curriculum. But enrichment, like the weather, is something everybody talks about and few do anything about. We don't really know what enrichment is. Does it mean accelerated coverage of a standard course of study, followed by advanced content in a given discipline— for example, completing elementary algebra in the eighth year and thus, in the twelfth year, having time for a course in calculus? Does it mean digging more deeply or extensively in an area—for example, studying original documents of some historical period? Or does it mean increased independent and creative work in some field of individual interest? Perhaps the very word enrichment is a misnomer; perhaps what is needed is not embellishment of existing course content but *different* content. Despite the plethora of "promising practices" suggested by and for teachers, these questions remain substantially unanswered.

Mathematics is one subject-matter field in which considerable experimentation with course content is now in progress. In Pittsburgh elementary algebra was successfully completed in the eighth grade by a group of carefully selected students. Similar results have been reported by other schools. In the University of Illinois Campus School the newly developed Illinois Mathematics Program (242) was used experimentally with superior seventh-grade students. Both of these programs are examples of rewriting the content of a course to expand the dimensions and thus provide both enrichment and acceleration. In St. Paul, Minnesota (207), however, the ninth-grade course of study was rewritten to include many concepts of modern mathematics and is being tried with one group of able students which will be compared with another such group taking the traditional algebra course.

An experiment in a tenth-grade geometry class, which included special mathematics units not normally taught at any stage of the usual course sequence, was reported by Lessinger and Seagoe (137). The experimenters found that the students in this program achieved better in basic geometry content, and in addition were superior to a comparison group in general mathematical understanding, flexibility of approach, and willingness to propose and defend original solutions.

A study of the effects of varied instructional procedures and content on attitudes toward mathematics and on mathematical achievement is being conducted in the junior high schools of Cheltenham Township (Pennsylvania) Public Schools with the co-operation of the Talented Youth Project (39). In the first year (1957) four seventh-grade high-ability mathematics sections were formed. They were matched on intelligence, arithmetic achievement, reading comprehension, and arithmetic teacher ratings. All four groups were pretested with a series of attitude and achievement measures. One group was taught without any modifications of the usual procedures. Another group was accelerated through a traditional arithmetic program, and by April of the seventh grade they demonstrated their readiness for the study of algebra by their scores on objective arithmetic tests and on a prognostic test in algebra. The remaining two groups followed the prescribed seventh-grade course of study, but spent time on a series of enrichment units covering history of numbers, number systems, powers and their meanings, and the like.

The following year, as eighth-graders, one of the enrichment groups moved into eighth-grade arithmetic, and worked on additional enrichment units dealing with such topics as measurement and statistics, operation of computers, logic, and topology. The second enrichment group entered the ninth-year Illinois Mathematics Program. The accelerated group continued work in algebra and completed more than half of second-year algebra by the end of the eighth grade. The fourth group continued as a control group.

In 1958 the entering high-ability seventh-graders were again divided into four groups: one to be accelerated through the traditional junior high mathematics program; one to work on a series of enrichment units; one to serve as a control group; and one to attempt the ninth-year Illinois Mathematics Program after a brief period spent on essentials of arithmetic.

All eight groups will be studied throughout junior and senior high school to determine the relative effectiveness of the various approaches. Evaluation will include measures of achievement, attitudes toward mathematics, and ability to handle new concepts and "discover" principles. In addition, the groups will be compared on the number of students who seek electives in mathematics and on the involvement of mathematics in their vocational choices.

## MOTIVATION AND ATTITUDES

As stated earlier, it has long been recognized that a child's IQ, or even his score on aptitude tests, represents only part of what determines his academic achievement or vocational selection. All teachers are familiar with the able but unmotivated student, and many report cards have gone home with the note "Should be doing better." This problem was studied by Terman (232) in his comparison of the vocationally most successful with the vocationally least successful adults among his gifted subjects. He found, through checking past records, that the two groups began to draw apart in achievement and personality ratings in their early high school years.

Although the problem of underachievement was recognized and school people knew that many able students, even some who did well in high school, failed to go on to post-high-school education, it was not until the publication of Dael Wolfle's manpower studies that educators and public became aware that about half the nation's able youth would not be academically prepared to fill our depleted talent reservoir.

Although financial difficulties explain part of our talent waste (steadily increasing scholarship aid should go far to remedy this), a large part of the waste is due to factors other than lack of money. In fact, we find that some gifted children begin to show symptoms of academic underachievement in junior high school, and some as early as the elementary grades. Who are these underachievers? What are their backgrounds? What are they like and why? What can the school do to help them? These questions have concerned researchers since Conklin's early studies (44). In summarizing the research literature on underachievement through 1957, Beasley (16) reports contradictory findings about the role of personal and social maladjustment in underachievement; she concludes that good or poor adjustment cannot be viewed as the specific phenomenon that in itself accounts for underachievement.

Studies now in progress or reported on shed some new light on underachievement. Drews (60), for example, found that the incidence of underachievers was very low in her group of gifted students. Most of the boys she studied were planning college careers; but waste was great among the girls, many of whom looked upon high school as terminal education.

Comparisons of gifted underachievers and high achievers by the research staff of the Portland (Oregon) Schools (191), and similar studies by the Horace Mann-Lincoln Institute in co-operation with Evanston (Illinois) Township High School (230) and with De Witt Clinton High School in New York City (83), revealed significant differences between the two groups in their self-concepts, school attitudes, and out-of-school pursuits. Some of the underachievers expressed negative views of those who make high grades, calling them grinds and suggesting that they did not participate sufficiently in nonacademic activities. The underachiever more often was cynical, felt victimized by adult authority, and perceived his family situation—with its strong parental domination—as conducive to poor morale. No differences were found between the two groups, however, in parental philosophy of child rearing. The underachievers were characterized by the perception of an excessive gap between their present status and the status to which they aspired. They often perceived this gap as too great to bridge through their own efforts and exhibited a belief in magic: some force outside themselves which would suddenly make things right.

In studies of the Clinton underachieving gifted boys* (83), inadequate father identification was frequently observed. These findings support the results of intensive case studies made by Kimball (124). She found among underachieving boys a greater tendency toward feminine identification and a more negative relationship with the father than was found among bright male achievers.

The above studies are descriptive, as are most of the earlier studies in this area; the causes of underachievement remain mysterious. In fact, it is probable that the causes are as diverse as are the underachieving youngsters themselves.

As mentioned earlier, some general social factors related to underachievement have been suggested: for example, bright children from homes of low socioeconomic status tend to be less motivated toward academic excellence than bright children from homes of high socioeconomic status; some ethnic groups present more problems of underachievement than do others—a fact probably related to the traditional attitudes of various ethnic groups toward intellectual pursuits (225). Even when these factors are held constant, however, great individual differences in achievement persist. A project now under way at Harvard (222) is studying the individual achievement differences between youngsters of comparable intelligence, comparable neighborhood, and comparable parental educational levels, in the hope of discovering in the life experiences of these children some generalizable factors that could account for differences in achievement level.

Since no single factor seems to differentiate adequately between high achievers and underachievers, Nason (170) approached the problem by studying the discriminatory power of the summation of various factors. The "patterns of circumstances" which he measured included personality adjustment, pupils' and parents' level of academic aspiration, pupil and parental choice of a future vo-

---

*Underachievement at the high school level is generally found to be twice as prevalent among boys as among girls (90).

cation, and pupils' inspiration or source of encouragement. He found that positive status on all of the circumstances assured membership in the top quintile on achievement, but that no single factor was a better discriminant than any other. However, low scores on the personality test he administered, if accompanied by high scores on the other factors, did not militate against high achievement. In general, the patterns of circumstances associated with different quintiles appeared to vary only in the *number* of circumstances *missing* from a complete pattern.

There is some indication that junior high school is the point at which the problem of underachievement gets a good start (83). A study of high and low achievers at the Bronx High School of Science (New York) (69) revealed that the most obvious differentiation between these two groups—which were matched in intelligence, entrance examination score, and other objective factors—was the grades they received in junior high school.

With the limited knowledge available today and without any clear understanding of what makes one child underachieve and another child from a similar background seemingly achieve up to capacity, what can schools do to help these underachievers? Certainly educational guidance, personal counseling, and remedial help would seem to be possible aids (14), but actually very little is known about the effectiveness of these procedures in combating underachievement. Are there any kinds of administrative or classroom modifications which might prove helpful? This question was raised at the De Witt Clinton High School in New York City (83). In co-operation with the Horace Mann-Lincoln Institute, a group of high-ability, low-achieving students entering tenth grade was identified. Half of these students were placed together in a homeroom with a specially selected teacher, who was their social studies teacher as well as their homeroom guide. For all other subjects they were distributed throughout the regular sections. A year's study of these students showed that although they were slow in improving, by the end of the year they did excel the control group in almost all subject areas. The following year, however, when the students in the experimental group were placed with a rather rigid social studies teacher who was inflexible in her demands for high standards of excellence in academic work and behavior, they made life miserable for the teacher. They were extremely supportive of one another in their negative behavior and tested the teacher's disciplinary limits at every step. Their grades no longer exceeded those of the control group, and in social studies actually fell below those of the control group, with an average drop of sixteen points.

The implications of this study point toward the need for continued careful selection of teacher personnel for such groups. Gifted underachievers apparently need teachers who are able to accept the students' limitations and who are sufficiently flexible to allow the students the leeway they need. Whether the high school years are long enough to provide the necessary support at first and then gradually to free the children from the need for such support is questionable. A look at the individual members of the group was quite revealing. For some of these youngsters the special class opportunity was just what they needed. A supportive teacher, a friendly atmosphere, and a reaffirmation of their own ability provided the impetus for them to move ahead. Some of them, however, had deep seated psychological problems which were not amenable to any kind of superficial group treatment. Certainly, in their case, more intensive personal help was necessary.

In 1956 the Board of Education of the City of New York, in cooperation with the School of Engineering of Columbia University, organized the Talent Preservation Project (229). Students identified as gifted—either by IQ scores above 130, or composite scores on the *Iowa Tests of Educational Development* at or above the 90th percentile, or both—were divided into several categories of underachievers on the basis of teacher grades received in the ninth grade. In addition to studying the various characteristics of these groups, the project has set up a variety of programs for working with the underachieving students. These programs range from group therapy, family casework services, tutoring, and special help with work-study skills to cultural enrichment such as trips to the theater, concerts, and museums. Although the design of the project does not make possible a comparative evaluation of the various approaches, it will be possible to assess the effect of special interest and help on achievement patterns of gifted underachievers.

A great deal of additional research is needed to discover ways in which the school can help underachieving gifted boys and girls. Before actual administrative planning for them, there should be much more careful academic, psychological, and possibly even psychiatric screening. It is probably important to differentiate between the underachieving youngster who, given some help and understanding, will rise to the occasion in the secondary school situation, and the youngster whose problems are too deep-seated to be amenable to any help at that late date. Extensive research is needed on identification of potential underachievers in the elementary and junior high school grades, so that they can be helped before they become too entrenched in their poor work and study patterns, and before their anxieties channel their defenses into underachievement.

The manpower waste is not limited to students who are identified as potentially able but who, for a variety of reasons, fail to fulfill their promise. It is even more marked in underprivileged groups, where the loss of potentially high-ability students is estimated in the hundreds of thousands each year, although they cannot be adequately identified by the testing procedures in common use (189). The work of the Southern Project (189), which involved identification of students who would not normally have been considered superior, followed by guidance and scholarship aid, made it possible for many more southern Negro students to go to nonsegregated colleges, where they were generally highly successful.

Along similar lines is the experiment now going on in Junior High School 43 in New York City (173). This school, located in a culturally deprived neighborhood, has an enrollment that is largely Negro and Puerto Rican. Out of this population a group was identified which would not be termed gifted by any standards generally applied, but which showed glimmers of potential ability. These students were put into special classes, and teachers and parents were carefully alerted to the intent of the program. Expanded curricular offerings, out-of-school cultural experiences, and special counseling facilities are provided for these children, who will continue to receive special help through the three years of junior high school and in the senior high school to which most of them will go. The final evaluation of this study will be determined by the number of students who go on to college and plan professional careers, as compared with a control group. The first evaluation of the program was reported by Wrightstone (271), who indicated that reading skills improved after one year of the program and that the first group to enter high school showed academic records superior to those of previous groups of students from the same junior high school.

Most educators view misplacement of talent as a serious waste. Misplacement might derive from the unwillingness of some able high-achieving students to pursue science, mathematics, or foreign language study, with the result that they are unprepared for professional work in these essential fields. There is widespread belief that many bright students enter the "soft" fields of business, home economics, health education, etc. Drews's (60) findings contradict this belief. She found that three-fourths of her gifted boys were planning their study for careers in science and engineering. And of 5800 Merit Scholar and Certificate winners (171), 60 per cent planned to study science and engineering courses, and another 25 per cent liberal arts. The number headed for business careers was limited to 2 per cent.

Mead and Metraux (159) studied attitudes toward science and scientists through content analysis of brief essays written by 35,000 students in schools across the nation. The students were asked to describe their image of a scientist and the kind of scientist they would or would not like to be (or to marry). In general, the authors found that the image of the scientist represented a deviation from the accepted way of life. The scientist was not seen as a normal, friendly human being who gets along with other people. Boys and girls reacted somewhat differently to the scientist. What boys reacted to positively (adventure, space, travel, and the like) did not appeal to girls. The positive reactions of girls emphasized humanitarianism, which did not appeal to boys. Girls generally rejected scientific careers for themselves and rejected a scientific career choice for their future husbands.

The extent to which able students may be deterred, through fear of rejection by their peers, from achieving intellectual excellence, was investigated by Tannenbaum (230) through an attitude test. He asked students to attribute various personal characteristics to brilliant and average students, who may or may not be highly studious and who may or may not be athletic. He also investigated the relation between the students' responses and their intellectual and socioeconomic status. He found that those students described as brilliant, highly studious, and nonathletic ranked the lowest when measured against the acceptable traits and general popularity characteristics. Studiousness was viewed as a handicap, especially by the girls; and brilliance, though viewed as desirable when accompanied by limited studiousness and athletic ability, became a handicap when associated with a high degree of studiousness and a lack of athletic ability. No significant differences in ratings were associated with the intelligence or socioeconomic status of the respondents.

## CURRENT TRENDS

What does research tell us about current trends in the education of superior children? In the past, surveys indicated that few schools were making special provisions for this group. Where schools did report special efforts, the efforts were usually through enrichment in the regular classroom. To what extent has the picture changed?

Recent surveys (21, 34, and 239) and school reports indicate a growing awareness on the part of educators of the importance of making special educational provisions for the gifted child. At the secondary level, especially in large schools, ability grouping through sectioning and honor classes is becoming more widespread (96). Such changes are slower at the elementary level, where classroom enrichment, grouping within classes, and part-time special classes are still the most popular practices. Least is being done in small nonsuburban communities. The outstanding programs involve at least some special or additional staff and consequently some additional cost (89).

A self-assessment survey of four hundred secondary schools in New York State (230) found schools attributing less importance to grouping and acceleration than to classroom enrichment as a means of providing for talented students. In general, schools did not consider their present enrichment procedures adequate.

Many school systems (271) have published guides for administrators and teachers which discuss identification procedures, administrative arrangements, and curricular suggestions. In some districts, individual schools may be engaged in a special program; in others, whole school systems are involved (191). Under a grant from the Fund for the Advancement of Education, the Portland (Oregon) Public Schools, in co-operation with Reed College, developed a comprehensive, district-wide plan. Special training for teachers through summer and in-service workshops, the addition of personnel, special classes and seminars at the secondary level, and enrichment units and special interest groups at the elementary level resulted in a unique program which stood up well under careful evaluation.

A new trend is seen in the efforts of state departments of education to undertake work in co-operation with public schools and sometimes with institutions of higher learning (157, 122). Not yet apparent in surveys or school reports, but a trend nevertheless, is the recent determination to make able students work harder, take more years of solid subjects, and spend less time in nonacademic pursuits. This determination is quite marked in the reports of the working groups at the National Education Association Invitational Conference (43) and in Conant's report on the American high school (41). The pros and cons of this trend should be thoughtfully considered.

## CONCERNS FOR SCHOOLS

The studies cited in this discussion give some idea of the kinds of questions being looked into at present. As noted before, some of the concerns have been stimulated not so much by educational re-evaluation as by manpower needs. There is some danger that the immediate cultural demands for more scientists and mathematicians will cause schools to urge able students to enter these fields at the neglect of other intellectual endeavors. Thoughtful consideration on the part of school people is needed if we are not to sacrifice both special talents and the long-range needs of our culture on the altar of immediate economic, military, and political demands.

The great research need today is in the fields of content and method. We need to know what will stimulate a love of learning among able children; what kinds of assignments will most effectively develop independence of thinking and effort; whether there are some subjects in which acceleration through the present curriculum is the most appropriate kind of teaching and other subjects in which greater exploration in depth or breadth may be the answer.

We also need to understand better the interrelationships of various aptitudes and talents in order to help students plan their programs. Should all intellectually able students take the same kinds of courses, such as three years of mathematics, three years of science, and at least three years of foreign language, in addition to the required English and social studies? Or should course offerings be more carefully differentiated in terms of special aptitudes and interests of students? Should students with high academic aptitude be encouraged to take art, music, or drama as a major subject?

All these questions are still open, as are many that relate to guidance and counseling, particularly for the underachiever. As schools become more alert to available research and act on it, at the same time becoming actively involved in the pursuit of research in their own schools, we will go a long way toward improving our educational procedures, not only for the gifted child or the academically talented child, but for all youngsters in our schools.

# 5

# INTELLIGENCE, SOCIAL CLASS, AND LIFE ADJUSTMENT

ELIZABETH MONROE DREWS
*Associate Professor, Michigan State University*

Ideas often die slowly, and many—some of the "old wives' tale" variety—relating to the meaning of intelligence have not even had the grace to "fade away." Although there are only a few exponents of phrenology (the study of lumps on the head to determine what and how much lies underneath), people continually (and usually erroneously) judge intelligence by appearance: "he has a bright eye"; "she looks smart." This fallacy is evident in current quips and cartoons. A recent cartoon shows a father—all nose, no forehead, and no chin—calling on the teacher. She looks up at him and says, "I'm so glad you came in, Mr. Jones; now I know I am expecting too much of your little boy."

Standardized tests are much more accurate than a casual glance or even a trained observation in giving us an approximation of an individual's ability. Even the IQ's and percentile ranks yielded by these tests, however, must be interpreted with great caution. Group tests are notoriously inaccurate when an attempt is being made to derive a single score for a single individual. The very young, the unhappy, and the excitable may get irreconcilably divergent IQ scores on group tests from one testing to another. Individual intelligence tests, such as the *Stanford-Binet Scale* and the *Wechsler Intelligence Scale for Children*, give somewhat more reliable IQ's than do group tests. Even the more reliable individual tests, however, do not offer enough information to determine, by a single score, present giftedness—much less identify potential giftedness. It is not uncommon for a child's IQ score to fluctuate fifteen to twenty points during the school year. By the time the eighth-grade level is reached, it is generally conceded (38), tests of developed ability are fairly good indicators of college success. As Tyler (241) says, it is perhaps best to emphasize present status rather than permanent endowment, both intellectually and in other dimensions.

## SPAN OF MENTAL GROWTH

Not only have opinions been revised with respect to the constancy of the IQ, but also there are new findings about the continuation of intellectual growth. Some thirty years ago it was thought that intelligence leveled off at about the age of sixteen and began to decline in the twenties. It has since became clear that intelligence test scores increase beyond the age of sixteen if schooling is continued. Owens (182), in a study with the Office of Naval Research, retested 127 college men who had taken the *Army Group Examination Alpha* when they entered Iowa State College. Results of the second testing, thirty-one years later, showed that they were intellectually more able in their maturity than they had been as young men. Bayley and Oden (15), in a longitudinal study begun by Terman, found that a group of approximately one thousand gifted adults who were tested on the *Concept Mastery Test* at approximately age thirty, and again eleven years later, were consistently higher on the second testing. That the *Concept Mastery Test* is a difficult test which allows sufficient ceiling for the most intelligent person to show increase in ability is particularly noteworthy. Often, growth in achievement or intelligence is not apparent because many tests have no upper limits that will measure such growth. At any rate, the comforting suggestion of these studies is that senescence and mental decline may come later and more slowly than we had once thought.

## TESTED ABILITY AND ACHIEVEMENT

Test scores are indications of the level a child has reached in his intellectual development. As such, they are useful tools. Despite the caution with which IQ's must be interpreted and the changes that occur in youth and maturity, scores do have predictive value. A student with high tested intelligence nearly always does better work in college than a student whose tests indicate average ability. He is also more likely to be successful as an adult. In other words, high intelligence and high performance are closely related, as a number of studies demonstrate.

Roe (202) for example, in her study of sixty-four outstanding scientists in the United States, was interested in finding out how intelligent these men were. She discovered that the usual tests developed for adults were much too simple, and asked Educational Testing Service to develop new and more difficult tests. The results of this testing demonstrated without question that this group of scientists was very intelligent indeed. The median score on the verbal test was estimated as equivalent to an IQ of 166.

Chauncey (38), of Educational Testing Service, was also interested in knowing the relationship between tested ability and achievement. He compared scores on the *Scholastic Aptitude Test* at college entrance with frequency of inclusion in *Who's Who* of the same people a quarter of a century later. The close linear relationship he found is illustrated in Table I.

TABLE I

RELATIONSHIP OF IQ TO INCLUSION IN WHO'S WHO

| *Scholastic Aptitude Test* IQ | Proportional Frequency in *Who's Who* |
|---|---|
| 110–119 | 1 |
| 120–129 | 2½ |
| 130–139 | 4 |
| 140–149 | 7 |
| 150+ | 14 |

Table I shows that those in the highest IQ range (150+) were 14 times more likely to be in *Who's Who* than moderately superior people (those whose IQ's were in the range 110-119).

Similar findings, arrived at without the use of standardized tests, were reported by Cox (46) in a study of the early mental traits of three hundred geniuses. Cox was aided by a number of competent research workers; from their joint efforts, based on analysis of available biographical data, IQ's were estimated and a mean IQ of about 155 was reported for the group.

## SOURCES OF GIFTEDNESS

Another widely held belief has been that most of our bright students come from high-level managerial and professional homes. To be bright and successful has been considered almost synonymous with being wellborn. It is true that at the turn of the century and before, most outstanding people seemed to come from the socially and economically elite. Galton (77) reported that most of the geniuses in his nineteenth century studies had illustrious parents or relatives. By the early 1900's, however, talented young people seemed to come from somewhat lower segments of the social pyramid as well as from the apex. Terman (233) reported in the 1920's that the bulk of the some fifteen hundred gifted youngsters in his study came from homes at the professional or higher business level. Similarly, Roe (202) reported that the majority of the outstanding scientists she studied, most of whom were in school in the 1920's, were from professional homes. Other families did not produce many gifted children, or else society "plowed them under." Only one-third of American children attended high school at that time, and undoubtedly children from average and poor homes constituted the major portion of those who left school early.

Today the base of intelligence has apparently broadened still more. Knapp and Goodrich (128) report that a majority of American scientists come from the lower middle class. Drews (60), in a recent report that traced gifted students from the eighth grade through high school, noted that three-fourths of the students came from average homes.

Young people who a few decades ago would have found it difficult if not impossible to do so, today are developing ability and are succeeding. The intellectually gifted no longer seem limited by home background and father's occupation. For example, Drews (60) found only a .04 correlation between the occupational choices of gifted boys and the occupations of their fathers. The son of a sewer cleaner had aspirations as high as those of the son of the state governor. Jones (117), reporting findings on his Berkeley (Calif.) growth study, indicated that these aspirations are not just fantasy. He found no correlation between the present occupational status of 36-year-old men and their socioeconomic status and ability scores in the ninth grade. He concludes: "Since the results of this study tend to emphasize the subject's abilities rather than social status factors in his childhood environment, they are consonant with the theory that to an important extent the upper middle class is recruited and maintained through ability factors" (117). These studies indicate that the poor but bright boy *can* make good.

## RISE IN TOTAL INTELLIGENCE LEVEL

Studies of the gifted over the last seven or eight decades appear to demonstrate that as the level of education of the masses increases, so does intelligence—at least measured intelligence. There is increasing evidence that we are "getting more cream out of the skim milk all the time" (a phenomenon which seems to arise from the fact that more people are in environments that foster intellectual growth).

Not only are more people exhibiting an above-average level of intelligence, but also there is some evidence that the total level of intelligence, at least in the terms in which it is commonly defined (vocabulary, information, and problem-solving skills), of the American, British, and North European population* is rising. This rising intellect may parallel an increase in bodily size and be another reflection of forces that have increased size, improved health, and extended longevity. As Snow (216) observed, ". . .perhaps no one as clever as James Clerk Maxwell or Newton is alive today, but thousands know more. We are a good deal heavier and taller, we live longer, but, above all, we know more."

This improvement of mind (if it is real rather than illusory) may stem directly from universal education and the availability, even inescapability, of mass media. The nineteenth century concept of the improvability of man, at least in a quantitative sense, may find here some measure of proof. Evidence seems to support speculations, made by social philosophers such as the classical scholar Highet (102) and the psychologist Murphy (168), that the human mind, as well as the human condition, apparently has improved for the two millenniums for which man has records. At least one large-scale study on school children (210) shows higher intelligence test scores today than a generation ago. Similarly, Tuddenham (240), who studied the intelligence of American soldiers, reports that "performance on a group test of the kind usually described as measuring 'general learning ability' or 'verbal intelligence' has markedly increased from World War I to World War II."

An optimist could easily interpret all this to mean not only that

*This hypothesis may hold for all parts of the world, but even fragmentary documentation is lacking.

more individuals are having opportunities to develop intellectually but also that the entire population is brighter than it once was.

## SOCIAL CLASS REALIGNMENTS

As mentioned previously, the apparent increases in tested IQ's and educational achievement may be results of both universal education and longer years of schooling. These increases may also be a result of another change, one that is related to the twentieth century's scientific revolution: the realignment of social classes and the emergence of a new class (61). In an age of technology, a new group of highly trained technicians and white-collar workers has sprung into existence. Rated on a conventional socioeconomic scale, this group is a grade below the professional and high-level managerial classes (a group often said to comprise about 10 per cent of the employed). Two significant things stand out with respect to the new group. The first is their number (estimated by some as 20 per cent of the total work force) which, when added to old-line white-collar jobs, has for the first time in history given us more white-collar workers than blue. Second, this group, with its high level of training and upward mobility, provides a likely environment for the production of mentally superior, high-achieving children.

Perhaps here is a partial answer to the tantalizing question whether today's gifted children are coming from different kinds of homes than did Terman's†. Since social structure and values—in other words, the home setting—have changed, it is clear that gifted children (as well as all other kinds of children) must be coming from different kinds of homes than they did three or four decades ago.

## GEOGRAPHICAL INFLUENCES AND SOCIAL CLASS

Geographical area also may influence an individual's social status.

---

†There has been much discussion recently as to where—what socioeconomic strata—our gifted come from. As was noted, early reports showed them to be coming mainly from professional and managerial classes. Drews (60) has questioned this and found the largest percentage of her gifted young people coming from homes below these levels. A re-examination of her material indicates that this difference may be due in part to the children of this large new class, the technicians.

Many studies of the stratifications in social class have been conducted in the East. It has always been farther from the bottom to the top, socially speaking, in the East than in other parts of the country. Knapp and Goodrich (128) stress the egalitarian philosophy of the Midwest and the West. Barker (12) found that the segment of the Midwest he sampled has only three classes and much fluidity among these. McClelland (147) indicates that in many towns people hold socially elite and valued positions not because of income or aristocratic forebears, but because they perform civic functions and are in general intelligent, hard-working people who contribute.

More and more it is what people have become, not how they began, that determines their rank in society. It would appear that the West has influenced all parts of America to some extent, and that the top and bottom are coming off the layer cake of social class structure. Europeans have remarked that we have always had a much shorter distance from bottom to top than they. This distance is now shorter than ever. Riesman (199) calls attention to the increasing "homogenization" of our society, while Lynes (145) speaks of togetherness on an institutional level—"corporations cuddling up to the colleges." Almost everyone says (when Mr. Gallup or Mr. Roper asks) that he is middle class, and it is beginning to look as if this is true.

It seems that society at large—perhaps because of the emergence of the new technological elite, perhaps because of a prosperity that offers satisfaction, and perhaps because of the influence of the Middle and Far West—no longer prizes the family coffer and the family tree as it once did. Inheriting money, a coat of arms, and a berth in the D.A.R. have lost much of their importance. Performance (a product of that magic amalgam of IQ and motivation) has to a great extent become the measure of men. That this valued performance is often of an intellectual nature is asserted by Whyte (247), when he mentions that his "organization men" place great value on the Ph.D. The thesis developed by Bullitt (32)—that ability outweighs parentage or wealth—is one held by many *au courant* social philosophers.

The observers who see the distance between lower and upper classes shortening, and a new aristocracy of ability arising, have commented on another phenomenon which ostensibly has been developing since World War II. This has been called togetherness and conformity and is said to be embodied in organization men and status seekers. The present generation is scolded severely and frequently for lacking the drive and the willingness to gamble, qualities supposedly instrumental in developing the youth of yesterday into the power elite of today (164). It is difficult to establish either the validity of these complaints or the extent of the infection. We do know, however, that bureaucrats now far outnumber entrepreneurs. Miller and Swanson (163) have discovered a change in middle class child-rearing practices and report that in bureaucratic middle class homes the Protestant ethic is relaxing and the pressure to produce is off.

In a world where the adults value co-operation, group decisions, and keeping in step but not ahead of the Joneses, there is some question whether the virtues of independence and dedication ascribed by both Terman (233) and Roe (202) to their gifted children of the 1920's would be found in equal measure in the mentally superior student of 1960. The gifted children of the 1920's were college students during the depression—a period described by Lynes (145) as a time when young people showed more idealism and effort than is apparent in today's noncommittal and security-conscious generation. Thus we may find a loosening of the grip of the Protestant ethic and a lessening of the urge to succeed in the sense that Webster defines it (aspiring to wealth and fame). Instead, "the dream is of comfort and not excitement, of security and not prominence" (145).

The critics who speak of excessive "adjustment" may be right if our young people are reflecting the patterns of their elders. Although the matter of overadjustment is a moot point owing to semantic problems as well as to a lack of validating empirical studies, there is little doubt that the gifted are both well liked and well adjusted. That they are the students preferred as friends was indicated by studies of friendship choices and sociability reported in Toronto (237), where four thousand eighth-graders were requested to make choices; in Urbana, Illinois (76), where elementary children in a college town were studied; and in Quincy, Illinois (139), where social leadership measures on intermediate-level children were obtained. Not only were the gifted rated as friends and leaders but also they met the empiric test: they were elected to offices far out of proportion to their numbers.

Drews (60) found that the gifted held four times as many offices as the average student. Furthermore, she reported that the more intellectual they were and the harder they studied, the more likely they were to be popular. This popularity held even when social class was controlled. Good performance seemed respected too, since the high-achieving gifted (straight A or nearly straight A students) held far more offices than the equally bright who simply got by (students who were content with a B or a mere C). Teachers, as indicated by recent studies of Getzels and Jackson (79), Holland (108), and Torrance (238), also seem to prefer this conscientious, sociable, responsible, high-achieving school leader who controls his impulsiveness and keeps his originality within bounds.

Studies concerned with adjustment show similar trends. It appears that the brighter he is and the better his school work, the more he is liked and the better his adjustment is. Drews (60) reports her gifted to be self-confident and aware of their above-average ability, and to show more positive attitudes toward self and school than do average students. She also reports the high-achieving gifted to be significantly more positive in their views of self and school than the low-achieving gifted. These recent findings support results of earlier studies. Terman (233) found that his successful men were better adjusted and more sociable than a group of gifted but less successful men. Such reports make ridiculous the use of the term adjustment as antithetical to intellectualism. Surely Sloan Wilson (254) must have had something else in mind when he wrote recently that our schools are confused and "not sure whether to make the child well adjusted or to teach him something."

There is no indication that school achievement of superior children is below the old par. In fact, as was mentioned before, there are many reasons to believe they are setting a new par. They are learning more things in less time and meeting teacher standards (the grades of the gifted girls in Drews's study averaged A-; of the gifted boys, B) as well as the criteria of objective tests. However, they may, as one of them put it, "have more desire to make good in school than to make good in life." School is finite, and the rewards follow performance in close sequence. Life seems infinite, and the rewards are uncertain.

Human nature being what it is, however, satisfaction with this quiescent state (the triad: adjustment, conformity, and togetherness) probably will soon pall. Some (135) suggest that it already has. As White (246) says, "Nirvana is not enough," and the healthy organism knows it. People thrive on uncertainties and difficulties. It is apparent that among many adolescents and young adults a rebellion is setting in—rebellion against conformity, rejection of mass motivation, and disregard of status symbols. The beats are apparent to all, but among many the offbeat lies just below the gray flannel.

Man seems to thrive on frontiers and to be a perennial pioneer. And the brightest of all seem to have the largest appetites for the unknown and the slightly perilous. This has been noted in many studies. For example, the superior student, when compared with his average age-mate, reads more science fiction and is "riper and readier" for space travel. Imagination is inextricably related to ability; and adjustment, when synonymous with regimented conformity, is not enough. As was observed by Goodenough (85), these gifted young people are more apt to be autonomous than suggestible, and, one might add, more apt to be brash than brainwashed.

# 6 STUDIES OF THE SUPERIOR STUDENT IN COLLEGE

COLLINS W. BURNETT
*Associate Professor of Education and Director of
Student Personnel, The Ohio State University*

Research studies on the superior and talented student involve a reciprocal relationship between high schools and colleges. For many years colleges have been interested in the efforts of high schools to work closely with outstanding young people. Colleges are aware that many able students will never arrive on the college scene unless they are identified and challenged in high school. Also, since the superior student's development is not confined to college years but goes on during high school too, college researchers have long realized the importance of what high schools are doing for this group of students. It is less difficult to develop a program for superior students in college if the processes of identification and motivation have already started in high school. On the other side of this reciprocal relationship, colleges have begun to intensify their research with outstanding students and to focus on implications that have meaning for high schools.

This chapter describes eight research studies which have been completed since 1951 under the supervision of the student personnel office, college of education, The Ohio State University, and relates their implications to high schools. The college of education at The Ohio State University has been active in programs and research dealing with the superior student since the 1930's when Pressey (196) developed the Degree with Distinction Program, which still continues on a modified basis.

In 1951 Heald (97) initiated the series of research studies on the superior student. The major focus of her effort was a follow-up study of 148 graduates who had been granted degrees of Bachelor of Science in Education *cum laude* and *summa cum laude* from The

Ohio State University between 1946 and 1950. She also wanted to obtain a profile of behavior characteristics of these students and to gather information that would improve the program for superior students. Her report showed that:

(1) Most of the men and almost one-half of the women had continued their formal education beyond the bachelor's degree.

(2) About one-half of those continuing their education had received scholarships, fellowships, or assistantships.

(3) At the time of the study thirty-two of the men and ten of the women had obtained master's degrees, and more than fifty others were working on advanced degrees.

(4) More than 80 per cent had taught and 50 per cent were still teaching.

(5) Although only a short time had elapsed since graduation, fourteen had written articles or booklets.

Students in this group stated that they felt they had received adequate attention while in the college of education. They did indicate, however, that they favored closer contacts with professors and advisers. They also wanted flexibility in the curriculum, with more opportunity for research, seminars, and guided reading. Suggestions also were made concerning acceleration, proficiency examinations, and encouragement of students to seek leadership roles in campus activities.

The suggestions made by these college students—flexible curriculum, more opportunity for research, opportunity to take proficiency examinations in certain courses, and encouragement to take leadership roles in activities—apply to high schools as well as colleges. Perhaps helping a superior student start a challenging research project in chemistry, biology, or history would not only motivate him in his high school work but also interest him in planning for college.

Danskin (54) investigated the study techniques of superior college students to determine whether those who have high academic achievement tend to use efficient study techniques. He devised an open-ended interview form which dealt with common study techniques at the college level and administered it to a total of 37 students (30 women and 7 men). In the group were 10 freshmen, 8 sophomores, 9 juniors, and 10 seniors.

The investigation revealed that the study habits of these 37 superior students seemed to be mediocre. In studying a text, only 9 turned topic headings into questions and read to answer the questions. Only 7 took working notes as they read. Most of the group seem to read with no particular study technique.

The group did better in the area of note taking. Eighty-nine per cent of the students took notes on class lectures regularly, although the notes were not well organized and seemed lengthy. Most of them did not know any means for determining what was important to include in the notes.

In preparing for and taking examinations, 81 per cent of the group waited until the last day or two before an examination to start the review. Only 3 students used the technique of predicting questions and then finding answers. Only 8 students planned a time budget while studying for an examination. In general it seemed that a good memory was the best tool these superior students had for studying for and taking examinations.

In reporting on place of study, 41 per cent of the group indicated that they liked to study in an easy chair or lie on a bed. About 86 per cent reported that they studied in the same spot each day.

Planning the use of time was also checked. Nearly half the group reported that they studied when they had time. About 11 per cent worked out a time schedule and followed it. One interesting point: About 38 per cent of the group did allow time for recreation. Superior students do not spend all their time in academic pursuits without some change of pace.

It is safe to assume that high-achieving students in the secondary school have no better study skills than their counterparts in college. Teachers in both high school and college are usually so intent on covering a certain amount of subject matter during the semester that little consideration is given to organized study skills which students need in order to profit most from learning experiences. Intelligent students who make good grades (in spite of poor study habits) can be challenged to develop skills that will enable them to accomplish more work in less time. Good students usually react favorably to a scientific way of doing things. The reading speed, comprehension, and retention process of the Survey Q 3 R method which Robinson (201) has developed at The Ohio State University is an excellent high-level work skill to use in stimulating superior high school students.

It would probably be unwise to add another course to the high school curriculum in order to teach the essential study techniques. A program of training for the teaching staff, however, can enable the teachers to develop a systematic approach which they will use with their students. Skills that involve reading rate and comprehension, note taking, studying for examinations, and budgeting time apply to most subject-matter areas; but special applications of these skills have to be made in foreign languages and mathematics.

MacLachlan (149) established criteria to study two groups of potentially superior students and two groups of potentially nonsuperior students. All of these students were enrolled in the first quarter of the freshman year. The potentially superior students who were placed in *Group I (N-40)* met the following criteria: (1) rank in upper third of high school graduating class; (2) *Ohio State Psychological Examination* between the 80th and 100th percentile; (3) high school activities including at least one major position of leadership and membership in at least three different organizations; and (4) a strong statement from the principal, counselor, or teacher about the student's outstanding promise.

*Group II (N-82)*, which was also potentially superior, met three out of the four criteria listed above.

*Group III (N-31)*, which was composed of potentially nonsuperior students, met three out of the four criteria set up for Group IV.

*In Group IV (N-17)*, the following criteria were established: (1) rank in lower third of high school graduating class; (2) *OSPE* score between 1st and 20th percentiles; (3) high school activities ranging from no participation in any organization to membership in no more than two; and (4) a weak recommendation from high school principal, counselor, or teacher.

The test for significant differences was used to determine how well *OSPE* scores served as a criterion for selecting superior students when compared with first-quarter grades. Differences significant at the 1 per cent level of confidence were found between Groups I and II, I and III, I and IV, II and III, and II and IV. There was no significant difference between Groups III and IV.

The difference between the potentially superior and the potentially nonsuperior groups with regard to campus activities was significant above the 1 per cent level of confidence. The other two criteria —high school rank and recommendations—were not evaluated.

The study revealed that the potentially superior groups tended to be a year younger than the potentially nonsuperior groups. Significantly, most of the fathers of students in Groups I and II were in professional and managerial positions, while the fathers of students in the other groups were mainly in the clerical-sales area.

Rydman (206) decided to validate the four criteria that Mac-Lachlan (149) used in her earlier study by determining to what extent these criteria would have selected students in their freshman year who later as seniors were awarded their degrees *cum laude* or *summa cum laude*. The four criteria were: rank in high school graduating class, score on the *OSPE*, participation in high school extracurricular activities, and recommendations from the high school principal or teacher.

Results of this study showed:

> The criterion of high school rank for selecting potentially superior students seemed to be substantiated, because 87 per cent of the students who received degrees with distinction were graduated in the upper third of their high school class. About 7 per cent of the honor graduates were in the middle third of their high school class and only one student was in the lower third of his high school class.

> The *OSPE* likewise seemed to be a good predictor of superior students. About 60 per cent of the honor graduates had total scores of 71 percentile or better; 83 per cent had scores of 51 percentile or better. It is important to note, however, that there were several low *OSPE* scores; one male student with a percentile of only 17 was graduated with a cumulative point-hour ratio of 3.21.

> Participation in high school activities showed a high degree of validity, because about 88 per cent of those who were studied participated in three or more activities.

> The fourth criterion, recommendations from the high school principal or teacher, was not supported by this study, which suggests that its value as a criterion is seriously open to question. Many recommendations were vague or couched in general terms; statements were omitted in a number of cases (206).

Myers (169) did a follow-up study of MacLachlan's research and used her same population to determine whether the differences between potentially superior and potentially nonsuperior students observed at the end of the first quarter of the freshman year were still noticeable three years later. His results showed:

1. Sixty per cent of the potentially superior groups (I and II) were still in college, but only 27 per cent of the potentially nonsuperior groups (III and IV) were enrolled.

2. Only 1.6 per cent of the potentially superior groups had been

dismissed for academic reasons, but 25 per cent of the potentially nonsuperior groups had been dismissed.

3. When compared on the basis of point-hour ratio, differences significant at the 1 per cent level of confidence were found between Groups I and II, I and III, and II and III, and between the combined potentially superior groups (I and II) and group III.

4. Again, differences with respect to participation in extra class activities, significant at the 1 per cent level of confidence, were found between superior and nonsuperior groups.

5. In terms of leadership on the campus, differences at the 2 per cent level of confidence were found in favor of the potentially superior students.

6. When advisers' ratings for those students in teacher education were studied in one sample (N-65) a difference in favor of the potentially superior students was found at the 1 per cent level of confidence.

All three of these studies—Rydman's, MacLachlan's, and Myers's —suggest that superior students can be identified by means of appropriate criteria. Whether the criteria that were successful in the college setting can be used with equal success in high school would have to be determined. In all settings, a multiple criterion seems not as prone to bypass certain superior students as is a single criterion. It also should be noted in this context that the term "superior and talented student" implies *more* than high academic achievement.

In a study with somewhat different objectives, Irvin (114) made an effort to determine to what extent superior students have personal problems and the nature of such problems. Three different groups, which were described as superior, average, and below-average (and containing 49, 31, and 20 students, respectively), were established according to predetermined levels of achievement on the basis of certain criteria: cumulative point-hour ratio, *Ohio State Psychological Examination* score, and frequency of participation in extraclass college activities. The superior group, for example, met the requirements of a cumulative point-hour ratio between 3.08 and 4.00, an *OSPE* score between the 80th and 100th percentiles, and participation in at least three different college activities.

The instrument used to determine the extent and kinds of problems was the *Mooney Problem Check List*. The most important general finding was that students in the superior group had about as many problems as those in the average and below-average groups. This finding is in opposition to that of Goldberg (see Chapter 4) and Drews (see Chapter 5). In analyzing the problems checked in the eleven different areas of the *Mooney Problem Check List* (for example, health and physical development; finances, living conditions, and employment; and social and recreational activities), it was found that superior students more frequently checked problems in the areas of social and recreational activities and of home and family than did students in the other two groups. Students in the average group, on the other hand, checked more problems in the areas of adjustment to college and of curriculum and teaching procedures than did students in the superior group.

Superior students, as compared with students in the below-average group, checked the following more frequently as specific problems: too little chance to read what I like; need for more worthwhile discussions with people; wanting to improve my mind; little chance to enjoy art and music; worried about a member of my family; doubting wisdom of my vocational choice. The last item tends to refute the notion that vocational counseling is unnecessary for superior students.

This study points up the fact that superior students in high school do have problems and need help. The high school form of the *Mooney Problem Check List* or some other appropriate measure may be used to determine the kinds and frequency of high school students' problems. Some of these problems will have direct implications for the curriculum. In order to fill the needs of superior students and to help them relate their schoolwork to themselves, teachers need to know what problems these students have.

The school counselor needs to be alert to the possibility that superior students in high school may not be sure of their vocational choices. Through tests, occupational information, and counseling, the counselor can help the student understand himself better. Knowing his own strengths and weaknesses may help the student to plan more intelligently for a vocation.

Two other studies should be mentioned. Campbell (35) developed a 70-point "academic potential" rating scale to select potentially superior students for scholarships in the college of arts and sciences at The Ohio State Univerity.

Points were awarded on the basis of high school rank, *OSPE* score, and leadership in high school. For example, a student who was graduated in the upper 5 per cent of his class received 30 points; a score on the *OSPE* between the 96th and 99th percentile entitled him to 20 points; and an outstanding leadership record earned him 10 points. The total for this student, on the 70-point rating scale, was 60 points.

One hundred twenty-three students who actually received scholarships to the college of arts and sciences were rated by Campbell on her scale. Using 41 as the cut-off point, she obtained two groups. The first group (sixty-three students) scored 41 or more points on the scale; the second group (sixty students) scored less than 41 points. For their first year in the university, the first group had an average cumulative point-hour ratio of 2.9, while the second group had an average cumulative point-hour ratio of 2.462. This .510 point-hour difference was significant at the 1 per cent level of confidence. Although the proposed scale did only slightly better in selecting superior students than methods previously used by the university, it seemed more objective and easier to use.

Wolfe (266) wanted to determine the attitudes of faculty and superior students toward programs for superior students. A questionnaire based on selected items for such programs (the items were suggested by experts and adapted from current programs in other U. S. colleges) was administered to the faculty of the college of education of The Ohio State University and to a sample of superior students. The results showed definite agreement between faculty and superior students on their attitudes toward developing programs for superior students. In seventeen out of twenty-two instances, there were no significant differences between the two groups. Where differences appeared, they were usually in degree of desirability rather than polar. Few differences occurred between student classes; where differences did occur, they were usually between freshmen and upperclassmen. Again, the differences were in degree of desirability rather than polar.

One conclusion from this study might be that it is not only safe but also desirable to invite participation by students in developing superior student programs. Students and faculty should be encouraged to plan co-operatively a program or a variation of the curriculum to challenge  superior and talented students. The seminar plan, acceleration, and advanced placement program developed with the help of a local college, independent study supervised by an interested teacher—these are all possibilities.

These eight studies of superior college students have been presented as illustrations of the kinds of research that have been done in this area. Some of the implications of this research will be of value to high school teachers, counselors, and administrators who are interested in ideas that will lead to more effective education of superior and talented students.

# SECTION III

# IDENTIFICATION

During the past few years, not only have educators revealed an increasing awareness of the necessity for identifying superior and talented students, but many have established practices in the school for doing so. Experience has shown that the identification of gifted students is best carried out by appraising and selecting students through a variety of techniques in many areas of their behavior. There are many factors, both intellectual and nonintellectual, which affect student learning in any classroom and which must be considered and evaluated in identifying and providing for the able students.

Identification enables the school to place each student in the best educational program it can provide for him. In order to place students intelligently, the school must assess each one's abilities, as well as his individual interests, drives, and aspirations. Without a careful, thorough, systematic screening program, some able students may be overlooked or placed in educational areas which do not challenge them. This is especially likely in the case of the high-ability, low-achieving, nonconforming student.

Recently, identification of able students has been greatly facilitated by the use of standardized group tests of mental ability and of achievement. The national educational climate and recent federal legislation have caused a new surge of interest in and increased use of standardized tests for locating able students. It is hoped that the increased use of such tests will be judiciously and intelligently directed.

The identification of superior and talented students requires an attempt to locate the individual differences which most pronouncedly affect students' school performance and are of such a nature as to lend themselves to differential treatment by the school. Schools undertake to identify superior and talented students so that data will be available (1) to assist all students to understand better their abilities, achievement, aspirations, and opportunities, and (2) to provide information about each student so that he may be placed in the educational program most challenging for him. If the identification program cannot justify the data collected in terms of one or both of these purposes, then the data have not been worth collecting.

Identification practices in schools utilize different *kinds* and different *qualities* of data or information. The different kinds of data include student behavior, student characteristics, and environmental conditions. In addition to kinds or sources of data, a school's talent identification program must also consider the quality or nature of the data. This calls for the use of longitudinal, normative, cross-sectional, and idiographic techniques of study.

All data upon which judgments are to be based should first be examined for their precision, validity, relevancy, and supplementary nature. Data are precise if they are reliable, consistent, and definitive; they are valid to the degree to which they relate to the criteria; they are relevant if they are pertinent to the decisions that must be made; they are supplementary if they supply missing information or help overcome some deficiency.

Learning about students and helping them is a continuous and complicated process. As the school identifies various types of students, it becomes better able to educate them effectively. Identifying students is simply a means to an end: making more intelligent provisions for individual differences.

The chapters in this section review some of the characteristics of superior children and some of the problems and practices in identifying them. Even a quick glance at the chapters reveals that no one definition of giftedness has been universally accepted by the workers in the field.

In the first chapter of this section, Henry Angelino discusses the characteristics of gifted youth. As he points out, many research studies operationally define the gifted as those students whose abilities place them in the top 1 per cent of students nationally. This poses questions: How many characteristics of students screened out by researchers are applicable to other superior or talented students not in the top 1 per cent? How many traits or characteristics ascribed to gifted students (top 1 per cent) by Terman, Hollingworth, and others apply to students who are in the top 5 per cent, 15 per cent, or 25 per cent of students nationally? Angelino also outlines the history of concern for the gifted and the characteristics attributed to gifted children by a number of researchers.

Bruce Shertzer, in Chapter 8, reviews some of the difficulties involved in identifying superior and talented students, considers the tools and techniques used in identifying such students, and outlines a step-by-step procedure that a school could use as a check list in its program for screening superior and talented students.

In Chapter 9, William Poland describes a study conducted at The Ohio State University to predict success in music as a career. He discusses the tests and other means that Ohio State has used in developing predictors of success in music and relates the significance of their results to high school identification programs in music.

Robert Iglehart, in Chapter 10, cites the difficulties involved in identifying talent in art, presents the characteristics of the talented art student, and suggests some provisions that facilitate the identification and development of art talent in high school.

Paul Brandwein, in Chapter 11, discusses the recognition of talent in science. He lists many varied methods that schools can use to identify the "science-prone" students and urges high schools to give these students an opportunity to conduct science investigations.

# 7 CHARACTERISTICS OF SUPERIOR AND TALENTED YOUTH

HENRY ANGELINO
*Professor of Education, University of Oklahoma*

Concern for the gifted is rooted in man's historical past. From the beginning of recorded time there have been attempts to provide appropriate types of education for the gifted. Generally, these more or less sporadic and unsystematic attempts were confined almost wholly to the upper classes.

Currently, there appears to be general agreement among thinking people that some special provisions must be made for the education and training of the academically superior and talented student, and that these provisions must be accorded top priority. This has been especially true since Russia launched her first outer-space missile. The widespread chagrin, the angry protests, and the charges and countercharges which followed the announcement of Sputnik I have focused attention on the entire American educational system—its hopes, promises, successes, and failures. This attention is particularly directed to the secondary schools and their presumed failure to educate and properly train our youth in the "solid subjects."

Quite suddenly, many people have become "experts" in the field of education, particularly education of the academically superior student. These people and others constantly remind us that we need more scientists, more mathematicians, and more technicians of all sorts so that we may become, once more, the leader in the world of science and technology. To be sure, America cannot afford to sit back and bask in past accomplishments or to daydream about glorious potentialities. It is quite true that our continued welfare depends on the full development of every single individual, including those whose abilities are in fields other than science.

This writer prefers to think that the current interest in the gifted and the talented is prompted by something more substantial than the immediate drive for safety and survival; rather, that it is prompted by concern for the individual himself because he is a human being and because, under a democratic system, he is entitled to individual consideration. Special education for the gifted is not only desirable but also necessary if Americans are really going to attain the democratic ideal of appropriate education for all children. Does this ideal not include the gifted? Is it democratic to have special education for the mentally retarded and the physically handicapped and not have special education for the gifted? As Americans we must always remember that every individual must be considered for what he is, as well as for what he may become. This does not exclude the gifted.

## HISTORICAL BACKGROUND

The concept of providing special facilities for the education of the gifted dates back to early classical times. In planning his Republic, Plato (188) recommended that the leadership responsibilities of the ideal state be placed in the capable hands of the philosopher-kings, who would be endowed with the greatest degree of rational intelligence. Plato stressed the importance of discovering and educating the most able youths as future leaders, and speculated on ways of identifying gifted children. He felt they should receive the education and training that would prepare them to be leaders of the state.

A number of Plato's ideas were taken over by the Romans, who specially trained their superior youths to become leaders in war and politics. In the sixteenth century a Mohammedan ruler had the "fairest, strongest, and most intelligent youths" selected for training as leaders (129). Intellectual superiority was highly regarded as a type of leadership during the Renaissance and Reformation and during the Industrial Revolution (228), but this view was not widespread enough to ensure systematic education.

Systematic education of the gifted appears to have been practically nonexistent in the seventeenth and eighteenth centuries. The political philosophy that "all men are created equal" ruled out the possibility of attention to individual differences. This attitude was reflected in the school curriculums of the times, as early American leaders generally endorsed this philosophy.

During the nineteenth century attention was again directed toward the gifted by the appearance in 1869 of Galton's *Heriditary Genius*. This work marked the beginning of an era in which appeared a number of books attempting to define the origins of superior ability. Among them were Galton's *English Men of Science* (1874), Lombroso's *Man of Genius* (1891), and Cattell's *Statistical Study of American Men of Science* (1906-10). These books raised the especially important issue of the relative contributions of heredity and education in the production of superior ability.

Lombroso's book, in particular, did much to keep alive the idea, held by the early Greeks and Romans, that genius is pathological. Lombroso believed that genius was associated with certain "physical stigmata" such as short stature, rickets, emaciation, stammering, left-handedness, and delayed development, all of which he claimed were indicative of atavistic and degenerate tendencies.

Most nineteenth century thinking, however, clung to the philosophy of the equality of all men and the theory that all native intelligences were equal and that differences existed only because of training. These beliefs left little room for any special education of the gifted.

In the United States, the earliest attempt to provide for the gifted in the public schools took place about 1867 in St. Louis, under William T. Harris. Harris introduced greater flexibility in the promotional procedures for the gifted, thus breaking the "lock-step" type of program. About 1900 some schools were using the multiple-track plan, which consisted merely of variations of the St. Louis procedure. By 1920 an increasing number of schools were using the enrichment plan; others, the individual instruction plan; and others, the acceleration plan. Between 1920 and 1940 the real emphasis was on enrichment (228).

In 1905 Binet published his mental test scale. In 1911 Goddard's revision of the Binet Scale appeared in the United States, followed in 1916 by Terman's. These scales soon demonstrated that they could uncover superior mental ability, and helped to modify attitudes toward ability prevalent in the nineteenth century. In 1925 appeared Volume I of the now famous *Genetic Studies of Genius* by Terman and his associates (233). Approximately fifteen hundred youngsters with IQ's of 140 to 200 were studied in terms of a number of traits and characteristics such as: racial or national

origins; sex; health and physical history; school progress; specialized abilities; intellectual, social, and play interests; and personality
and character traits. The findings reported in this study and in
follow-up studies form the core of current scientific knowledge about
the intellectually gifted (33, 46, 234).

In 1926 Hollingworth's monograph *Gifted Children* presented a
general summary of the field (111). In the 1930's and early 1940's
many more studies of gifted children appeared, contributing much
to our growing knowledge of the intellectually gifted (110).

In the post-World War II era, provisions for the gifted were
again at low ebb, enrichment being the most common practice. A
nationwide survey of secondary schools in 1954 (116), however,
indicated that an increasing number of schools were becoming aware
of the need to make special provisions for the gifted.

The sudden upsurge in efforts relative to the gifted may be traced
to the competition between Russia and America for the world's
scientific and technological leadership. Russia's overtaking of America in production of both scientists and satellites has awakened
the general public to the necessity of looking more closely at its
treatment of superior and talented youth.

## CHARACTERISTICS OF THE GIFTED

What is the gifted person like? Is he the strange person, the
puny, sickly, bespectacled individual that popular opinion says he
is? Or does he differ from this stereotype?

A definition of the term "gifted" is in order. To the writer, a
gifted individual is one with an IQ of at least 135 on a commonly
used intelligence test. Of course, there are pitfalls involved in des-
ignating giftedness by an arbitrary IQ score. However, even
greater pitfalls lie in using mere words and phrases—as so many
do—in attempting to define and identify the gifted (1, 58, 256).
This highly subjective approach says much but means nothing.
Therefore it seems more desirable to include in one's definition of
giftedness a certain level of potential measured by some acceptable
instrument such as an intelligence test, even though IQ is not the
only criterion of giftedness.

Some individuals with high IQ's also have special abilities or
talents. In themselves these talents are not necessarily character-

istic of giftedness. No matter how talented along a particular line a person is, he is not really gifted (intellectually) unless he has a high IQ. For example, a person who can play several musical instruments well may not be gifted: he is talented, but not necessarily gifted. Special talents are often mistaken for unusual mental capacity. It is true, however, that intellectual giftedness and some special ability or talent are often found together.

Any attempt to educate the gifted must be based on a thorough knowledge and understanding of their entire backgrounds, physical characteristics, and social and emotional traits. Also, educators must have an adequate measure of intellectual endowment and be able to use perceptively the numerous kinds of quantitative data available. Only facts can dispel the prejudices, misinformation, and false beliefs concerning the gifted which are held by far too many people.

There are enough facts available to make it possible to view the gifted in their proper perspective. It is important to remember, however, that the gifted are far from being a homogeneous group; actually they show wide variations in almost every respect. There are intragroup differences in achievement, as well as in other areas.

The characteristics of the gifted have been reviewed ably and thoroughly by Catherine Cox Miles (162). Rather than to repeat her findings, the important consideration here is to explore interaction between an individual's inherited potential (innate ability) and his total environment. "Heredity times environment," then, is the basic issue. The various stimuli provided by a person's environment really nurture genius. Sidney Pressey, in a recent article, emphasizes the role of nurture in the final expression of genius: "At any age, development of any ability is fostered by a favorable immediate environment, expert instruction, frequent and progressive opportunities for the exercise of the ability, social facilitation, and frequent success experiences" (193). The earlier these factors enter the picture, the better. To develop into genius, superior original capacity must grow under favorable circumstances.

One of the most ambitious and extensive studies of the gifted is the Stanford study of Lewis M. Terman and his associates, begun in 1921 and reported in *Genetic Studies of Genius* (233, 234). This study involved over fifteen hundred children ranging in age from three to nineteen and in IQ from 140 to 200. (Included in the group were sixty-two children whose IQ's ranged from 135 to 139.) These children represented roughly the upper 1 per cent of the school population. Although what is true of this group should be true of gifted children generally, all the characteristics may not apply equally to all gifted children.

## Racial and Ethnic Origins

In America, gifted children have been found most frequently in ethnic groups with high social, economic, educational, and professional achievements. There are certain ethnic groups that are known to contribute more than their share of superior children. Among these groups are the Jews, English, Scots, Scandinavians, and Chinese. Certain other racial and ethnic groups, such as the Negro, Mexican, American Indian, and southern Italian, contribute few superior children. However, the fact that gifted children have been found in every racial and ethnic group emphasizes the need to provide opportunity for superior children born in families where the means (environment) for full development is lacking.

The majority of the students in the Terman group came from old American stock, families with New England and Middle West backgrounds. There were fewer from foreign-born parents. However, children of immigrants as well as Negro and Mexican children were found in his gifted group. In New York City, where Leta Hollingworth did pioneer work with the gifted, gifted Jewish children were proportionately far in excess of other groups. Wherever they are found, the Jewish groups rank high, their numbers of gifted being far greater than the expectancy. Although it appears that particular cultural conditions and certain ethnic stocks do produce a proportionately higher percentage of gifted children, final conclusions about the relation between ethnic origins and giftedness cannot be reached until a larger sampling (including a sampling from the mother country of each group) has been covered.

In regard to IQ's among the Negro population, more Negro children of high ability would be found if more were looked for. Past studies of Negro children with high IQ's indicate that race in itself is not a limiting factor and that gifted Negro children are not different from the gifted of other racial groups (265).

There is no conclusive evidence on which racial or ethnic groups produce the most gifted children or children with other special abilities or talents. All children should have, from birth, the best possible environment in order to develop their potentialities to the optimum.

## Socioeconomic Level

Gifted children may come from any home, though they are more often found in homes whose backgrounds and socioeconomic levels are superior. In Terman's group, the gifted showed greater than average proportions of native American parentage, urban parentage, and Jewish parentage, and a noticeable shortage of Negro, Indian, and Latin ancestry. Studies also show that the socioeconomic environment of gifted children is generally superior. The parents of the gifted children follow more mentally demanding occupations than those of unselected populations. Their neighborhoods and homes are above average. In Terman's group, for example, the professional class produced ten times its quota of gifted children.

The educational level of the parents of gifted children is also higher than the average in most instances. In the Terman group, the parents averaged twelve years in school, the grandparents ten years. These parents exceeded the average for their generation by four or five years. Also, the number of eminent ancestors was far greater than one would expect from chance. It seems characteristic of gifted children to be born in families whose ancestors were able and held positions of responsibility and trust in their communities.

For the most part, then, home backgrounds and economic levels of the gifted are superior to those of the general population.

## Vital Statistics

When considering vital statistics, as well as medical and physical data, it is found that gifted children, age for age, exceed the growth norms. This is particularly true for height, weight, ossification of carpal bones, and age of pubescence. Studies show almost complete agreement that the gifted tend to be slightly above average in nearly every physical aspect (103, 184, 233, 234). The gifted tend to develop more rapidly through childhood and youth than do average youngsters, and they are advanced in both speech and locomotion, as compared with control groups. Pubescence, too, comes somewhat earlier.

Illness rates and infant mortality rates are very low in families of the gifted. The frequency of insanity in these families is lower than the average. Life expectancy also seems to favor the gifted over the average. Taking the group as a whole, medical reports show that the gifted have superior health and relative freedom from defects. Other things being equal, there appears to be a direct relationship between physical health and mental ability in groups of individuals. These findings correlate with results of other studies, which show that the great majority of the gifted come from home environments in which parents have above-average education and socioeconomic standards. These homes are able to provide better food and living conditions, and they show more concern for the welfare of their children than do the homes of the majority of children. The conclusion is, then, that in physical characteristics the gifted child ranks above the general population.

## Educational Achievement

Most gifted children find school learning rather easy. Almost half the children in Terman's group, for example, had learned to read before they entered school, so that the regular class work was not difficult for them. Once in school, about 85 per cent of them were accelerated, skipping one or more half-grades; and in the opinion of their teachers, the children should have been accelerated even more. Scores on achievement tests in school subjects revealed that the majority of these children had already mastered subject matter one to three grades above their placement.

Gifted children like academic work and make the best progress in this dimension. The so-called hard core subjects are easier for them than for other students. The children in Terman's group tended to excel in *all* the academic subjects, contrary to the popular idea that gifted individuals are one-sided in their school work. Their teachers rate them as superior to their average classmates in debating, language usage, composition, general science, reading, mathematics, and other abstract subjects. They seem less superior in activities not so highly correlated with intellectuality, such as

98                 WORKING WITH SUPERIOR STUDENTS

physical training, sewing, cooking, manual training, shopwork, and
penmanship. Parkyn (184) and Witty (256) report similar results
regarding the superiority of the gifted in hard core subjects. Their
achievement-test results favored the gifted in all subject-matter
areas.

## Out-of-School Activities and Interests

Terman's gifted students also excelled by displaying a wide range
of interests in their out-of-school lives. Terman's children, at all
ages, read more than did average children. Here, in fact, was the
greatest contrast between the gifted and the average children, since
the gifted read twice as much as average children of similar ages,
and they generally read superior materials mainly from science,
mathematics, history, poetry, drama, serious fiction, and travel
books.*

Gifted children in Terman's study pursued play activities somewhat similar to those pursued by their age group in general, although they tended to prefer games played by older children. They
preferred older playmates and were less likely than average children
to show any sex preference in choosing playmates. They lost interest
in the so-called childish games at a much earlier age than the
average child. The games enjoyed most, and most often played by
both the gifted and average children, were the active social games,
although the gifted also enjoyed more or less quiet games that required thinking.

The vocational aspirations of the gifted, in Terman's study, tended to be much higher and more realistic than those of average
children. Also, they preferred occupations near the occupational
levels of their fathers.

## Character and Personality Traits

Evidence that gifted children are above the average in character
and personality traits comes from parents and teachers and from
the results of objective tests. When compared with others, the gifted

---

*Current research by Abraham (2) and Kirshner (126) shows that today's gifted
children may not read any better than average children of the same age.

show up more favorably on tests of ideals in character, personality, and social standards. They demonstrate less boasting, less cheating, and considerably greater trustworthiness under stressful conditions. They are more self-critical.

W. D. Lewis in a study of the characteristics of superior students concludes that the majority of his gifted "are very normal children making normal adjustments and there is no evidence here that abnormality and queerness is the typical characteristic" (138).

Two facts related to the gifted group stand out clearly. First, the deviation of gifted from average children is in an upward direction for almost every trait measured. We can find no law of compensation in operation whereby the intellectual superiority of the gifted is offset by inferiorities of the nonintellectual dimensions. Second, the upward deviation is *not* as great in all traits. It is greatest in those aspects of behavior most closely correlated with intelligence, such as originality, intellectual interests, and high scores on achievement tests. In school, the gifted perform best in the academic, or solid, subjects. Average children, on the other hand, have more success in subjects requiring less conceptualization.

Other studies of similar groups, though less extensive, corroborate the findings of Terman's work. Studies by Hollingworth (110) in New York, Witty (256) in Kansas City, Worcester (268) in Nebraska, Duff (62) in England, and Parkyn (184) in New Zealand emphasize that, regardless of where they are, most children with high IQ's show the same general superiority. In short, the conclusions reached by these investigators were that favorable parental and home backgrounds, above-average health and physique, outstanding academic achievement, and superior emotional stability characterize the gifted groups.

Scheifele (209) has compiled an imposing list of the intellectual, physical, social, and emotional traits found among gifted children. Although all gifted children do not necessarily possess all these traits, her list is useful as a guide in identifying gifted inviduals.

## The Gifted in College and Later Life

In college, Terman's gifted students continued to maintain their status intellectually, academically, and socially. They attended college in larger numbers, received better grades, obtained more degrees, and received many more honors than any group with which they were compared.

The really important aspect of all these studies of the gifted is what actually happens to the children as they grow up and assume adult responsibilities in society. The follow-up studies by Terman and his group (234), Witty (256), and others help answer this question.

The survey of Terman's gifted group by Terman and Oden (234) showed that by 1945 approximately 90 per cent of the men and 86 per cent of the women had gone to college; of these, 70 per cent of the men and 80 per cent of the women graduated. Advanced degrees were taken by 51 per cent of the men and 29 per cent of the women.

Despite the fact that their mean age at graduation was more than a year below the average, both sexes participated in more than their share of extracurricular activities. Not only were their grade averages superior, but their records in nonacademic honors were well above those of the average. There were some exceptions, of course. These were attributed to poor or inadequate work habits, lack of interest, emotional maladjustments, or a deliberate neglect of certain studies in order to pursue special interests or projects.

In their follow-up reports, Terman and Oden include a mass of data about their subjects, over 95 per cent of the survivors of the original Terman group. The average age of these subjects was slightly over thirty-five years. In general, these reports indicate marked school success through college and graduate school. The majority of the subjects, particularly the men, were found to be rather well established in their lifework.

Occupationally, the status and accomplishments of the gifted group were highly satisfactory from the standpoint of both earned income and level attained. Nearly half the men were relatively well established in various learned professions (as college professors, doctors, lawyers, and the like). About 20 per cent were in the higher-level business occupations (managerial and executive). A small minority (less than 4 per cent) were employed as clerks in stores, factory workers, truck drivers, and the like.

The women, however, had not reached the high occupational level of the men. A great many of them were married and completely engrossed in their homes and families. When the 1940 follow-up was made, of the total number of gifted women, nearly half

(42 per cent) were housewives and not included in the gainfully employed. By 1955 the percentage of housewives had increased to 60. As a whole, both occupational level and income were lower for gainfully employed women than for men.

A breakdown of the women's occupations shows that about 35 per cent of the working women were in office and business jobs, about 21 per cent in public school teaching, and 11 per cent in college teaching or other professions requiring a graduate degree. Other professional and semiprofessional occupations accounted for 29 per cent. Only 4 per cent went into a variety of nonprofessional occupations. Educators who are concerned with the public school teaching shortages will be especially interested to note that 35 per cent of these gifted working women chose office and business jobs, while only 21 per cent entered the field of public school teaching. Surely, efforts to interest more of these gifted women (as well as gifted men) in the teaching profession would be worthwhile.

## THE UNDERACHIEVER

Always with the educator is the problem of underachievement—the failure of a person to produce or succeed up to the level of his potential. In the 1940 follow-up, Terman and his associates made a detailed analysis of the case histories of the 150 most successful men (designated as Group A) and the 150 least successful men (designated as Group C) in the original study. They were attempting to get at some of the nonintellectual factors affecting success in adult life (234). Although all of Terman's gifted group had measured at or above IQ 135 on the tests, their productivity differed greatly. Group C failed to live up to the promise of their early years. Terman indicated that personality factors were particularly important as determiners of achievement.

Men were chosen for Group A or Group C on the basis of their success in adult life. The criterion was "the extent to which a subject made use of his superior intelligence"—as evidenced largely by academic marks and professional recognition for subjects who had completed a graduate course of study, and by earned income for those who had gone into business or semiprofessional pursuits (234). The greatest contrasts between the two groups occurred in the educational and occupational areas. Of Group A, 90 per cent graduated from college, as contrasted to 37 per cent of Group C. Nearly 76 per cent of Group A, but only 15 per cent of Group C, completed a year or more of graduate work. Also, students in Group A were most often accelerated in school. Parents of students in Group A were conspicuously different from parents of students in Group C in the following respects: superior educational and occupational level; more encouraging attitude toward higher education; greater marriage stability; and the "qualitative" aspects of their homes.

In occupational classification, Group A was far ahead of Group C. More than two-thirds (68 per cent) of the former as compared to 9.33 per cent of the latter were engaged in what were classified as "learned professions." Over 30 per cent of Group A, but only 7.3 per cent of Group C, were in semiprofessional and managerial positions. None of Group A, but over 48 per cent of Group C, were in clerical jobs, skilled trades, and retail business. Only six were unemployed, and these were from Group C.

As mentioned above, students in Group A generally had a more satisfactory home background. In terms of parental education, over 50 per cent of the A fathers and 15.5 per cent of the C fathers had college degrees. The difference in the mothers' education was not so great: 18 per cent of the A mothers and 11 per cent of the C mothers had degrees. The Group A students demonstrated superior school work during the high school years, participated in more extracurricular activities, and had better scores on achievement, when compared with students in Group C.

It appears that the main reasons for differences in adult achievement are found in the psychological dimensions—greater drive to achieve, more perseverance towards goals, more self-confidence, and greater all-around social and emotional adjustment.

## REALIZATION OF POTENTIAL

Abilities develop and change throughout life, since they are part of an entire organism which is affected by the dynamics of a total life pattern. A person's measured potential at a given age may not be realized at maturity. Reports concerning the accomplishments of gifted adults confirm the view that equal IQ's in childhood do not guarantee equal achievements in maturity. IQ is always a factor in accomplishment, but it is only one factor among many. Interrelationships among factors may prove to be as important to achievement as possession of the factors themselves. Terman's follow-up studies show the importance of favorable environment as well as of heredity. Even the highest IQ's, 170 and above, do not of themselves guarantee highest achievement.

It appears that our cultural values, beliefs, and ideals sometimes get in the way of certain types of accomplishment. The influence of an industrial, technological era—with its emphasis on aggressive competition and athletic prowess—often discourages literary and artistic gifts in the formative years, particularly among American male children. How many boys, for example, may have been dissuaded from developing deep interest in the fine arts or humanities by the dominant attitudes and values of the father, the community, or the larger subculture? This may explain why so few of the males in Terman's group pursued careers in the creative arts as compared with the number who became scientists, doctors, lawyers, and executives. This is even more likely today, because of concerted efforts to urge the gifted into the science area. It seems that our society is determined to discourage males from intellectual pursuits that might prevent them from becoming the male prototype: ultramasculine, tough, experienced, and sophisticated.

Occupations considered inappropriate for males are generally considered appropriate for females, and vice versa. Girls are not encouraged to go into scientific and engineering careers: our values are not yet geared for such an attitude. Many of the professions and occupations formerly pursued entirely by males are still difficult for women to enter today. Two points bear reinforcement: (1) Giftedness does cross sex lines and does not favor one sex over the other. (2) Giftedness does not emerge automatically; and a potentially gifted child must have, in the words of Pressey, "early encouragement, intensive instruction, continuing opportunity as he advances, a congruent stimulating social life and cumulative success experiences" (193).

The great task of educators, parents, and everyday citizens is to discover superiority wherever it may be, encourage it, and develop it to its fullest potential regardless of race, creed, or sex. In addition, ways must be found to prevent the failures—those underachievers who go through life never realizing what they might have been. Educators look upon these tasks as great responsibilities as well as great privileges. They do not want to fumble the ball—the outcome of *this* game is too important.

# 8 IDENTIFYING SUPERIOR AND TALENTED STUDENTS

BRUCE SHERTZER
*Associate Director, North Central Association
Project on the Guidance and Motivation of Superior
and Talented Students*

One of the most important goals of public education in the United States is to help all students develop to the fullest extent of their abilities. Heavy losses in human resources result when superior and talented students are not promptly identified and encouraged to make the most of their abilities and talents (267). Trained and educated minds have always been in demand and counted upon to perform an important function in American society. The increasing complexity of the world we live in makes the development of such minds not only important but also essential.

John Gardner, of the Carnegie Corporation of New York, has aptly named this era the "era of the great talent search." The chief reason for identifying talent is to enable the individual to view himself and his world in a way that permits him to accomplish his best—not only *do* his best, but *be* his best. In order to attain this goal, schools must first carefully identify their superior and talented students. Since talent is so complex, this is a difficult task; but it is not impossible. Difficulties may arise because of discrepancies between test results and teachers' judgments. Or they may be due to the interpretation or connotation of the term *talent*. McClelland illustrates this well: "The term *talent*, to begin with, is ambiguous. Sometimes it refers to an aptitude or ability *in* the person, and sometimes it refers to talented performances *by* the person—i.e., behavior which goes beyond the ordinary in meeting some criterion of desirability" (147).

Identification may be defined as assessing the abilities and talents of students in the school and selecting those students who meet the criteria established by a program. This assessment may include standardized tests and inventories, observational techniques, teacher judgments, and screening of previous records of behavior. Selections are made by statistical weighting of the test data, by subjectively evaluating the data or—most commonly—by both approaches.

Much research has been conducted in the area of identifying able students, and there is an abundance of literature reporting investigations and methods of locating talent in the schools. French (70), Conant (43), Henry (100), DeHaan and Havighurst (58), Kough and DeHaan (132), and Brandwein (22) have all devoted attention to this subject.

An identification program has certain advantages for the school in which it is conducted. First, the procedure of developing criteria and machinery for identifying able students focuses attention on the need to provide special programs for superior and talented students. Second, the identification process will produce a specific list of superior and talented students, including information about their potentials, strengths, and shortcomings. This list and information will make teachers, counselors, and administrators more sensitive to the individual differences among students in the school, and more willing to devote time and attention to challenging students who have demonstrated superiority.

## PROBLEMS INVOLVED IN IDENTIFICATION

Problems often arise when a school initiates a program for screening superior and talented students. As has already been implied, discrepancies between results of different intelligence tests, discrepancies between test results and teachers' judgments, and disagreement about the definition of talent may cause difficulty in initiating and carrying through a program for identifying superior and talented students. In addition, six other problems may arise:

1. *Failure of teachers to recognize potential ability in students coming from socioeconomic backgrounds different from their own.* Some schools have reported that the aspirations, attitudes, and actions of potentially superior students from social and economic groups above or below that of the teacher may cause the teacher to overlook or ignore their potential ability.

2. *Failure to recognize potential talent or ability in minority groups.* Not all talented youth in the white majority have been discovered and encouraged, but by far the largest untapped source

of potential talent is the minority groups such as the Negro or Spanish-American. Many studies have documented the fact that a large pool of Negro talent is not being used. In the state of New York, where the Negro population is 12 per cent of the total, the percentage of college students who are Negro is roughly ⅓₈th of 1 per cent. One reason is that the majority of Negro students do not take the college preparatory curriculum in high school. It may also be that school counselors fail to recognize Negro students as future physicians, teachers, attorneys, chemists, engineers, technicians, and other professional workers.

3. *Failure to identify and encourage academic achievement in superior girls.* Although girls outnumber boys as high achievers in high school in a two-to-one ratio, twice as many able boys as girls enroll in college (269). Inasmuch as most girls will be employed for twenty-five years during their lifetime, this wastage of talent is even more serious. James P. Mitchell points out that between 1960 and 1970 "the number of women workers will increase at nearly twice the rate of men" (165).

4. *Possible inadequacy of present tools and techniques to screen and identify superior and talented students.* Critics of present tests of mental abilities point out that the tests measure potential only and that there is no guarantee that a student's performance will be commensurate with his potential. Predictions based on test results, these critics assert, rest on the assumption that the characteristics measured by the test will not change from the time of assessment to the time of actual behavior. They also point out that present standardized tests favor students from the upper strata of society and are unfair to students not reared in the particular culture in which the test was standardized.

Those who consider present tools and techniques adequate to assist in identifying able students, while cognizant of the limitations of the tests, believe that such measures help predict student achievement with better than chance success. They believe that the intelligent use of standardized tests, combined with other techniques for identifying talent, is superior to waiting for selection to take place in the general setting of the school.

5. *The possibility that identifying superior and talented students will create an intellectual elite.* Some educators believe that the identification of the gifted will automatically deprive the average

student of leadership opportunities and that those identified will become intellectual snobs, creating a sort of class barrier in our society.

As Goldberg points out, however, American society has a number of elites:

> Indeed, no western society is without its elites. The real question has been: What kinds of elites can American society develop and tolerate within its values framework? In a democratic society, elites must emerge from accomplishment, not from self perpetuation. Furthermore, the very variety of elites protects American society against the dominance of any single one (84).

Also, if an intellectual elite does exist in a school, it may not be the result of the identification process; it may be a consequence of the actions of teachers, counselors, and administrators.

6. *Lack of trained counselors to carry out the responsibility of identifying superior and talented students.* Even though many part-time counselors are being replaced with full-time counselors, the average counselor is trying to work with twice as many counselees as he can effectively handle. In 1958 schools in the North Central Association Project on the Guidance and Motivation of Superior and Talented Students reported a ratio of one full-time counselor for each 750 students in their schools. This is three times the counselor-student ratio of one full-time counselor for each 250 students recommended by the U.S. Office of Education and the American Personnel and Guidance Association. In 1959 the project schools improved in this respect, reporting one full-time counselor for each 550 students. Partial solution to this problem lies in freeing these highly trained people from the numerous clerical functions that might well be handled by others.

## TOOLS AND TECHNIQUES USED IN IDENTIFICATION

There are a number of techniques and practices for the identification of superior and talented students. The following paragraphs summarize these procedures.

### Standardized Tests

The most commonly used means of predicting ability is the standardized test. Under this rubric are included tests and inventories of mental ability or scholastic aptitude, achievement, specialized aptitudes, skills, interests, and personality.

The type of standardized test most frequently used in identifying students is the group test of mental ability. This is used as a screening device to find students who have potential talent and whose performance, the school believes, will be commensurate with that talent. Many schools prefer to use a group mental ability test that yields a multiple score, such as a verbal score, a quantitative score, and a total score. They believe that a multiple score enables school counselors to understand better the nature of each child's intelligence. Quite often, after the administration of group mental tests, schools give an individual intelligence test, such as the *Stanford-Binet Scale* or the *Wechsler-Bellevue Intelligence Scale,* to recheck selected students who have reading difficulties or whose class achievement does not match their performance on a group intelligence test.

The next type of standardized test most frequently used for identifying talented students is the achievement test. Batteries of achievement tests are available in English, science, mathematics, social studies, foreign languages, and reading. Reading achievement is of particular importance in selecting superior and talented students, since reading is a skill that is vital throughout their academic careers. From achievement test results, counselors discover how much students have learned and to what degree they integrate or transfer learning from one area to another. Since achievement test scores are a reflection of learning that has gone on before, they give the counselor additional data on which to base an estimate of the student's progress in the future. Achievement test scores help the counselor to diagnose the student's strengths and weaknesses and to place him in those classes which will challenge him most. When well-constructed standardized tests of achievement are administered and interpreted wisely, the results can be of great assistance to the school in screening its superior and talented students.

Another type of standardized test sometimes used in searching for talent is that of specialized aptitude. Warren defines aptitude as "a condition or set of characteristics regarded as symptomatic of an individual's ability to acquire with training (usually specified) knowledge, skill or set of responses such as the ability to speak a language, to produce music, etc." (245). Test publishing companies have produced various instruments for assessing musical, mechanical, clerical, social-intelligence, artistic, and physical aptitudes. Surveys reveal, however, that few schools use these instruments in their identifying process.

Standardized batteries of interests and of personality are less frequently used by schools in screening for superior and talented students. Perhaps greater attention should be given to the assessment of interests and personality, since individuals are interested or motivated in achieving those things which satisfy their needs and goals. Such inventories could provide a key to classroom behavior. Some educators, believing that adolescents' interests are fluctuating and unstable, have doubted that much significance could be given to pupil interests. But a recent study by Robert M. White,* U.S. Department of Health, Education, and Welfare, has revealed a stability of interest among young people.

## Past Performance

Many schools, in compiling a list of superior and talented students, use student's past grades as an identification technique. They reason that if a student has previously performed better than the average student, he has the necessary ability and incentive to be included in the school's superior and talented student program. Grades are expressions of teachers' estimates of the level of students' achievement in classes. Since there is no accurate yardstick for judging classroom achievement, making these judgments is difficult. The variability in standards and meaning of grades from one teacher to another limits the value of school grades as predictors of success. School grades can be significant, however, when they are considered as a series of estimates. Grade average continues to be the best single predictor of future grades in high school and most colleges.

Schools which use grades as one means of selecting superior and talented students normally establish a cutoff point, such as a B average. Many assign numerical weights to the grades and require a specific total score for inclusion in the program. Some schools have assigned numerical weights to different subjects,

---

*Robert M. White, Personal Communication, March 2, 1960.

giving academic subjects three points, shop or homemaking courses two points and physical education one point.

## Teacher Observations

Many schools use the recommendations of teachers in selecting students for their superior and talented student programs. Quite often a student will exhibit behavior indicative of high intellectual ability even though he has neither received high grades nor scored highly on an intelligence test. Such students may come from educationally deprived backgrounds, may be maladjusted or underachieving, or may have some other type of educational handicap.

Teacher nominations should be used to add students' names to a list of intellectually superior students, but should not be used to exclude names that have been included on the basis of test scores or grades. Experiments have indicated that the most practical way of securing teacher nomination is to provide each teacher with a list of behavior characteristics indicative of intellectual ability. The teacher is asked to use this list to evaluate systematically the students with whom he comes in contact. He may consider each student in terms of each characteristic (131, 132).

Most of the students indentified by teacher observations will be the same ones identified by tests and grades. Teacher observation of behavior characteristics, however, will probably help to locate one or two additional intellectually superior students from a group of 100 to 150 students. The actual number will depend on the effectiveness of the testing program and the grading system.

The teacher nomination technique can be particularly useful for identifying students who have special talents and skills, such as artistic or musical ability, since there are few standardized measures of these abilities. Again, a list of the behavior characteristics that indicate some special ability can be used by teachers to evaluate their students. Some schools have programs especially designed for students talented in art, music, drama, or some other area.

## A STEP-BY-STEP PROCEDURE

Although each school must develop its own methods of identifying superior and talented students, the following step-by-step procedure outlines points which all schools must consider.

1. *Establish responsibility for the identification process.* Many schools delegate this responsibility to a committee composed of teachers, counselors, and an administrator. The committee is given authority to carry out its responsibility and assign tasks.

2. *Establish the objectives to be achieved with the students who are identified.* Is the school interested in fostering social leadership, scholarly competencies, scientific accomplishment, or appreciation of the fine arts? The objectives of the program should be summarized in definitive written statements of the skills, understandings, and attitudes the school wishes to develop in its talented youngsters.

3. *Define the group of students to be identified.* Is the school's program designed to benefit the top 1 or 2 per cent, the top 5 per cent, or the top 15 per cent of students, nationally? What proportion of the local school's population will be chosen? Will provisions be made for students with special talents or abilities? Before students can be identified, the school must know how many and what kinds of students are being sought.

4. *Collect and organize the results of standardized group tests of mental ability.* Consult Buros's *Fifth Mental Measurements Yearbook* for the selection of a group test of mental ability. After the test has been administered and scored, the names of students whose scores meet the criteria established (step 3) should be placed on the first working list for the committee on identification.

5. *Use an individual test of intelligence.* An individual mental ability test should be administered to any student whose score on the group test seems questionable. The original list should be revised (names added or deleted) according to the results of the individual testing.

6. *Collect and organize the results of standardized tests of achievement and specialized aptitudes.* A second list should be compiled, including the names of students who meet the criteria established in step 3 on standardized tests of achievement and specialized aptitudes.

7. *Obtain the past grades of students.* A third list should include the names of students whose cumulative grade averages meet the criteria established in step 3.

8. *Obtain teacher recommendations of students.* The names of

students recommended by teachers should make up a fourth list. As mentioned earlier, the teacher recommendations can be based on a list of behavior characteristics indicative of intellectual ability.

9. *Organize a composite master list of students to be considered.* A master list of the names of all students mentioned on any of the four lists described in steps 4, 6, 7, and 8 should be drawn up, and points awarded to the students on the basis of their appearance on the various lists. For example, a student might receive two points for a mental ability test score at a certain percentile, one point for his past grades, and one point for a teacher recommendation.

.10. *Select the students who are to participate in the program.* After deciding the total number of points that will merit a student's inclusion in the program, the committee should compile the final list. This becomes the list of superior and talented students in the school. Each student on the list should be carefully considered in terms of physical and emotional health.

11. *Review the list each semester.* The list should be kept flexible, since students will withdraw from the school, capable new ones will enter, and some who were not originally selected will become eligible. Identification is a continuous process and is the responsibility of everyone—teachers, counselors, administrators, and parents.

## CONCLUSION

In this article a brief review of the process of identifying superior and talented students in the school has been presented. The principles on which identification is based include the following:

1. A systematic search throughout the school's population is necessary. If the screening process is not conducted in a careful, well-organized way, many capable students will be overlooked. The search should be conducted as carefully, yet as humanely, as possible.

2. Factors other than mental ability should be recognized and considered during the screening process. Such factors as the student's reading level, social characteristics, physical and emotional health, and general pattern of behavior should be considered in developing a list of talented students. Many types of evidence

must be used. Educators have yet to develop a single, faultless measuring instrument for identifying the superior and talented.

3. Identifying superior and talented students is the responsibility of all teachers, counselors, and administrators of the school. It must be carried on concurrently with the school's total program and must have responsible direction.

4. The identification process should be initiated as early as possible. Most authorities in talented student work recommend that identification be initiated in the elementary school years; some place the level at grade 3 or earlier. This necessitates effective communication of identification needs, procedures, and information to administrators, teachers, and the public. Early identification makes possible valuable cumulative information.

5. A continuous screening of superior and talented students should be in operation in the school. This enables the school to detect and challenge the "late bloomer." Factors of either an emotional or environmental nature that might impede identification at any given time could thus be offset.

6. Flexibility should be maintained in the screening or identification program. School officials should be willing to add students who were not previously identified in the program. Schools will also find that some students are unable to cope successfully with the program; such students should be dropped.

The identification program is a major step toward liberating potentially able students from the "lock-step" process of education. It is the first step in a design to help superior and talented students undertake a productive role in our society. In this identification process the school must not fail to view each student as an individual with talents which are incredibly complex, but which must be nurtured.

# 6 PREDICTING SUCCESS IN MUSIC STUDY

WILLIAM POLAND

*Director of the Music Theory Testing Program,*
*School of Music, The Ohio State University*

Failure has marked attempts to select those individuals with high probability of success in the various careers in music by measuring talents presumed to be innate. No one has succeeded in separating talents from environmental forces or learned attitudes, skills, and information. The most complete attempt to do so is represented by Carl E. Seashore's *Measures of Musical Talent* (1939). Scores on such tests, however, have shown essentially no relation to success in music study or professional life. The most recent comprehensive review of music tests is by Lundin (144), whose basic data and criticisms are well documented. The only important test published since Lundin's book is the *Music Achievement Test* by Aliferis and it seems no more successful than the previous tests (133).

Most of the music tests were constructed between about 1920 and 1940. The theory and practice of testing and the statistical methods of evaluating test results have changed considerably since then. In music as in other areas, armchair speculation is gradually being replaced by conclusions arrived at scientifically. More is known to-day about the relationship between the physical and psychological dimensions of sound. But musical talents remain unspecified. If someone performs well, he is said to be talented; but the expression "talented" seems to have as many meanings as it does users. If the writer seems to treat the concept of talent rather harshly, it is because of his belief that current usage of the term tends to regard superior performance within the framework of a faculty psychology. There is no doubt that some young people have neural or neuro-muscular structures that make certain kinds of behavior easy for them to acquire. If this is what is meant by talent, then innate talents exist and eventually we may be able to measure them directly rather than by way of performance.

Even if talents could be readily measured now, it would not be enough to know that a child is talented. The development of talent depends on the acquisition of many skills and much information. Further, innate and acquired abilities must be accompanied by a desire to put these abilities to social use. By the time a child reaches the age at which relatively stable predictions are possible, the innate and the learned are so completely confounded that the only feasible solution to the problem of finding the musically talented—a problem in prediction—appears to be a longitudinal study of success and failure in music. Ideally, this study should begin with the first signs of a child's musical interest and continue through adulthood, a span of thirty to forty years. Although it is possible to design such a study, schools cannot wait forty years for results.

Certain conditions seem to favor the development of talent in any given field. Pressey (193) set forth the following conditions:

1. A prevalent cultural interest in the field

2. Exceptional early opportunity and encouragement to develop the ability

3. Superior individual guidance and instruction beginning at an early age

4. Opportunities to use the special ability as it develops

5. Association with others interested in the same field

6. The stimulation of many successes, for which the individual gains recognition

Pressey draws a parallel between the cultural attitude toward musical achievement in mid-eighteenth-century Vienna and the attitude toward athletic attainment in the present-day United States. He demonstrates that in Vienna, the six conditions existed for musicians; in the United States, they exist for athletes. Universities have a responsibility to help develop interest in cultural fields. They can conceivably forward the arts as effectively as they have forwarded football.

Since a school of music is principally a producer of teachers, it seems reasonable that it could help to improve the setting for the development of musical talent by turning out a better teacher. One way to produce a better product is to improve the raw material. A school's raw material is pupils. Since the school's job is to turn pupils into students and students into culturally responsible, successful musicians, it must start with the most promising pupils. The problem is one of prediction.

The school of music at The Ohio State University became interested in this problem several years ago. Prediction actually involves preparing for the future on the basis of information from the past. The first task was to define success in music, since the fundamental criterion for admission to a school of music is high probability of success in music. It rapidly became apparent that no definition was possible. It is possible to point to successful musicians, but any attempt to define their success in terms of specific criteria only produced a mass of anecdotes—no criterion data.

Most professional musicians graduate from a conservatory or university school of music. Charles Spohn (217) traced the pattern of institutional instruction in music in the United States. The trend is clear. Increasingly, success in music is tied to the ability to graduate from a university school of music. What are the criteria for success in such a school? Three universities (Harvard, with a liberal arts background; University of Michigan, with a conservatory background; The Ohio State University, which grew from a department of music education) are examples of schools that graduate successful musicians. It is reasonable to assume that each school attracts a population of students differing in some important respects from the students in the other schools. It is equally clear that the schools' graduates would have characteristic differences. Also, the schools' curriculums differ, and there is no reason to assume that predictors for success at one of these schools would work equally well at the other two.

The concept of national norms is at least implicit in all the well-known music tests. In the light of the differences in atmosphere, curriculums, and aims of the major music schools, it seems obvious that the only norms with any real meaning would be norms for a given situation. John R. Hills (106) worked with tests to predict success in mathematics in several universities. He concluded: "There may be no unique trait, or constellation of traits which can be called mathematical ability. . . the implication that there is no unique mathematical aptitude is derived from the fact that certain of the abilities measured in this study are related to success in some curriculum-criterion-institution contests but not in others." Substitution of the word *music* for Hills's *mathematics* reveals the basic assumption made by The Ohio State University school of music study in 1954.

It was decided to try to construct a group test that would predict success in a single course—the first quarter freshman course in the fundamentals of music. Most classroom music courses depend on the information and skills learned in this course. It was hoped that such a test, plus tests given to all students applying for entrance to The Ohio State University, would predict performance for the first quarter of work in the music curriculum. In another context, however, The Ohio State University had already constructed the basic test needed.

In the spring of 1951 the school of music inaugurated its annual Music Opportunities Day. High school students considering a career in music were invited to spend a day on campus. As part of this program, the music theory staff prepared and presented in test form a set of items representing the kinds of skills and information they thought necessary for beginning college level courses in music theory—the kinds of things Ohio State's school of music wanted its students to be able to do when they entered. There was no attempt to construct a predictive test. The test results were reported to students in terms of weaknesses and strengths, in the areas tested, with instructions for improving their weaker areas. It was decided to see if this test, designed to give pertinent information to high school students, would help the school of music predict the probable success of its first-quarter freshmen.

It had been the school's policy to give individual examinations in aural comprehension and sight singing to each entering freshman, so that firsthand knowledge about the aural and informational characteristics of each student could be obtained. In the fall of 1954, Ohio State gave the entering freshman class regular individual examinations and the group test from the spring 1954 Music Opportunities Conference. The group test scores had a Pearsonian correlation of .77 (N-75) with first-quarter music theory grades, while the individual examination scores had a correlation of only .53 with course grades. In other words, the group test accounted for about 60 per cent of the factors influencing grades, while the individual examinations accounted for only 25 per cent. When both scores were used in multiple regression equation form, the individual audition scores did not make a significant contribution to the prediction made by the group test scores alone. On this evidence the individual examinations were discontinued.

Why did the group test—requiring only pencil-and-paper responses—predict better than the individual examination that used "real musical responses"? The type of judgments made by the experts on the basis of the individual examinations are known as clinical. The group test covered a wider sample of the students' skills and information and was uniformly administered; the results were quantifiable and therefore adaptable to statistical treatment and control; the tests were empirical. Theodore Sarbin reviewed (1944) the literature comparing the clinical and empirical methods of prediction and decided overwhelmingly in favor of the empirical method (208). The point is that the information collected was better quantified in the group test. In more formal language, the group test enabled Ohio State to order events into classes and to make predictions with optimal accuracy. The individual examiners no doubt also tried to order events into classes, but they tended to rate students on an individual basis. R. B. Cattell (37) said that intuitive judgment is a stereotyped distortion of data by a unique mind. Apparently the experts who judged the individual examinations were making too many intuitive judgments.

The test sampled—and apparently rather well—what experts thought music students ought to be able to do at the time of entrance. The first group test was not designed to relate to any subject but music theory. It was felt that samples of prospective students' musical backgrounds should be collected in other ways. The music faculty was asked to make statements about the kinds of things they thought students should know or be able to do before coming to the school of music. Two new tests were constructed on the basis of these statements. One of these tests was concerned with identifying standard works by title and composer. The other test was concerned with a variety of information about composers, compositions, musical personalities, and technical matters. All the test items were put into multiple choice form, and all three tests were administered to high school student guests during the spring 1955 Music Opportunities Conference. The three tests were presented as indicators of what the faculty would like the students to know and be able to do. The results of the spring 1955 testing were used as reliability and internal item analysis checks. The school of music then modified the tests and used them with the fall 1955 freshman class. After further revision, the three tests were administered to the fall 1956 freshman class. This test battery makes it possible to predict music theory grades and first-quarter music point-hour ratios with correlations in the 80's, music history grades with a correlation in the 70's, and applied music grades with a correlation in the 50's. In the last three years, revisions and cross-validation on the tests have continued. The latest correlation with first-quarter music theory grades is $r = .81$ ($N = 85$).

In 1958, on the basis of information derived from the tests, the freshman year in music theory was reorganized. The sophomore year in music theory is currently being reorganized. To bring the courses up to date, certain leads offered by analysis of the test data have been combined with the work of Pressey (194) on accelerated college students and that of Skinner (214) in elementary arithmetic. Within the theoretical framework of the ideas of Donald Hebb (98)—who has succeeded in accounting for Thorndike's trial-and-error learning and the Gestaltists' insightful learning as two extremes of an essentially single process—studies have been conducted on new methods of organizing and teaching the material of elementary music theory.

Some of the results of this work are especially significant in terms of public school music programs and their encouragement of the musically talented. It appears that the public schools could enhance students' probability of success in music by making it possible for such students to develop speed and accuracy of response in the verbal, notational, and aural elements commonly referred to as the fundamentals of music.

Clifford Williams (249) says, "Talent testing in the areas of art, music, and mechanics is so closely tied to experience that it is difficult to detect ability in children who have received little or no training." It is equally difficult to detect musical ability in high school students who have received little or no training. Under the present system at Ohio State, however, such detection of ability is not necessary. Ohio State will conditionally admit students to the school of music who make substandard scores on the placement tests. Records show, however, that only one in ten admitted with substandard scores has survived the sophomore year.

As soon as the data that have been collected are processed, it will be possible to predict success in any course or course group in the first two years of the courses of study in music. Sixty-two persons have graduated for whom complete records have been maintained. For these sixty-two, predicted first-quarter music point-hour correlated .72 with graduating point-hour. Indications are that in two more years Ohio State will be able to predict graduating point-hour about as well as it now predicts point-hour for the first quarter.

Development of the test battery will continue by integrating an analysis of music course content with data about the changes in students as they progress through the curriculum and into professional life. The question will be asked repeatedly: "How do information and skill acquired at a given point in a student's progress relate to success at later points in his career?" Efforts to assess this relationship are important, since The Ohio State University school of music and more than two hundred sister institutions have primary responsibility for the education of musicians in every phase of their professional development. A well organized prediction program, based on pertinent tests, careful record keeping, and critical technical and statistical analyses of data, can materially help these institutions meet this responsibility.

## CONCLUSION

A major reason for the failure of published standardized tests in music is that not enough is known about the relationships between specifiable musical skills and information on the one hand, and school or professional success on the other. Curriculums, methods, and goals are not standardized and perhaps should not be. Under such conditions, it is not surprising that no large testing program in music has yet been effective.

Recognizing the difficulties of predicting talent in general and the past failures in predicting musical talent in particular, a small-scale prediction program was initiated. The intent was to evolve a set of measures of functional consequences of inborn and acquired abilities of those interested in music as a career. The first stage of this investigation was concentrated at the point where high school students showed interest in seeking admission to a university school of music. At this point, relatively specific criteria may be set for the applicants.

Success in identifying musical talent is too much to claim for the results, but success has been achieved in predicting who can succeed in The Ohio State school of music curriculum and in isolating some of the skills—all subject to improvement under instruction—which contribute to this success. It appears that the public schools can make major contributions to success in music by developing these skills in students who show interest in music. This amounts to a recommendation to foster musical literacy, and leads directly to the suggestion that serious consideration be given to creating, for music, the six conditions (outlined on page 116) that favor the development of talent.

# 10 IDENTIFYING ART TALENT

ROBERT IGLEHART
*Professor of Art and Chairman, Department of Art,*
*University of Michigan*

The problem of early identification of those gifted in the visual arts has received sporadic attention over the past several decades. None of the various testing instruments developed during this time has proved useful, nor does the writer know of any serious use of such instruments. Attempts have ranged from an effort to measure the student's level of general art appreciation, as in the *McAdory Art Test,* to personality diagnoses based on projective techniques, as in the *Rorschach Ink Blot Personality Test.* Although in each instance it has seemed clear that something was being measured, the nature of the characteristics under investigation has remained regrettably obscure.

The most recent and comprehensive study of testing techniques was conducted at Cooper Union Art School in New York City, which annually selects and awards free-tuition scholarships to its entire freshman class. The three-year study yielded negligible results.

The reason for the difficulty in developing effective selection techniques is not hard to understand. Talent in any creative field consists of a delicately balanced constellation of gifts and characteristics. Talent is, for example, more complex than a factor such as mechanical aptitude (for which there are successful instruments of identification) and more specific than general intelligence. Many art educators insist that success in art is generally proportionate to IQ and academic achievement. This may be an accurate conclusion for a specific situation, but it does not tell us much more than that a reasonably intelligent pupil will do as well in art as in other fields. And it does not begin (nor does it pretend) to assess the specific components involved in creative ability.

The writer believes there would be general agreement that the

123

three primary (and interrelated) components of talent in art are (a) general intelligence, including the ability to arrive at new values and ideas; (b) a general sensitivity and imaginative response to experience, particularly in the visual area; and (c) the manipulative skill required in the expressive act.

The central characteristic of the creative artist is his ability to reorganize experiences into new and meaningful forms which, in turn, create new values. Thus, in terms of function, no real separation of a, b, and c is conceivable. Visual perception, for example, is an act of the whole consciousness. The manipulative skill, most easily observed and identified, is probably the least critical and most educable component of art talent.

Brewster Ghiselin, in speaking of the creative process in the mature artist, says: "The technical processes merge indissolubly with the creative process, as soon as the use of substances and forms begins to be guided by a sense of their sufficiency or insufficiency in formulating insights and attitudes" (80). This would seem to be equally true of both the mature and the aspiring artist, and makes technical skill appear to be, in mathematical terms, a necessary but not a sufficient condition. Hence, tests of technical skill or of taste (such as the *Meier-Seashore Art Judgment Test*) seem too limited to disclose any significant range of characteristics or to allow for major changes in current attitudes, philosophy, and taste—changes which may themselves be initiated by unusually creative and inventive personalities.

Since neither technical skill nor knowledge about art is in itself a reliable index of creative talent, perhaps the solution lies in an attempt to investigate a constellation of factors within a constellation of personality traits. Some attempts in this direction have been made: current projective techniques have been used to a small extent and, in at least one instance, new tests have been planned in the hope of identifying a pattern of creative response. At the University of Michigan, for instance, a series of experiments is under way—sponsored jointly by the art and psychology departments—from which it is hoped coherent patterns of response may ultimately emerge.

Even if reliable means were found to identify the intelligent, imaginative, and potentially creative student, there would remain an area of judgment which no objective instrument could reach. Imagination has been likened to a "twilight zone" between the end of the receptive process and the beginning of the expressive one. Once that "twilight zone" has been entered, critical perceptions and evaluations come into play.

Accurate identification of the gifted art student necessarily involves observation not only of his working process, but also of the tangible product—drawing, painting, sculpture, or the like. Here, real judgments can be made only by the competent and knowledgeable artist or art teacher. No evaluation can be made by direct comparison with the work of the adult artist, but there are at least two overt characteristics that can be looked for:

1. A persistence of interest in the visual arts—not merely in their technical but in their creative and experimental aspects; a tendency to reject stereotyped solutions and to seek out novel (but not necessarily successful) means

2. A persistence of expressive effort; a longer-than-normal attention span; a capacity for independent, self-motivated work

A marked gift in creative art will of course be typically associated with other gifts and with superior intelligence. It will come to fruition only if combined with a willingness to hold values often in conflict with those of the school or society.

The high school counselor can contribute to the development of young people with art talent. He should see that, in addition to a competent art teacher and art program, the following are provided: (a) extracurricular activities that afford opportunity for the self-expression of the interested and able; (b) some means of obtaining counsel from serious local artists, nearby college art faculties, or both; and (c) opportunity for the students to visit college art departments to receive counsel and observe classes and student work.

# 11 THE RECOGNITION OF TALENT IN SCIENCE

*PAUL BRANDWEIN*

*Senior General Editor, Harcourt, Brace and Company, and Director of Education, Conservation Foundation*

Educators have given increasing attention in recent years to the identification of science talent among students. As a result, a body of data has evolved about the characteristics of the science-prone student.

The data support the following three propositions:

1. There now exists a body of knowledge sufficient to enable interested teachers at the high school level to identify students with high-level ability in science.

2. There now exists a sufficiently large accumulation of tested methods at the high school level to enable interested teachers to furnish opportunities to students with high-level ability in science, so that these students may be stimulated to enter scientific careers.

3. There now exists a body of recommendations concerning the first two of these propositions that require thought and action—especially action.

In regard to the first proposition, useful information about identifying talent in science may be acquired from a number of sets of experience. The following* are examples:

1. The special experiences gained by high schools throughout the country and described in various publications (95).

2. The experiences gained by the Cleveland (Ohio) Board of Education in conducting its Major Work Program, and the Portland (Oregon) experiment with the gifted.

3. The experience gained by high school teachers whose students have had continued and marked success in science. (There are also the special experiences of teachers whose students have been suc-

---

*These are in no way inclusive, but merely selected references.

cessful in the various science scholarship examinations. Lists of such teachers are available. For instance, the names of teachers who have had considerable success in the Westinghouse Science Talent Search may be obtained from the offices of Science Service, Washington, D. C.)

4. The experience gained by participants in the National Science Teachers Association project, Future Scientists of America (planned to stimulate activities for students with interests in science).

5. The experience gained by the examiners who have prepared and conducted examinations for the Westinghouse Science Talent Search, the Bausch and Lomb scholarships, the College Entrance Examination Board's science testing, the National Merit Scholarships, and others. (Studies already exist which relate success in these examinations to success in college and future research work. Similar studies relate achievement in high school to science achievement in college.)

6. The experiences gained by the College Entrance Examination Board and the Educational Testing Service in devising a *Test of Understanding and Reasoning in Science*. (Early forms of this test have been used with some success in identifying students with high-level ability in science. There is also the experience gained through statewide testing in Oklahoma by Science Research Associates. Able students who might otherwise have been missed were identified.)

7. Experience gained by investigations of giftedness in general: for example Hollingworth (110), Terman (233), Witty (256); of the origins of scientists: Knapp and Goodrich (128), Roe (202); of the nature of creativity: Roe (202), Barran (13); and of the nature of high-level ability in science in the adolescent years: Brandwein (22, 23, 24, 25).

8. Experience gained through operational research such as the North Central Association Superior and Talented Student Project (175).

These are just a few of the experiences that could be examined to gain perspective on the identification of students with high-level science ability. When present methods of identification are analyzed, it becomes apparent that we tend to predict ability in science on the basis of high verbal and mathematical ability. Indeed, we almost equate ability in science with developed ability in the verbal and mathematical areas. Although high general intelligence (including verbal and mathematical ability) is a part of high-level ability in science, it is definitely not the only characteristic of such ability. The other characteristics are designated by the writer as the *predisposing factor†* and *the activating factor*.

The *predisposing factor,* as we have used it, is observed in scientifically talented young people as they work in the face of discomfort (illness, failure, opposition, or disapproval). Emotionally involved, they remain dissatisfied with the results of their endeavors. In short, these youngsters are highly motivated.

Besides developed ability in verbal and mathematical areas (intellectual involvement) and the predisposing factor (emotional involvement and motivation), the *activating factor* must operate for the scientifically talented youngster. That is, the youngster must have the opportunity to express himself in science; his interest must be activated by the opportunity to work; his vast intellectual appetite must be nourished by an expert dietitian—the teacher.

Even if we lack methods of identifying the scientifically gifted student, these students will grasp the opportunity to work creatively, if the opportunity is made readily available. They will, in short *identify themselves*; they will ask for recognition. They will place themselves in a position to be stimulated, to go on to college, and to take advantage of opportunities.

Anyone who studies methods of dealing with students who are gifted, talented, or science-prone (those with highly developed abilities in science that are the result of the interaction of heredity and environment) knows that the problem is being attacked with some success in certain areas identified with the schools' endeavors to educate their young people.

Imagine that there was a fifteen-year-old lad who could easily run the 100-yard dash in twelve seconds. What would be done? He would be developed; he would practice after school; he would be coached carefully; his parents would co-operate with eagerness and care; his school and his community would be proud. We build stadiums for such people.

Very few would say of this runner: "According to our curriculum he has to run the 100-yard dash in twenty seconds in the ninth

---

†The jargon may be discarded, but "drive" is not a satisfactory substitute.

grade; in fifteen seconds in the tenth grade; in twelve seconds in the eleventh grade. Only in the twelfth grade may he run the race in ten seconds. He should take these courses: 100-Yard Dash I, 100-Yard Dash II, and 100-Yard Dash III, in sequence." This, however, is precisely what we do to science-prone youngsters. They are forced to follow the same curriculum that others follow. We acknowledge their abilities by awarding them high grades in the regular courses; but we do not generally award them any special opportunity, as is done in art, music, and athletics.

This does not mean that either acceleration or enrichment is sure to develop scientific aptitude. As one examines today's courses in science and mathematics and the way they are generally taught, it soon becomes evident that they are a history of science—an analysis of the past to shed light on the future. It is necessary for young people to read history in textbooks and to repeat experiments by way of workbook and manual; for the knowledge gained is essential to the preparation of all cultured men, whether they are artists, scientists, or mathematicians. A course in great experiments, great natural laws, or great scientific principles (our present courses in science and mathematics) is just as valuable as a course in great books. However, this is hardly sufficient. In essence, one becomes a writer by writing, a painter by painting, a scientist by "sciencing," and a mathematician by "mathematizing." The earlier one writes, paints, "sciences," or "mathematizes," the earlier he begins to create and become competent in his field. A course in which youngsters have an opportunity to create prepares our science-prone students—who are expected to become, among other things, our "doers" or "creative minds," our innovators and inventors—for a future in science. To originate, it seems clear, one should practice originating. It is entirely possible, practical, and desirable to give students the opportunity to do *original investigating* at the high school level. This "course" might well last throughout the years of high school, and would be a "course" (or a course in investigation of science) that would run concurrently with the usual courses in the history of science—for example, general science, biology, chemistry and physics. Recognition of talent in science must be supplemented by giving youngsters the opportunity to do original work in courses in science; it must go beyond merely acknowledging their special ability in courses in the history of science.

There is no single practice for encouraging scientifically talented students which would be appropriate for all the schools in the United States. Nevertheless, several useful practices (130) have already been developed, and other practices are being experimented with.

The basic assumption underlying the provision of special opportunities for young people talented in science is that when opportunities for high-level work in science are available, young stars with interests in science and with high-level ability will come forward and identify themselves. The important follow-up to this self-identification is the *mating* of those who have shown themselves to be gifted with additional and more demanding opportunities for scientific development.

# SECTION IV

## PROGRAM ORGANIZATION

This section is concerned with the organization of programs for superior students. In order to succeed, a superior student program must be carefully organized and administered. When every faculty member has a part in its development, understands the plan for a program, and assumes responsibility for the maximum development of each identified student, an environment will have been established that is conducive to the successful operation of the program.

The point of such programs is not to coddle students or to take over their responsibilities and obligations, but rather to challenge them to function at the level of their abilities, interests, and aspirations. On this basis, a program can be developed that will provide for the optimum intellectual and emotional development of each student. Each faculty member has a function to perform: to assist each identified student to achieve the purposes of the program within its framework and structure.

There are three basic administrative approaches that have been used to place superior students in situations where the instruction will be at a more appropriate level or of a more appropriate kind: acceleration, ability grouping, and enrichment. Traditionally the method of providing for superior students has been acceleration of grade placement. Recently the most popular plan has been classroom enrichment. Surveys of current programs, however, show that more schools are moving toward ability grouping, with the better programs providing for enriched and challenging instruction within these selected groups.

Regardless of the administrative organizational pattern, a superior student program must have certain essentials:

1. The program must be built within the total fabric of the school. It will be most effective if it is developed and integrated as part of the total school, rather than as a separate entity outside the context of the school's educational philosophy.

2. One member of the school must be given responsibility for the operation of the program. Without such centralization of responsibility a continuous and systematic program will not be possible.

3. Basic information about each student in the school must be gathered. Effective program design depends on knowledge of each student's background, experiences, abilities, and aspirations.

4. School-wide resources and personnel must be assessed in terms of the contribution they can make to the program. Techniques and methods for utilizing the resources and personnel must be developed.

5. An adequate system of records is essential, including (for each student) the results of individual inventories, cumulative records of school grades and attendance, test scores, reports of home and family conditions, and remarks about progress and curricular experiences.

6. Teachers for the program must be carefully selected. A teacher must respect individual differences among superior students; he must have the ability to challenge such students, and naturally must not feel threatened by their penetrating questions.

7. Any administrative device—that is, enrichment, acceleration, or special grouping—selected by the school must stimulate and extend the interests of superior students and challenge their abilities. The program must utilize a wide variety of appropriate materials, since they are the means of teaching or building a feeling of responsibility and self-reliance in students.

8. Community resources and agencies must be inventoried and used to extend the experiences of the talented students. Free and frequent exchange of ideas, information, and services must be encouraged between the school and the community.

Which administrative device—acceleration, enrichment, or ability grouping—can most productively and appropriately order and significantly illuminate subject matter for superior and talented students? This challenging question must be approached scientifically, and its answer worked out according to the specific characteristics of the groups of gifted students under consideration. The best approach will often be a combination of all three devices: acceleration, enrichment, and ability grouping.

The nature of the superior student, the learning process, and the learning situation (including the teacher and the psychological climate of the classroom) all have implications for the educator in establishing a program to challenge the gifted. Educational practices for the superior student should be consistent with the school's educational philosophy and should be set up with reference to the total school and community situation. Too many superior student programs, organized on a pattern that was successful in another school, have disregarded the particular needs and characteristics of their own students, parents, and communities.

In the first chapter in this section, Chapter 12, Robert DeHaan deals with the factors essential to building and developing a program for superior students that is a vital force in the school. He expresses the need for co-operation among teachers, counselors, and administrators. He anticipates that this co-operation will effect an integration of the total resources of the school and community. This co-operation will enable the school to experiment with different methods and make imaginative use of all its personnel and resources in the process of building a program for superior students.

In Chapter 13, Jack Kough discusses the administrative provisions for the gifted. He delineates the three broad administrative approaches and treats the advantages, disadvantages, materials, methods, and practices of each one. His descriptions and practical suggestions will assist educators who are investigating the various administrative approaches.

Willard Abraham, in Chapter 14, offers some guidelines for program development. He points out that a school's program must be consistent with its philosophy and goals and that each staff member should be able to relate to specific functions within the program. Abraham emphasizes that a school should: (1) formulate the philosophy and objectives of its superior student program *before* organizing the program into basic functions, and (2) organize basic functions so that the program is effectively co-ordinated, understood by all concerned, and adequately implemented.

# 12 ESSENTIALS OF A TALENT DEVELOPMENT PROGRAM

ROBERT F. DeHAAN

*Chairman, Department of Psychology,*
*Hope College, Holland, Michigan*

Most educators agree that it is necessary and desirable to reassess and improve the educational opportunities for gifted and talented students. The purpose of this paper is to outline some of the essential elements of a program designed to meet the needs of these students.

## FINDING A DESCRIPTIVE TERM FOR GIFTEDNESS

It is difficult to find a suitable term to designate students whom we ordinarily call gifted students. Teachers and parents often react strongly against the term "gifted child." "Gifted student" or "gifted child" implies that there is a higher human value attached to these students than to average or slow students. It also implies that the gifted deserve a preferred position on the educational scene and should have superior education.

Educators need a better descriptive term for giftedness, one that is acceptable to teachers and parents. The author suggests "students with gifts." This designation, although a little clumsy, does indicate that primarily, students are to be valued as persons and not for the gifts or potentialities that they possess.

## OUTLINING OBJECTIVES FOR THE PROGRAM

What kinds of persons do we wish our talented students to become? What skills, understanding, and attitudes do we wish them to attain? What do we want them to achieve? When educators seriously consider such questions as these, they are in effect setting up the educational objectives or goals for their talent development program. The more explicitly these objectives are stated, the more they will influence what is done in the program. Furthermore, when objectives are explicitly stated, it becomes possible to measure at a later date whether or not, or to what degree, they have been attained.

Objectives should be stated in behavioral terms and in terms of the end product of the educational endeavor, namely the student. Teachers sometimes confuse goals with methods when formulating their objectives. Although the two are never completely discrete, it is desirable to state goals in terms of what the student will be able to achieve. Methods should be stated in terms of what the teacher will do to make such achievement possible.

Both long-range and short-range objectives should be established, with deadlines and timetables for meeting the objectives, including regular times for critical review of progress.

## ESTABLISHING A BROAD, GENEROUS DEFINITION OF TALENT

There are many different kinds of talent, and the definition of giftedness adopted by a school should include a wide spectrum of talents. Too often educators have dealt with only a narrow definition of talent—that is, in terms of IQ alone. This excludes some children who need special attention but who may not receive it because their IQ does not measure up to a certain criterion.

There are several talents that make up the spectrum. From the school's point of view, academic aptitude is probably one of the most important. High academic aptitude consists of unusual verbal skills, numerical ability, memory, and reasoning ability. Academic aptitude is sometimes mistakenly regarded as an indication of general intellectual ability. It is probably more accurate, however, to think of it as a rather specific ability—the ability to do the kinds of tasks that are required in a school situation.

Closely allied to academic abilities are the abilities that go into the making of a scientist. Scientists generally have the abilities listed above, focused by a deep and abiding interest in the study of nature.

Another important set of abilities might be called creative abilities. These abilities consist of such personal and mental traits as flexibility in thinking, ideational fluency, associational fluency, and originality.

Leadership consists of a set of loosely correlated aptitudes which enable one person to influence other people. Leadership ability, sometimes called social power, is an important aptitude that should be dealt with in an educational program designed for students with gifts.

Artistic talent is another family of talents. Students differ in their abilities in the visual and plastic arts and in their abilities to write creatively, to act, and to compose and perform music. These aptitudes also belong to the spectrum of human talent.

The practical arts—such as craftsmanship, mechanical skill, and physical ability—should also be included in a complete compendium of gifts and talents.

There is no universal definition of giftedness. Educators may wish to include in their own operating definition whatever aptitudes or abilities seem important to them in terms of their school's values, the resources of the school, and the nature of the community. When a question arises as to which talents a school should select to be developed in an educational program, educators might well decide, on the basis of the historical significance of such aptitudes in human culture, the value that is placed on such aptitudes in contemporary society, and the contribution of such a talent to a full life for the individual.

Educators should concern themselves with as wide a spectrum of giftedness as possible. They should also develop a generous definition of talent. That is, the program should not be limited to the top segment (for example, the top 1 per cent) of students; youngsters with lesser degrees of talent should also be included. Schools concerned with students whose abilities appear to be in the upper 10 to 25 per cent of the population will probably develop more satisfactory programs than schools that are concerned with only the upper 1 or .5 per cent.

## PROVIDING FOR SYSTEMATIC, CONTINUOUS SCREENING

Talents do not spring forth full-blown, but must be discovered and nurtured. Discovering talents is an active educational process. A warm, accepting relationship between adult and young person is necessary for the nurturing and maturation of most talents. Some teachers, however, wait passively for talents to appear. This is a mistake, since latent talents often need to be coaxed into existence.

Ideally speaking, screening for talents should begin in kindergarten on the first day a child enters school and should continue throughout the student's educational career. Certain students may be "late bloomers," whose aptitudes do not display themselves until fairly late in their educational careers. Every teacher should be continually on the lookout for signs of talent in each student.

Actually, teachers are talent scouts. Each teacher sees a particular student in a somewhat different perspective. Students react differently to each teacher. Perhaps this difference in response may account for some students' being late bloomers. A relationship with a particular teacher may be just what is needed to bring out latent talent in a given student. Broadly speaking, there are two major systematic methods for discovering talent, plus an intermediate third method. The first method is by objective tests; the second is by teacher observations; and the third is by informal testing situations constructed by the teacher.

## Standardized Tests

Objective tests are probably the best instruments for discovering academic talent. Intelligence tests and academic achievement tests administered throughout the career of a student will probably do the most satisfactory job of detecting academic ability. The results of objective tests, plus academic grades of the students, can now be used in the eighth grade to predict, with a fair degree of accuracy, a student's college achievement.

## Teacher Observations

Standardized tests of creative ability, leadership, talent in the fine arts, and ability in the practical arts are not nearly as well developed as tests of academic aptitude. For all practical purposes, such tests do not exist; teachers themselves must make special note of abilities in the nonacademic areas of talent. Teachers need assistance, however, in carrying out this assignment. They need to know what kinds of behaviors to look for. They need to be helped to recognize their own personal bias in dealing with pupils, so that no talented students will be overlooked.

It is a common practice in industry for supervisors to rate their subordinates. Studies have indicated that when the supervisor is interested in rating and does his rating carefully, when he is well adjusted personally, when he is sympathetic and understanding of people, when he is aware of his own capabilities and limitations, and when he is trained and experienced, he will do a good job of rating. These characteristics of a good rater can apply to teachers as well.

## Informal Testing Situations

Informal testing situations supplement the teacher's observations and are especially useful in discovering talents in the arts, social relations, and practical skills. It is important, in such informal tests, to develop a method of rating a student's work objectively. This requires time, but situations tests will richly repay the school that introduces them. Not only do they help discover talents in students, but also they are generally good teaching devices.

## TEACHERS' RESPONSIBILITIES

It is important for all teachers to study the characteristics of students with gifts. Especially important is the problem presented by the underachieving pupil. Such pupils present a real challenge to the ingenuity and perseverance of a teacher.

Often teachers expect a predetermined answer to their question of *what to do* for their gifted pupils. Such an answer is not possible. Teachers themselves can usually discover *what to do,* however, by studying the characteristics of their bright and talented students. The answer often suggests itself as teachers get to know their students better.

Teachers need technical help from guidance, curriculum, and administrative consultants in carrying out their part of the program for the development of talent. A summer workshop and a year-long in-service program are two of the best ways to insure intensive study of the needs and capacities of the students with gifts. Modifying the curriculum for the better students cannot be done at odd moments of the teacher's day. Teachers need to study the curriculum as intensively as they study students. This requires time and effort over an extended period, with the help of guidance, curriculum, and administrative personnel.

# THE METHODS OF CLASSROOM ENRICHMENT, SPECIAL GROUPING, AND ACCELERATION

The heart of the problem of developing talent in students is the selection and organization of learning experiences that will pace the learner at an optimum rate of advance in areas of learning (besides the common learnings) in which he has special abilities. Such learning experiences are loosely called enrichment. Enrichment consists of learning experiences that are advanced, that require mental functions more complex than average, that require greater than average speed at higher levels of generalization and abstraction, and that are designed with the needs and capabilities of particular students in mind.

Enrichment can be carried out within the classroom without help from outside, in special groups set up for special learning experiences, or by means of acceleration. A school system that flexibly uses all three of these methods will undoubtedly have a more successful program for developing talent than a school that dogmatically rejects some and holds to others.

## Classroom Enrichment

Classroom enrichment is the "work horse" for a program of special education for gifted and talented students. When a school system begins any program for students with gifts, every classroom and every teacher should become a part of it. This means that in their own classrooms teachers should make a special effort to satisfy the needs and capabilities of more advanced students. Responsibility for doing so should not be shifted to other teachers and special groups.

Minimum classroom enrichment can be provided by giving able students special projects and opportunities to advance into more complex and more challenging work that they can handle with a minimum of supervision. Students can do this work, either alone or in small groups, after completing their regular assignments. Such enrichment is tacked on, so to speak, to the regular curriculum.

A more meaningful kind of enrichment consists in modifying the whole concept of the regular assignment, and substituting for it a concept of the assignment tailored to the learning style and pace of the individual student. If this were done, enrichment would become an integral part of the assignment, for gifted students and for other students as well.

Obviously, it takes a well-qualified teacher to integrate enrichment into the curriculum. Classroom enrichment is easy to administer from the principal's point of view. It requires practically no schedule or room changing. It has the disadvantage, however, of being difficult for the teacher to manage in a large class and in classes with wide diversity of talents. Thus, although it is desirable for every teacher to carry out enrichment in her classroom, by itself enrichment is probably not sufficient for a complete program of educating talented students.

## Special Grouping

Special grouping is the second important administrative method of arranging for the education of students with gifts. The purpose of special grouping should be to provide learning experiences that for some reason cannot be provided in the regular classroom. Special grouping ranges all the way from a small, temporary committee whose task is to prepare a special report, to a large, specialized career school, such as the Bronx High School of Science in New York City.

## Acceleration

Acceleration, the third method of providing advanced learning experiences for students with gifts, is designed to pace the learner at a faster rate than rigid grade-level organization allows. Some examples of acceleration are: early entrance into kindergarten or first grade, flexible grade arrangements that permit three years work to be completed in two years, and early entrance into college.

# USING AUXILIARY EDUCATIONAL SERVICES

Classroom teaching of students with talents needs to be supplemented by the other educational facilities available to schools—particularly the family, guidance services, and educational facilities in the community.

Educators must impress parents more effectively than they have regarding parents' roles in the education of their own children. Parents can probably do much more than they are presently doing to stimulate their youngsters intellectually and to motivate them to desire education. The most important source of motivation for youngsters to go to college appears to be the family. Also, recent studies indicate that parents can do a great deal consciously to instil in their children motivation to achieve. When schools discover youngsters with talent, parents should be brought into the long-range planning for such youngsters and encouraged to do everything they can to enhance each youngster's education at home.

The guidance and counseling services of the school are also important in helping students with gifts plan their educational programs and vocational careers. The vocational guidance of students with many talents is sometimes rather difficult because there are so many choices they might make. These students should be given a great deal of time to think over their choices. It is probably best for them not to settle quickly upon a choice, but rather to leave their choice open to a broad family of vocations.

The community also offers some unusual opportunities for enhancing the education of students with talent. The science seminars sponsored by the Joe Berg Foundation* are perhaps the most concerted effort made yet to utilize community resources to enrich the science program of students. The pattern set by this program can be followed in other areas of talent development, such as art and social science.

## CONTINUAL PROGRAM ASSESSMENT

The educational program for talented students should be continually and carefully examined for areas that need improvement. This evaluation should be based on clear objectives outlined early in the program. No evaluation is possible unless the educators have decided beforehand what their program should be and what their students should attain, and unless at the outset they have established plans for such evaluation. Only with such plans (preferably represented by a carefully delineated research design) can a program be measured and a decision be made as to whether or not the original objectives have been achieved.

*See "An Action Program in Science for Superior and Talented Students," p. 295.

# 13 ADMINISTRATIVE PROVISIONS FOR THE GIFTED

JACK KOUGH
*Vice-President, Science Research Associates*

If an educator is to provide intelligently for the gifted in his own school, he should know about the educational techniques that have proved helpful in other communities. Current gifted child literature may only confuse the earnest educator. When he learns of the multitude of school activities for gifted children, he may find it difficult to decide what kind of program would be most appropriate in his own system. This chapter is designed to dispel such confusion and give the busy educator an overview of gifted child programs.

There are many different approaches to helping gifted children, but all of them are based on three major administrative arrangements. We shall examine these various approaches, first in outline form, then in some detail. The educator will thus be able to survey the various programs and possibilities at a glance, and then to consider each program and how it might work in a particular school system.

The basic administrative arrangements that may be used for gifted child programing are:

    I. Classroom enrichment
    II. Grouping
        A. Specialized schools
        B. Special classes in regular schools
            1. Classes recruited from one school
            2. Classes recruited from several schools
        C. Special groups for only part of the school day
            1. Grouping in the curricular areas
                a. Multitrack programs

This chapter is reprinted from Jack Kough, *Practical Programs for the Gifted* (Chicago: Science Research Associates, Inc., 1960), Chapter 2.

        b. Honors courses

        c. High school seminars

        d. Special courses

     2. Grouping for noncurricular school activities

  D. Grouping for out-of-school activities

  E. Grouping within the regular classroom

III. Acceleration

  A. Skipping of grades

  B. Early admission to the education program

     1. Early admission to kindergarten or first grade

     2. Early admission to college

  C. More rapid progress through the normal educational sequence

     1. Ungraded primary

     2. Two grades combined in one, or three in two

     3. Advanced placement program

     4. Extra courses for extra credit

     5. Credit by examination

A short description of each of these administrative arrangements follows.

## CLASSROOM ENRICHMENT

The most widely used technique for encouraging the gifted student is to provide him with an educational diet richer than that of other students in the same classroom. The bright youngster remains in the classroom with other youngsters of less ability but is given special attention, either individually or in a small group of gifted students in his class. This type of program is generally called classroom enrichment, as distinct from ability grouping and acceleration.

In a certain sense every form of helping the gifted involves enrichment. All programs for the gifted are designed as an intellectual challenge to the rapid learners. Classroom enrichment, however, has come to mean particularly a program designed for gifted students who remain within their usual age-grade group.

The classroom teacher may make modifications in his instructional program in two ways in order to challenge his gifted students. First, he can provide opportunities to explore more deeply any subject being studied by the class. In a unit on the American Indian, for instance, the gifted youngster may go further in exploring Indian legends or the present condition of Indians in the United States. This method gives depth to the child's learning experiences. Or, the teacher can provide breadth by assigning subjects that are not normally covered in the classroom, including completely new fields, such as foreign languages.

It is important to remember that enrichment opportunities in depth and breadth are provided *in addition to regular classroom work*. The classroom teacher who enriches the educational diet of the brighter youngsters also must be sure that these youngsters acquire the normal skills and the required information taught in that grade. The gifted students probably will master such learnings very rapidly; some may have done so even before entering the class.

Enrichment does *not* mean adding more of the same kind of materials or activities to the child's program. It does not mean, for example, that the gifted boy or girl should work thirty of the same type of mathematical problems while the average child does fifteen or twenty. The gifted child may develop the requisite skill by working only three or four problems. Classroom enrichment *does* mean that in the same classroom, with children of varying abilities and interests, the gifted child is provided with a greater variety of new learning situations, materials, and activities to give him the depth and range of educational experience that he requires for his fullest development.

## Advantages of Classroom Enrichment

The decision to use classroom enrichment as the fundamental technique for helping the gifted child is often based on very practical administrative considerations. In most smaller schools it is impossible to have special classes for the gifted and it may be difficult to work out an acceleration program that allows the best students to move more rapidly. Even in larger schools the enrichment program has many advantages. Enrichment within the regular classroom requires few if any additional expenditures or administrative alterations.

Another advantage—the most important for the total class—is that an enrichment program allows the gifted students to stimulate the other students intellectually and even to assist in the teaching process. Those who favor classroom enrichment feel that the presence of gifted children in a classroom tends to lift the intellectual level of all classroom activities.

Proponents of classroom enrichment also argue that the child who is bright is not necessarily more advanced physically and socially. Therefore he is more comfortable, both emotionally and socially, if he remains with his own age group.

Another argument for classroom enrichment is the philosophical one that it is more democratic than other administrative provisions for the gifted. It does not segregate the gifted child, but enables him to develop in a real-life situation among those of differing abilities.

Still another advantage claimed for classroom enrichment is that it often is the first major step toward more individual instruction for all the students in the class. Any teacher who learns to enrich the curriculum adequately for bright youngsters is learning how to individualize instruction and he should be able to apply this learning in teaching average and slow youngsters.

Some teachers and administrators favor classroom enrichment because they feel that within this general technique it is possible to use methods that are equivalent to grouping and acceleration: to group the top students in the class for some areas of curriculum work, or to accelerate the learning experience of individuals within the classroom.

## Disadvantages of Classroom Enrichment

Those who feel that classroom enrichment is not adequate question whether it is really democratic to lump together all youngsters simply because they happen to fall within the same age span. They argue that classroom enrichment, theoretically sound though it may be, usually forces both the bright youngster and the slow one into the pattern of the average student. The bright youngster, then, is bored and does not achieve to his full capacity, while the slow one is frustrated because he cannot meet the class standards.

Those who oppose classroom enrichment discount its democratic value because they feel that home and community contacts allow gifted youngsters adequate opportunity to develop healthy social attitudes.

Others point out that a gifted child in a group of average children may develop a sense of superiority because of the ease with which he can excel, whereas if the gifted student studies and competes with other bright youngsters he will gain better perspective of his own abilities.

The greatest disadvantage of the classroom enrichment approach, however, is the heavy burden it places on the teacher. Extra time is required to detect those students who are gifted, extra ingenuity is called for to make curriculum adjustments. If a teacher is not able to meet these demands on his time and ingenuity, or is not adequate in intellectual ability and training, the gifted children in that classroom probably will not receive any real help. In an age of specialization, opponents of classroom enrichment say, the need for teachers specializing in work with the gifted should be recognized.

Even if a teacher does try to make modifications for the gifted, most teacher time and help must be devoted to those who are having difficulty learning the skills they are expected to have in that grade. Thus the slow learners will take a disproportionate amount of the classroom teacher's time and attention, while the rapid learners will receive a minimum amount of help. In such a situation the gifted student may miss important learning opportunities, may not be adequately motivated, and may develop poor work habits.

## Evaluating a Classroom Enrichment Program

Since it is difficult to measure the effectiveness of a classroom enrichment program, this technique has sometimes been called an educational smoke screen. This smoke screen may conceal the fact that many school systems actually are doing very little for the gifted child. Almost any school administrator can praise some teacher and the wonderful work he is doing with a particular youngster. He can indicate the "results" of classroom enrichment in his school, but this "case study proof" does not necessarily mean that the school has a classroom enrichment program to meet the needs of all the gifted students.

The following yardsticks may be applied to determine whether a school has an organized classroom enrichment program or a mere smoke screen:

1. Has each classroom teacher identified and listed the students who are gifted? If teachers are unable to do this, a well-planned classroom enrichment program is not operating. If only some of the teachers have done it, the gifted child program is not reaching all of the gifted youngsters in the school.

2. Can each classroom teacher describe the specific curriculum modification being made for each bright youngster? Again, if each teacher cannot do this, there is not a complete classroom enrichment program.

3. Does some person have supervisory responsibility for the entire program? Such a person may help classroom teachers in the identification process and provide motivation, ideas, and materials as the program progresses.

## Classroom Enrichment—a Total School Program

An effective classroom enrichment program involves the entire school staff. Since there are likely to be gifted children in every classroom, every member of the staff must be familiar with the total school program, its methods, and its goals. Teachers with specialized training, or those who have shared responsibility for developing and implementing an enrichment program, may act as consultants to help other teachers plan and sustain enrichment programs in their own classrooms or subject areas. At regular intervals opportunity should be provided for the exchange of ideas and practices. Teachers should be encouraged and assisted to appraise their own class programs as well as that of the school as a whole.

## Classroom Enrichment in the Elementary School

*Classroom organization.* The physical arrangement of the classroom is an important aspect of any enrichment program. Movable desks that can be arranged to facilitate special work groups give the teacher more freedom in planning study arrangements. Tables that accommodate four or five students who may be working on a special project allow children enough room and privacy to work freely. Such subgrouping is especially important for classroom enrichment in large classrooms.

Children may be divided into subgroups for regular study assignments, for committee work or special enrichment activities, or as a permanent arrangement for working within the regular classroom curriculum. Grouping within the classroom has two effects: by decreasing the size of the study group, it enables the teacher to spread his time more effectively; and it gives students the opportunity to work with others at their own interest and ability levels.

In some classes the teacher will work with gifted students individually rather than in small groups. Special emphasis will vary for each classroom, depending on the students' interests and abilities and the teacher's special preferences and talents.

In the elementary school the particular topic studied is frequently not as important as the specific skills or set of skills developed. Thus, whether to study Australia or China as a unit in social studies is not nearly as important as how to provide individual pupils with opportunities for intensive experience in the methods social scientists use in solving problems confronting them. The goal is to develop an inquiring mind.

*Materials.* The classroom can become a treasure chest of exciting ideas for children of all levels of ability, and also provide a starting point for helping the child with superior learning ability and wide-ranging interests. Interest corners may be built around selected interest areas. Maps, charts, pictures of distant lands, bas-relief re-creations of ancient cities—all help to extend children's experience in new directions. The most important source of enrichment can be the classroom library. Books should be of various types: art, poetry, fiction, non-fiction, and biography. Encyclopedias, dictionaries, and other reference books also should be immediately available to all students. The teacher should encourage the use of these books to help open new avenues of interest and stimulation.

*Curriculum.* Once the stage is set for a classroom enrichment program, the next important step is to review the curriculum. For an effective enrichment program, the curriculum should aid in the development of the initiative and creative ability of those children who in an ordinary classroom situation would not extend themselves intellectually.

On the elementary level certain basic skills such as arithmetic, reading, grammar, and spelling must be taught. When teaching these skills, many teachers prefer the bilevel curriculum method. The bilevel method involves two programs with two sets of materials: one set for the gifted group and another for the regular class. Both programs operate in the classroom at the same time. (In some classrooms a third level may be added for students with learning difficulties.) Especially useful in such programs are multilevel curriculum materials published by commercial companies. With such materials, students start at their own level and progress as fast and as far as their learning capacity allows.

A number of research studies have shown that learning which grows out of a child's own experience is greater and more lasting in value to the child than learning which is adult imposed. To capitalize on these findings, many schools have developed special curriculum units which correlate students' interests and the regular study program. This unit method provides the most flexible base for a classroom enrichment program. The unit offers a wide range of varying activities in which each student may participate as fully as his capabilities permit.

For example, a seventh-grade unit that has as its purpose acquainting students with the physical characteristics and governmental structure of the city in which they live can complement work in the basic subject areas and provide long-range activities for the classroom. Trips to museums, industries, and city buildings broaden students' interests and their understanding of their city. Gifted students may be encouraged to develop their own special projects as suggested by the unit.

In one school where such a unit was offered, the high-ability group worked on a group research project to report on the origin, structure, and growth of their city's major industry. The project involved a great deal of outside research, visits to the plant, and preparation of reports for class presentation. While the entire class worked on the general unit, the gifted children explored this one avenue much further.

Such projects introduce to the gifted students the methods of research, analysis, and reporting. These students learn the value of good work habits and of co-operating with others to complete a project. They learn to use primary sources, to gather and evaluate various kinds of data, to set standards for judgment, to view their own work critically, and to accept the criticism of other students in the group.

The teacher who does not use the unit method of teaching can also make provisions for the brighter student. If a fairly rigid curricular sequence is followed, the gifted children should be allowed to complete the basic work of any day or week as rapidly as they can while still maintaining high standards. The extra time should then be devoted to special enrichment activities.

Success or failure of classroom enrichment on the elementary level depends largely on the enthusiasm, ingenuity, and interest of the teacher and administrator. Thousands of gifted children never develop their talents because of the absence of adequate enrichment in their schools.

## Classroom Enrichment in the Secondary Schools

Because education on the secondary level is curriculum-centered rather than a skill-learning process, enrichment is more easily incorporated into the program. The curriculum at this level is flexible enough to be broadened and extended to meet the educational requirements of any student.

Many classes in large secondary schools are actually ability groups. For instance, an advanced chemistry course is usually elected only by above-average pupils. This situation permits an intelligent inquiry into any subject area by the research method (isolating the problem, setting up hypotheses, collecting and organizing data, arriving at tentative conclusions, and evaluation). It also emphasizes the importance of discussion and group exchange techniques and the interrelation of the disciplines in making analyses.

The research method and the process of creative thinking give direction to study in any subject area and enable students to see relationships between subject areas. In social studies, for example, economic, political, and sociological problems can be dramatized through study of literature and the visual arts. Superior students in a social studies class might find John Steinbeck's *Grapes of Wrath* or the motion picture *Friendly Persuasion* exciting study material in exploring divergent economic, political, and social realities.

In a world history class, a group of students might form a current events forum to review political problems for the class. Mock United Nations sessions and "Meet the Press" round-table discussions enable gifted secondary school students to explore topics of current interest and to find an outlet for their ingenuity. Simultaneously the entire class becomes geared to a higher level of study activity. Students can begin to comprehend, through their own research and the analysis of fellow students, the relativity of facts and ideas; they learn to approach any conclusions critically, to respect views founded on values other than their own, and to regard any "answer" as open to further inquiry.

Foreign languages and the sciences are perhaps the subjects most frequently selected for broadening the educational experience of superior students on the secondary level, since top students usually elect these subjects. Ability grouping often occurs automatically, eliminating most of the students who have not the ability and interest to continue academic training beyond high school.

Foreign language programs can be enhanced for the superior student when emphasis is placed on learning to speak and understand a language as well as to read and write it. Such enriched foreign language programs enable the student to acquire reading and writing fluency with greater ease. At the advanced high school level the superior student may be encouraged to read in a foreign language literature which deals with a subject of special appeal to him.

Special honors groups within the regular classroom can provide gifted students with the opportunity for more intensive study in the subject field. Students in a freshman mathematics course, for example, can be encouraged to approach mathematics from a more creative point of view—as in the study of number systems, mathematical concepts and structure, and statistics. Honors groups in elementary English composition courses might study the fundamentals of logic—inference, induction, and analogy—as these apply to written statements. These special classroom groups are particularly important when a class includes students with a wide range of ability levels.

## GROUPING

Many educators feel that the best way to accommodate the needs of all students is to bring together students of similar ability for all or a portion of their educational experience. Such groups, in which the range of individual differences is reduced, permit teaching methods and learning experiences that are most appropriate to the ability level of the students.

Although the process of grouping has been called by many names (ability grouping, segregation, multilevel or multitrack curriculum, homogeneous grouping), the aim has always been to provide greater opportunities for students of similar intellectual capacity.

Some grouping is a normal part of most school programs. On the elementary level there is classroom grouping for curriculum work such as reading and for special activities or projects. On the secondary level there is subject grouping as well as the elective system, which automatically groups students of similar interests or abilities. Grouping as a superior student programing device, however, involves planned procedures for identifying gifted students and activities designed especially for this group.

## Advantages of Grouping

The most widely used argument in favor of special grouping is its efficiency both in facilitating learning and for in-service teacher training. Learning activities can be adapted to the individual student's needs. When placed with a group on his own intellectual level, the student is forced to appraise his own abilities more realistically and is motivated to work harder as a result; he is stimulated and challenged to progress beyond his age-grade level; he can explore new areas and exchange ideas with confidence of group acceptance rather than with fear of group rejection.

In a homogeneous ability group the teacher is able to intensify and enrich an area of learning and to bring greater depth to each student's educational experience. Total curriculum planning is simplified and individualized instruction facilitated in a group where abilities and interests are similar.

Many proponents of special grouping say that, in a country where individual achievement is encouraged and social and economic mobility are possible, the educational system must encourage the fullest development of its young people. This, they feel, can be achieved by grouping that enables every student to receive the educational experience best adapted to his intellectual abilities, aptitudes, and interests.

## Disadvantages of Grouping

Those who oppose grouping stress the possible danger of setting up an elite by singling out students for special attention. When the brightest students are removed from a class, there is a loss of stimulation that might have vitalized the learning experiences of less able children. The superior students, isolated from classmates of average ability, may become overly concerned with achievement and competition. Opponents of grouping fear that gifted students' personality development and social growth are threatened when they do not have the opportunity to develop their leadership traits in a heterogeneous group.

Many opponents feel that since special grouping frequently requires additional classrooms, extra materials, and specially trained teachers, many school systems cannot realistically meet its demands.

## Types of Grouping

*The specialized school.* In some communities there are separate schools for the gifted. In such schools academic requirements are considerably stiffened but the benefits of a normal school environment are maintained. There are often special schools for students with certain interests or abilities, such as schools of science or fine arts. Since separate facilities are feasible only where population is highly concentrated, special schools exist only in large metropolitan areas.

The New York City school system has four specialized, nonzoned high schools which admit qualified students living anywhere within the city limits. The Bronx High School of Science, along with the usual secondary curriculum, offers intensive studies in mathematics and science to students with appropriate interests and abilities. Students do extensive outside reading and research: they may take advanced courses under the Early Admission to College and Admission to College with Advanced Standing programs.

The Hunter College Elementary School in New York City, a public nursery, kindergarten, and six-year elementary school, is well known as a special school for gifted elementary children.

The University of Chicago Laboratory Schools offer a full twelve-year enrichment program, accelerated so that eight years of the regular public school curriculum are covered during the first seven years. Students are ready to enter college on completion of eleven years of study.

Admission to special schools is based on intelligence test scores, achievement test results, and special aptitude test scores, as well as on demonstration of social maturity and emotional stability.

Special schools such as the Hunter College Elementary School and the University of Chicago Laboratory Schools achieve a dual objective: they provide gifted youngsters with the kind of intensive and varied learning experiences they need to develop intellectually and creatively, and they operate as special training centers for teachers.

*Special classes in regular schools.* A second grouping method involves special classes for gifted students within the regular school. These classes form, in effect, a separate school experience within the physical facilities of the regular school. Gifted students are separated for all purposes, except perhaps in health education classes and in extracurricular and recreation activities.

*Classes recruited from one school*—In large metropolitan communities, gifted student groups can be drawn from the population of one school. In New York City, for example, eight high schools have special grouping in all subject areas for gifted students. When this is possible, transportation and administrative problems are minimal.

*Classes recruited from several schools*—In most communities there are not enough bright students in any one school to organize gifted child classes. In such communities gifted students from several schools are brought together to a centrally located school where a gifted child group has been established. The Cleveland Major Work Groups is a successful program of grouping gifted students recruited from several schools. Major Work students participate in all the noncurricular activities of their respective schools and maintain contact with other students.

Although this method requires some administrative modifications in terms of additional contact with parents, transportation planning, and other adjustments, the Cleveland experiment and similar programs demonstrate the feasibility of such a system for communities wishing to establish special gifted group classes.

*Special grouping for only part of the day.* The most common form of selective grouping is separation of gifted students into specialized groups for part of the school day. Students selected for special grouping spend a part of the day in the regular classroom with youngsters of varying abilities and the remainder of the day in special classes of gifted students. Gifted student classes may emphasize enrichment experiences either in the specific curriculum areas or through study outside the regular school curriculum.

*Grouping in the curricular areas*—Most part-time special grouping is in subject areas, such as mathematics, chemistry, English, and social studies.

The MULTITRACK PROGRAM, gaining momentum in American secondary education, enables a school to offer required courses on various levels of ability. The gifted students are in the top track and cover advanced material more rapidly than students in the other tracks. High school freshmen in a special history class, for example, may use a college-level history text, while students in regular freshman history use a ninth-grade text.

With the development of new multilevel learning materials for the elementary level, the multitrack system is coming into wider use in teaching basic skills and subject areas in the elementary school. Existing multilevel materials not only stimulate and challenge the gifted students but also provide successful learning experiences for students of less ability. As more multilevel materials are developed, the problems of individualized teaching for students of varying abilities will decrease.

HONORS COURSES in secondary schools and colleges allow gifted students to develop their talents and pursue advanced study in selected areas. Many schools offer continuing two- or three-year honors programs in mathematics and the sciences. Honors courses stress independent research and experimentation. In mathematics, for example, students may be encouraged to prepare and submit their own problems; in biology, physics, or chemistry, they may do extensive laboratory experimentation.

HIGH SCHOOL SEMINARS, which introduce methods of critical thinking, inquiry, and discussion in the study of history, English, and the social sciences, are becoming increasingly popular. As with honors courses, seminars are usually small and selective. Individuals have to meet certain ability or achievement requirements, or both, to participate in these more difficult academic experiences.

The variations of SPECIAL COURSE WORK for gifted students are innumerable. In a Chicago high school, for example, courses that combine English and social studies (an adaptation of college inter-departmental studies) are offered to gifted groups. Freshman English students use the *Foreign Relations Series* (booklets on foreign relations for high school students) as source materials in developing reading, writing, and speaking skills. Students learn to read critical-ly for precise meaning. In presenting pro and con arguments on policy decisions, they develop skills of logical argument and clear presentation of ideas. Because the class is encouraged to think creatively in an area where there are no ready solutions, students gain a sharper understanding of the function of language.

*Grouping for noncurricular school activities*—Generally, grouping for noncurricular school activities has been in areas such as drama-tics, art, music, and crafts. Some school systems, however, offer elective courses for high-level students in academic areas that are not included in the regular curriculum. A school in Pennsylvania, for example, offers concentrated foreign language study to interested high-ability students.

Special grouping allows students with genuine talent a variety of experiences beyond those provided by the regular school program. Research into the evaluation of various media and mastery of specific techniques, as well as the development of individual talent, can be stressed in a non-curricular program.

*Grouping for out-of-school activities*—There are numerous school- or community-sponsored programs that provide out-of-school activ-ities for gifted children. Special study clubs meet before or after school; art and music programs are conducted by community groups; and industry sponsors science fairs.

*Grouping within the regular classroom*—Grouping within the elementary classroom is a common method, particularly for the teaching of reading. This method illustrates an overlapping of gifted student techniques. A teacher may group students effectively and apply enrichment techniques to the gifted group. Such grouping depends on the ingenuity and ability of the individual teacher rather than on administrative decisions.

## ACCELERATION

Any procedure which allows a student to progress more rapidly and complete a given school program in less time or at an earlier age than the average student may be termed acceleration. Acceleration is based on the philosophy that the student who learns more rapidly and easily should not be restricted to the same pace as other students in his age group, but should be allowed to move forward to more challenging work.

Acceleration is one of the oldest accepted procedures for extending the educational horizons of gifted youngsters. In some forms it requires a minimum expenditure of school funds and involves almost no administrative problems.

Many forms of acceleration, both group and individual, are utilized in schools. Acceleration can take place at any point in the educational process from kindergarten to college. Grade or course skipping, combining two years' work into one, summer school attendance, extra courses for credit, college courses in high school, and credit by examination are all forms of acceleration.

## Advantages of Acceleration

Many educators feel that acceleration is the best way for students to progress academically in relation to their ability and intellectual maturity. These proponents feel that the gifted student should be encouraged to advance academically at his own rate rather than at the pace of average students of the same age. Not only does the bright student develop more rapidly intellectually, they say, but he also tends to mature physically, emotionally, and socially much faster than other youngsters.

In this age of rapid technological advances, many educators are increasingly concerned with what they consider a lag in the educational process. Acceleration as a gifted student technique, advocates feel, hastens the beginning of a student's most productive period, whereas a prolonged school training period forces the bright student to delay entry into a life career.

Another frequently voiced argument for acceleration is the economic one: fewer school years mean less expense to parents, schools, and the community.

## Disadvantages of Acceleration

Educators who oppose acceleration as a gifted student technique fear that students who mature early intellectually may not be as mature socially and emotionally. They cite the many adjustment problems that are likely to result. They also argue that the accelerated gifted child will be deprived of the opportunity to develop leadership qualities that he would have in his own age group.

Other opponents feel that acceleration results in serious learning gaps in academic areas. They feel that students' creativity is exploited and that they are urged to extend their knowledge of specific facts rather than to explore and reflect on general concepts.

## Skipping of Grades

Probably one of the oldest acceleration methods, skipping was practiced prior to the twentieth century. Skipping is based on the assumption that the youngster who is sufficiently bright can forego the learning experience of a given grade and accept the challenge of the next-higher grade.

This type of acceleration can be dangerous: it often leaves the student with gaps in one or more academic areas; it sometimes places him in a group beyond his emotional, physical, and social maturity. Recent acceleration programs include skipping only in a limited number of special classes.

## Early Admission to the Educational Program

Early admission to kindergarten or college is a form of acceleration frequently used in programs for the gifted student. Such plans are based on recognition that gifted youngsters are more advanced and can benefit from educational experiences before most students are ready for such experiences.

*Early admission to kindergarten or first grade.* Many educators advocate providing for gifted youngsters as early as possible in the educational sequence. Experimentation on the early admission of bright children to elementary schools yielded favorable results. Mature four-year-olds have been allowed to start kindergarten; five-year-olds have been placed in first grade; and bright children who have learned to read at home start school in the second grade, when they are six. Under this system the heterogeneity of classes is reduced and a class tends to be an ability group rather than an age group.

*Early admission to college.* In recent years there has been experimentation with early admission to college. Perhaps the most significant experiments in this type of acceleration are conducted under the Early Admissions to College Program, initiated in 1951 with Ford Foundation support. Some colleges and universities now admit eleventh-grade and even tenth-grade students who show sufficient ability and maturity. Although evaluation studies show that highly competent students can succeed in college study even though placed with classmates a year or two older, few high schools have accepted the program.

Early admission programs in the high school usually function by close collaboration with a nearby college or university. Students in the Portland (Oregon) project take special accelerated courses planned in conjunction with Reed College. The University of Chicago (one of the initiators of the Early Admissions to College Program) provides for acceleration in its laboratory schools. Since the first eight years of regular curriculum are covered in seven years, students will normally enter the college program after eleven school years.

## More Rapid Progress Through the Normal Educational Sequence

Another type of acceleration found in many gifted child programs allows the student to move through the entire curriculum in less than the usual amount of time. This method may be used at any point in the educational sequence.

*Ungraded primary.* A promising approach to individualized instruction, the ungraded primary plan allows youngsters to complete the three years of primary curriculum in varying lengths of time. A bright child may move through the three-year program in two years; an average child will finish in the normal three years; and a slow child may need four years to complete the primary grades. This system tends to group youngsters according to their ability automatically and makes the subsequent grades somewhat more homogeneous.

The ungraded primary method may also be adapted to grades four through nine, but few schools have experimented with it at the middle and upper elementary levels.

*Two grades combined in one.* Another acceleration method combines two or more grades into a lesser number of years. Through such specially planned classes, bright students can complete the full educational sequence in a shorter time. The approach is similar to that in the ungraded plan. In the New York public school system, 62 junior high schools offer special programs that allow academically superior students to complete three years' work in two years' time. Two Baltimore junior high schools also use this method.

*Advanced placement program.* A well-defined system, the advanced placement program enables capable students to take courses for college credit while still in high school. The plan has gained much greater acceptance among high school administrators than the Early Admissions to College Program. Students remain in high school for the normal number of years, but enter college with enough credit to complete four years of college work in three years or less.

Secondary schools are assisted in planning and teaching courses in eleven college-level subjects by the School and College Study of Admissions with Advanced Standing (underwritten by the Ford Foundation). Starting in the tenth grade, students may complete up to one year of college work while still in high school.

*Extra courses for extra credit.* Another variation of acceleration is the practice of allowing students to take high school courses beyond the number required for graduation. Although no college credit is given for these courses, they add an extra dimension to the student's educational experience. Language, public speaking, dramatics, and laboratory science courses not required in the regular curriculum often help to prepare the student for college or for a specific vocation.

*Credit by examination.* Widely used with servicemen after World War II, the credit-by-examination method allows students to receive high school or college credit by passing an examination. Students may use their accumulated knowledge gained through extraschool study, travel, and independent research. One school allows students to take departmental examinations in mathematics before receiving regular classroom instruction. If they pass, they receive credit for the course. The possibility of adapting this method to the high school program deserves consideration.

# 14 GUIDELINES FOR PROGRAM DEVELOPMENT

WILLARD ABRAHAM

*Chairman, Department of Special Education,*
*Arizona State University, Tempe, Arizona*

In developing programs for superior and talented students that make sense to them and to their parents, teachers, and administrators, the writer has frequently cited, as the first guideline, a four-word rule of thumb: locate, motivate, educate, evaluate.

No program for superior students can evolve unless it first finds the superior children who need special help. Nor can such a program succeed if it fails to motivate the underachiever—the youngster who is not working up to his capacity, the so-called able but unambitious student. The third step in the rule of thumb—to educate—is the central goal of all superior and talented student programs. To evaluate, to adjust lists of names, activities, and techniques of teaching, is the final but never finished step in providing for able youngsters.

Another frequently used guideline is the necessity of synchronizing students' abilities, achievements, and aspirations. Often a bright child goes unrecognized because either his achievement or the level of his aspiration (or both) is not commensurate with his ability. If sufficient teaching and guidance time were devoted to this child, he might break through the restraints of his own achievement and aspiration barriers and demonstrate the high ability he possesses.

A third guideline is based on the realization that there is no such thing as a third-grade class and there are no such persons as a fifth-grade teacher or an eighth-grade child. Individual differences characterize every student in every class. In the past, some teachers used the same techniques, bibliographies, grading system, and homework assignments for all; but now it is more important than ever that full recognition be given to the differences

161

found among the students. These differences are of many kinds—
differences in abilities, interests, family and cultural backgrounds,
place in the family, aspirations, and health (mental and physical).
Teachers must now be prepared to adjust their plans according to
*who* comes in the door, *what* his needs are, *where* he has been
before he enters, and *why* and *how* he became the kind of person
he is.

Child-study techniques are the fourth guideline for the development of programs for superior and talented students. These techniques enable educators to study individuals and accumulate data
that will make possible a program tailored to the individual's needs.
The school must ask two questions: "What kinds of students do
we have?" and "What kinds of adults do we wish to foster?"

To discover the kinds of students it has, a school may use a
variety of accepted techniques, adapted to the children, the school,
and the community; these techniques must always be in the hands
of competent persons. Of particular importance are the things children say, the things they write (in autobiographies for example),
and the way they act in various settings, as skillfully observed by
the teacher. Among the devices for collecting this information are
standardized tests (intelligence, achievement, personality, and other
types), teacher-made tests, anecdotal records, parent conferences,
child interviews, health records, and home visiting. The more
complete cumulative records or folders and case studies may also
be used.

Special training and skill are required to utilize three additional
child-study techniques: sociometry, play therapy, and painting.
These techniques can make significant contributions to what teachers and counselors know about children, but they can also be dangerous devices in the hands of the incompetent person or the novice.

As for the kinds of adults the school wishes to foster, the
answers seem obvious, but perhaps they are not. The school wants
its students to become "well adjusted," "socially acceptable," "contributing members of a community," "happy," "prosperous," and so
on. Perhaps there is agreement on the words, but not on the
meanings behind them, for some of the greatest dreamers in art
and science have been none of the above. It may be, then, that
a shy person is also well adjusted, that an imaginative one should

challenge our basic beliefs, and that a creative one is very difficult to live and work with.

The present-day expectancies of both parents and school people as to how children should act and what they should become have evolved from a background which includes a depression, two world wars, and a world of turmoil. Today the problems of the world are of a different nature, and youngsters (average as well as gifted) must adapt themselves to concepts of space, missiles, and interplanetary travel. Educators developing programs for the gifted must take full cognizance of the background from which the young now come and the new world which they will enter.

A fifth guideline, closely related to the child study suggested above, is the information provided by delving into the attitudes of superior and talented students. Having been children in a different age, we sometimes lose touch with the thoughts and interests of today's gifted youth. A questionnaire used in Arizona (2), followed up by a series of interviews, recently revealed many things about gifted children. For example, they have many friends, love sports, like to read (and they read well, although their choices are frequently very trite), behave and misbehave as most other children do (and their parents punish them with no special regard for their IQ!), like most of their teachers, appreciate firmness tempered with a sense of humor, and have few unusual fears or worries.

There is need for more careful study of why some of these children drop out of school, what needs they have for guidance, which of their teachers and counselors they come to for help, and how they feel about what they're studying and the approaches used by teachers to those subjects.

A four-year-old who says "I have a wonder on my mind" and wants to share it, a seven-year-old who pretends not to hear, a nine-year-old who refuses to raise his hand to answer a question after being repeatedly rebuffed, a thirteen-year-old who deliberately misses answers on tests so he won't be different, and a sixteen-year-old who is bored, frustrated, and angry are all examples of bright children whose performance is affected by their attitudes. These attitudes may be submerged and difficult to identify, or they may be on the surface for the teacher or counselor to evaluate. If attitudes can be identified, they will reveal much about the student's needs and make it even more imperative that programs be designed with the individual in mind.

Although educators must be on guard against making false generalizations about groups of people, the recent work of Drews (60) and Getzels *et al.* (79) will help them recognize students' attitudes, discover the causes, and make program adaptations on the basis of them.

Another important guideline for programs that are meaningful to young people is information about why some programs have been ineffective in the past. Why have bright students dropped out of school? What are the reasons they give? What are the *real* reasons?

Although lack of money in the family is often given as the reason for dropping out of school, how often does it cloud some more basic issue like parental discouragement, poor teaching, inadequate guidance or none at all, or uninspiring courses of study, curriculums, or school atmosphere? It may require almost psychiatric "digging" in a dropout follow-up study to uncover some of the basic causes, but the altered programs and subsequent reduced dropout rate will be a positive reward for such efforts.

Guidelines also appear in obvious but important factors like these: the number and characteristics of the superior and talented students with whom the school will be working; the readiness of the community and of parents for program changes (and the parents' group includes parents of youngsters who are *not* superior and talented!); and what the guidance people know about the children, their parents, and the community.

Help is also available from research reports reviewed in *Exceptional Children, Review of Educational Research,* and other journals, as well as from the insightful writing and experimental work done by individuals who are devoting much of their time to the study of this area. In addition many school districts are making contributions by their efforts to develop new programs with care and to evaluate their on-going programs.

Just as specific homework assignments should be made for particular children, so program adaptations should be made for particular schools and communities. No matter how successful and attractive a school's program may appear, it may not fit the needs of another school. Drafting a superior and talented student program becomes a unique project, based on what a particular school needs and wants for its children. The program cannot be completely separated from the rest of the school program, nor can the gifted youngsters be completely separated from the rest of the children. Herein lies much of the program's significance: all children can ultimately profit from program adaptations that are sensitive to the needs of the superior and talented.

The most obvious guideline of all, of course, is the idea of educating each child to his capacity. Although—as a result of the phenomenal rise in school enrollments in recent years—the individualized approach may be sought but too seldom attained, it remains the basis for most philosophies of education, the objective still most eagerly sought. It is now more important than ever that superior and talented students be included in this objective—that is, that they receive individual attention. Through the North Central Association Superior and Talented Student Project and other endeavors, more attention is being given to this important group, whose loss society can ill afford. For the exciting and swiftly moving future, the loss of major segments of this talent from the realms of politics, medicine, teaching, science, and other fields is both wasteful and dangerous.

On the basis of limited information, some educators have expressed the fear that too much attention and money are being concentrated on the education of our brighter children. Examination of existing programs indicates that this is not the case, however, and that there is no immediate danger that it will be. In fact, the real danger lies in neglecting a superior and talented student who is bored or otherwise dissatisfied with school, is tempted by the immediate dollar to drop out, or is not being challenged to his capacity. For him, we must continue to seek realistic guidelines for effective programs—and then take the important step of developing these programs.

# SECTION V

## GUIDANCE SERVICES

In recent years, the recognition of the vital significance of human relationships in the learning process has fostered a new direction in education. The purpose of education has been extended to include attention to the emotional growth of the individual and to his relationships with other people. High school guidance is now concerned, among other things, with fostering personality adjustment and growth. Realizing that traditional pedagogic techniques are inadequate to handle some of the emotional blocks that may prevent students from accepting or integrating school learning, educators have provided counseling and group work media to deal with such impeding or thwarting factors.

School counseling programs are ordinarily organized around the educational, vocational, and personal problems of students. The objectives of the program may be superficial, relating to the correction of situational difficulties; or they may be more extensive, aiming to influence the personality structure of the student. The extent to which a student's life is influenced varies according to his own situation and according to the depth and scope of the guidance service employed in the schools. Usually, however, guidance aims to treat the specific normal and disturbing problems which interfere with the development of the individual student, or around which decisions must be made.

The school administrator must accept the responsibility of providing guidance services for superior students. These services should be based upon a complete study of the superior student: his capacity for learning, his physical and mental health, his school record, his social adjustment, and his aptitudes and interests. Because guidance services are, by the very nature of their purposes, kept mainly on an individual rather than a mass basis, they may be adapted to the problems of superior students. In general, the school's regular guidance program will assist superior students in many ways. The traits of superior students—perseverance, alertness, interest in problems, great mental energy, good humor, sustained attention, mature use of language, quick comprehension, and responsiveness— make them receptive to the ordinary guidance techniques. Few if any special guidance provisions beyond those normally provided will be necessary.

Counselors in the North Central Association Superior and Talented Student Project report that their major concerns with superior students include:

1. *Getting superior students to achieve up to capacity:* This problem is more common among superior boys than among superior girls. In determining whether a superior student is working up to capacity the counselor must have three sets of data: (a) the student's ability level as measured by good tests of scholastic ability, (b) his achievement level as measured by grades and standardized achievement tests, and (c) the established relationship between ability and achievement for the superior population of which the student is a member.

2. *Defining educational and occupational areas in which superior students are interested*: This problem is sometimes complicated by a conflict between the student's choice and that of his parents. Also, recent stresses in international relations have made it difficult to establish criteria for selecting superior students' occupations. Should they prepare for work that fulfills the immediate needs of society, or should they select the occupations most appropriate to their own interests, abilities, and aspirations?

3. *Dealing with social and personal adjustments of superior students:* This sometimes involves adjusting parents' ambitions to

the interests of superior students, or resolving the intellectual differences between the superior student and his family. There are few instances of serious social maladjustment accompanied by brilliant achievement. However, when such an instance does occur, the counselor faces a decision requiring considerable wisdom. Should he dissuade a superior boy from intellectual pursuits because the boy's social development seems to be retarded by his unusual concentration? Or should he permit the student to grow more and more absorbed in his intellectual interests? The argument for developing social skill is that even the artist or scientist can be more effective if he is at ease with people. The counselor should probably make an effort to bring the student out of his withdrawal and help him establish effective social relations.

4. *Overcoming the classroom teacher's lack of sensitivity:* Counselors are sometimes approached by superior students who believe that teachers expect them to do an unreasonable number of unchallenging tasks. Most teachers are becoming increasingly concerned over what and how to teach superior students. Some superior students, however, report that they are afraid to recite in class or ask questions other than superficial ones. Apparently, some teachers feel threatened by the probing questions of their superior students.

5. *Helping superior students organize their time and activities:* In some cases, a student's underachievement may be traced to his inability to schedule his time wisely. Such students lack either the skill or the motivation to distribute the 168 hours in each week so that each hour is spent wisely. Superior students are involved in many school, church, and community activities, and they frequently occupy leadership roles in these activities. Many need help in planning for the demands of these roles and in assigning values to the activities in which they engage.

The chief tasks in counseling superior and talented students are to assure that they are exposed to educational experiences which challenge their abilities and to guarantee them the fulfillment of all their varied intellectual potentialities. These tasks can be accomplished through the following guidance activities: (a) helping superior students select appropriate courses; (b) organizing school, home, and community facilities to provide a continuity of enriching experiences; (c) designing class and out-of-class activities that supplement the regular curriculum of the school; and (d) supplying to individual students information on which wise decisions may be based. Through such guidance activities, stimulation and challenge for superior students to develop in many directions will be possible. The Carnegie Foundation for the Advancement of Teaching (36) states that the superior and talented student

> . . . has the potentiality of developing in many directions. He should be encouraged to develop his intellectual talents on as broad a front as possible, and one of the central aims of his high school program should be to preserve such intellectual breadth. Under no circumstances should he be urged to make early vocational choices which eliminate some of these intellectual potentialities at the expense of others. If his heart is set on a certain profession, he should, of course, be allowed to entertain that objective. But even so, he should be encouraged to develop his potentialities on as broad a base as possible.

Lawrence Derthick (59), U. S. Commissioner of Education, recently reported a study in a New York high school which demonstrated the effectiveness of good counseling for superior students. In this study, 27 per cent of the superior students who had counseling made honor grades, while only 10 per cent of those without counseling did so. Also, 53 per cent of the superior students who had counseling went on to college, as compared with 35 per cent of those without counseling.

The abundant literature on guidance and counseling includes little that is specifically written on guidance and counseling for talented students. This is not surprising, since the objectives of guidance for the superior and talented are not fundamentally different from those for other students. Until recently, most counselors made few attempts to delineate techniques applicable to superior students because personal nuances are so subtle, and variables in counseling so myriad, that an attempt to detail counseling practices for a particular group of students seemed somewhat futile.

The dearth of writing about counseling and guidance for superior and talented students also is attributable to two other facts. First, no research study has yet yielded results reflecting differences in *kind* between the problems and needs of superior students and those of other students. Second, there is still a great need to provide basic services for all students, and the efforts of the school counselor are expended to that end. Yet, these facts notwithstanding, good counseling and guidance practices must be based on a sound understanding of the differences among students, even if these differences are only in degree.

In this section, guidance services for superior students are considered, especially insofar as they differ from the guidance services normally provided. In the first chapter, Louis G. Schmidt reports the problem areas of superior and talented students. Problems of occupational choice, motivation, underachievement, self-concepts, aspirations of girls, and parental understanding are pointed out as concerns for the superior student and the counselor. The counselor can and must encourage and support the gifted student in using his abilities in a constructive manner.

Roland Ross, in Chapter 16, discusses some of the general principles of guidance services for superior students. These principles might lend direction to the guidance department in a school's talent development program. Ross states that the central tasks of guidance services are to challenge the student to risk failure, but at the same time to free him from fear of failure.

In Chapter 17, Frank Womer describes how school testing programs can aid counselors in identifying superior students and providing guidance and instruction for them. He lists some cautions for counselors in using and interpreting test data.

Calvin Daane, in Chapter 18, analyzes high schools' provisions for organizing and disseminating college information. This informational service seems highly important, since it is unfortunately true that many superior students have been unable to go to college, or to the college of their choice, simply because of the absence of an effectively organized program of college information and college counseling—one which gives students the information they need to make decisions.

In Chapter 19, Herman J. Peters discusses how counseling services provide for talented students. He suggests the establishment of counseling priorities, describes the proneness for counseling which can be developed in bright students, and outlines how the counseling process helps bright students to establish attitudinal and aspirational goals commensurate with their levels of ability.

# 15 PROBLEMS OF SUPERIOR AND TALENTED STUDENTS

LOUIS G. SCHMIDT

*Associate Professor of Education, Department of Guidance and Counseling, School of Education, Indiana University*

It is doubtful that superior and talented students have problems that are entirely different from those experienced by average students in the normal counseling setting. However, superior and talented students do have some special intellectual needs which require educational planning beginning early in their school experience and continuing from the elementary school through college. Part of this planning is the sole responsibility of the counselor, but he must co-operate with the rest of the staff in the important jobs of identifying the superior and talented and assisting them to take advantage of the many opportunities provided by the school program.

Almost everyone agrees that youngsters with intellectual potential for outstanding contributions in science, business, industry, and the arts should be located as early as possible. For the sake of society as a whole, they should be provided with special educational opportunities which will help them fully utilize their potentials. Equally important, superior students should achieve for the sake of their own self-realization. Today American leaders are distressed because the nation faces a serious manpower shortage in college-educated people. Business, industry, educational institutions, and the professions are competing for the services of college graduates. Although the numbers of college graduates are not sufficient to fulfill the demands of society, our nation does have an adequate supply of youth who are capable of earning college degrees. The National Manpower Council describes the situation as follows:

> Today, less than half of those capable of acquiring a college degree enter college. About two-fifths of those who start college, many with superior ability, do not graduate. For every high school graduate who eventually earns a doctor's degree, there are twenty-five others who have the intellectual ability to acquire that degree but do not (267).

172

There are a number of reasons why bright students fail to attend college: For some, high educational attainment is not valued by their families and friends; some believe they lack the financial resources to attend college; some have not chosen vocational goals that require a college degree; others doubt their ability to succeed in college; many lack the ambition required. Of this last group, Terman said:

> They deliberately choose not to enter the usual American ratrace for what is usually regarded as success. Nor can I find it in my heart to condemn those who make this choice; it may well be that their fewer honors and lower income are fully compensated by greater contentment and a lower incidence of anxiety and ulcers (100).

On the other hand, studies on creativity (22, 79, 228) report the total immersion of students in their tasks and their enjoyment of work. Anne Roe (202) tells of the dedication her scientists feel toward their work.

In the last two or three years, there has been much progress in identifying talented students. These youngsters usually perform well on measures of intelligence, regardless of what the particular instrument or criterion may be. Counselors can assist faculty members to find material in the research literature which will help them identify and understand the potentially gifted youngsters in any local school situation.

Adequate and constant evaluation of the curriculum is necessary if a school is to provide activities which challenge superior students to achieve up to their abilities. The counselor has an important role in this process of studying the curriculum and recommending changes. Through his interviews with pupils and his interpretation of the cumulative records, the counselor is in a unique position to help the school meet the objectives of its program for talented students. He can advise the administrators and faculty members of the enrichment practices and curriculum changes that will stimulate the gifted youngsters. This is possible only if the counselor makes a careful study of ways of developing superior programs, in addition to studying the individual students in his school.

To help him understand the superior and talented student, the counselor must use every available tool and technique of guidance. He must consider ability and achievement test scores, school grades, anecdotal reports from teachers, autobiographical materials, and additional information obtained from parents and other interested people. The study of superior students is a continuous process, since situations change very rapidly. For example, some youngsters who at an early age seem superior are merely precocious, and very soon are found in the middle of the group.

Information on superior and talented students which the counselor has gathered should be made available to all teachers on the staff. Whether this material is in a cumulative record form or some special form for superior students, it should be located in a central place. Accessibility is very important, since teachers might ignore the material if it were not readily available. Lines of communication between the counselor and the teacher should always be kept open. It is not enough for a counselor to identify the superior students in a class and then assume that his responsibility to the teacher and to the student has terminated. A student's movement toward or away from the educational goals that have been set should show in his records, and this information should be shared with the teacher. The counselor and the teacher can then develop methods or practices that will enable such students to make the most of their opportunities.

The importance of counseling services in the elementary schools cannot be stressed too strongly. Unless a talented child is recognized early in his school experience and a challenging program provided for him, there is great danger that he may develop poor study habits, habitual daydreaming, dislike for all subjects, dislike for a particular subject, or boredom. He may be caught in a situation in which the repeated exercise of easy tasks lulls him into a state lacking in motivation. In many cases, by the time the superior and talented youngster reaches the secondary school it is too late to change his poor attitudes, bad habits, and low aspirations.

## PROBLEMS OF OCCUPATIONAL INFORMATION

Educational guidance and particularly the provision of occupational information are important in the counseling of superior and talented students. A child who is identified as potential college material early in his elementary school experience can be encouraged to plan well in advance for college. His parents, too, should be aware of the child's potential and brought into such planning. For superior and talented students, long-range goals are often a strong motivating force, stimulating them toward better school achievement.

An early occupational choice may not be a wise decision for a superior student. The best vocational guidance encourages the superior and talented student to acquire a broad cultural education in his early school experiences and to defer narrowing occupational interests until post-high-school and early college years. With the rapidly changing work scene in the United States, the best vocational preparation a superior and talented student can receive is adaptability to change in every phase of living. The need for adaptability is illustrated by the manufacture of products that were unheard of five years ago, by the increasing mechanization and automation of jobs, and generally by the changing character of our national economy.

It is also important to remember that most superior students are capable of succeeding in a great number of occupational pursuits. Counselors sometimes have difficulty knowing where to begin with a superior and talented student who scores well in almost every area measured by a general achievement or aptitude test. For many of these youngsters it may be important to encourage them to acquire a broad training and to avoid a specific occupational choice until near the termination of their formal schooling.

## PROBLEMS OF MOTIVATION

Counselors are regularly faced with the problem of motivating superior and talented students. Bright youngsters from homes of low socioeconomic status tend to be less motivated towards academic excellence than those from higher socioeconomic backgrounds. Certain ethnic groups have more problems of underachievement and lack of motivation than do others.

Counselors have long known that a child's IQ or his scholastic aptitude is only part of the explanation for high achievement in school work. The term "not achieving up to ability" has been used frequently, on report cards and elsewhere, to describe youngsters not working up to their potential. The exact causes of underachievement are still unknown. They are probably as complex and diverse as the underachieving youngsters themselves.

As previously indicated, there is some evidence that junior high school is the point at which the problem of underachievement gets a good start. It is essential that counselors detect underachievement in superior and talented students wherever it begins, and implement a program for its correction. Group counseling sessions or work with individual students may be helpful. These approaches must center on finding and alleviating the causes of underachievement. The underachievement itself is only the symptom.

The counselor cannot solve the problem of underachievement alone. The teacher-student relationship must be such that underachieving youngsters can gain the support they need to develop their ability and receive encouragement to move ahead. Much additional research is needed to discover the most effective ways in which counselors, teachers, and schools can help these students. For example, it is important, but difficult, to differentiate between the underachieving youngster who will succeed in the secondary school situation with the help and understanding of professional counselors and teachers and the youngster whose problems require psychiatric or special remedial help.

## PROBLEMS OF SELF-CONCEPT

Although research about the self-concept patterns of superior and talented students is limited, some evidence is now available concerning the underachieving superior and talented student. The underachieving superior and talented student views himself differently than does the achieving gifted student. Counselors often fail to determine how a gifted student perceives himself and his special abilities—information which must be considered in helping these students solve their problems. The brilliant student who tries out for the football team and fails, for example, may develop a poor estimate of himself. Because he has found that he is not "best" in all areas, he may transfer this poor self-concept to other areas of his endeavor.

Work with gifted underachievers who have negative concepts of themselves indicates that such students have not had rich and satisfying relationships with adults. These students may believe that the adults who are giving such encouragement do not truly understand the problem. Teachers and parents can produce further negative results if they do not handle this type of student carefully.

## PROBLEMS OF GIRLS

A study (269) of the top 10 per cent of Indiana high school graduates revealed that there were twice as many girls as boys in the top group. College enrollment figures, on the other hand, showed that twice as many boys as girls entered college. One of the chief reasons for this situation was that many girls renounced intellectuality because it didn't pay off socially to be a "brain." Some of our brightest women students make every attempt to conceal their intellectual ability because they fear intellectual achievement will frighten away prospective husbands.

Bright girls need more encouragement and they need to have opportunities to identify with models of women scholars who have gone on to be successful scientists, professors, and business figures. These models should exemplify femininity, as well as competence (60).

## PROBLEMS INVOLVING PARENTS

The parents of superior and talented youngsters often need assistance in understanding their children's problems and in helping their children develop socially and intellectually. The counselor should play a significant role in giving the parents the information and assistance they need.

The counselor should attempt to discover parents' attitudes toward giftedness in their youngsters before too much information is revealed. It is also helpful to understand the particular needs and problems of the parents before suggestions can be made to them about their superior children. Parents who understand and accept their responsibilities toward them can do much in the way of fostering mental health as well as aiding the youngsters in the pursuit of special interests and helping in the development of new ones.

## CONCLUSION

Although the superior and talented student does not have problems entirely different from those of other students, he has certain special problems relating to his superiority. He needs, to a greater degree than do most students, encouragement to use his talents and abilities in a constructive manner. Obviously, a first step is that his ability be recognized by his teachers, parents, and peers. Further, the student must learn to see himself as an individual with special abilities—a healthy yet modest acceptance of this reality is a first step in building a positive and accurate self-concept.

Miriam Goldberg states some of the problems faced by superior students:

> The gifted, and especially the very gifted, youngster may be faced with the problem of communicating with his peers. He may find himself an outsider, and unless helped by the home and the school to understand and accept his uniqueness as an asset, he may become an anxious, fearful individual, unable to utilize his potential abilities (84).

To be effective in these matters, schools must employ competent counselors to assist the superior student to appraise, understand, and accept himself and his special abilities and aptitudes. The counselors will also help this student make appropriate vocational and educational choices, and they will help parents understand their responsibilities toward him.

# 16  GUIDANCE SERVICES FOR SUPERIOR AND TALENTED STUDENTS

ROLAND G. ROSS

*Program Specialist, Guidance, Counseling, and Testing Section, U.S. Office of Education*

Education has been defined many times and in many ways. Most of these definitions have certain common elements, such as mention of the factors of natural drive and interest and of provisions for the expansion of natural powers. The many definitions of guidance are also similar in some respects. For example, most of them describe guidance as designed to help meet the special educational needs of pupils which cannot be met through normal instructional practices or administrative procedures.

While the guidance program must function within the framework of the total educational program, it should provide the structure and be the vehicle by which natural drives and interests and special needs of pupils can be planned for. The guidance program is especially adaptable to this highly important task—a fact which is universally recognized, but not as universally implemented.

Basic to the development of specific guidance services for superior and talented students should be a school-wide statement of the underlying principles that will govern the school's gifted child program. These principles might include the following:

1. Every student possesses talents which, if identified and developed, will result in maximum satisfaction for himself and for society.

2. It is essential that every member of the school staff acknowledge and accept his responsibility for helping each child develop his talents to the fullest extent possible.

3. To provide an adequate program with full consideration of the individual differences of students, the staff must have the abilities and skills needed to perform in their chosen fields. The teacher's breadth and depth of academic knowledge is directly proportionate to his ability to provide varied instruction suited to individual needs.

179

4. The right of the individual to choose courses must be tempered by his level of development and the maturity of his judgment. Although the basic goal of guidance services is students' self-direction, the self-understanding and environmental opportunities of the students must be considered before they are allowed complete freedom of choice.

5. To provide for individual differences without first identifying the nature and extent of these differences may be worse than making no provision at all.

6. The school can more adequately provide for individual differences if community resources are widely used.

7. Provisions for individual differences should start with an emphasis on known strengths. Although every effort should be made to understand students' weaknesses, their strengths are the main concern in a program for the superior and talented.

8. There is nothing more unfair to individual students than attempting to treat each one exactly alike. Students are not exactly alike in any respect, and their individual differences should be fully considered.

9. The teacher-student ratio is in inverse proportion to the extent to which the teacher can effectively identify and provide for individual differences.

10. We can know students in terms of their separate talents, but we cannot understand students unless we view their talents as part of their total educational pattern.

11. Education in a democracy must teach both individuality and conformity. Success is measured by the extent to which students demonstrate individual variability within a framework of basic conformity. Overstressing conformity leads to mediocrity of performance.

The principles listed above are not exhaustive, but merely suggestive of the guides which a school will incorporate into the early stages of its program development.

John Hersey has said:

> The most important unsolved problem in education is discovering and releasing the maximum potential of each child. We need poets, senators, and businessmen, as well as scientists and engineers. If we discover what our children have in them early enough, we will have more than enough of everything (70).

This, then is the challenge: discovering and releasing our human potential.

Through counseling, testing, and planned group experiences, the individual gains understanding of himself and his relationships with others in a rapidly changing world. Only through this understanding can the gifted student make realistic plans and learn techniques for meeting life situations. The guidance process can develop the following: (a) respect for every person, (b) empathic insight into problems of others and insight into their own problems, (c) a positive attitude with attention focused on assets, (d) a desire to take initiative and (e) recognition of the need for self-direction.

The elements of a well-integrated guidance program function with maximum effectiveness only when professionally competent personnel are involved. For example, the individual inventory can be a collection of meaningless statistical data in the hands of a novice. No amount of educational, occupational, social, personal, or other types of information is of value without a trained counselor who can make interpretations, and an educational program that will meet the needs of children located by such approaches. Evaluative studies not related to the total educational program have little value. Counseling, carried on by professionally competent personnel with ample time for their work, is the catalyst in the whole guidance program.

A great deal (58) has been written about the characteristics of superior and talented students. Some of the characteristics which have been identified are the following:

1. Self-discipline
2. Originality
3. Spontaneity in learning
4. Love of the surprise in learning
5. Outstanding ability to concentrate
6. Ability to generalize
7. Ability to conceptualize, to think abstractly

The school administrator, with the assistance of the school staff, has the important responsibility of providing this group with a favorable climate in which to function; without such a climate, talent may never come to fruition.

The teacher's obligation to encourage all students applies particularly to the superior and talented group. Encouragement, multiplied over and over, will release their intellectual potential. These students need especially to be guided into creative activities. Creativity is not so much an aptitude as an attitude or state of mind; it is characterized by inventiveness and curiosity. Such qualities do not just appear. They must be fed and nurtured, since the development and utilization of creativity is hard work. Although creativity is an elusive quality, and one demanding careful nurture, we cannot afford to neglect its development in our able youth. Helping them become creative is a shared responsibility: counselors, teachers, administrators, parents, and the community must co-ordinate their efforts to this end. The security of our way of life depends on the release and full utilization of potential in our youth.

Our talented and superior students need help in order to choose from the multiplicity of opportunities that are open to them. They should be encouraged to experiment, to be willing to risk failure or surrender success. Gifted youth must neither fear failure nor seek refuge in conformity. There is an exquisite and delicate balance between freedom for creativeness and maintenance of orderly living within the classroom. Only a superior teacher can recognize and achieve this balance.

# 17

## SCHOOL TESTING PROGRAMS AND SUPERIOR AND TALENTED STUDENTS

FRANK WOMER
*Associate Professor of Education, School of Education, University of Michigan*

There are two ways in which a school testing program can be used to help superior and talented students. First, it identifies them; second, the data obtained through such a program can be used to guide and instruct them. No program designed to encourage maximum utilization of human talent can be any better than its techniques for identifying that talent. Also, the operation of such programs within American schools must be rooted in guidance and instructional activities.

## THE SCHOOL TESTING PROGRAM

Before examining some guideposts for the use of testing in working with superior and talented students, we should consider what is included in a typical school testing program. The following types of tests are the most common:

1. *Intelligence* (scholastic aptitude). It is generally wise to administer three or four measures of general intelligence between kindergarten and twelfth grade. Several test score estimates that are relatively close to each other increase one's confidence in the results. Widely divergent scores may suggest a need for additional testing, perhaps with an individually administered test.

2. *Aptitude.* Aptitude batteries attempt to break down general intelligence into specific mental abilities such as verbal reasoning, numerical reasoning, and abstract reasoning. Or they may attempt to assess special abilities such as mechanical or clerical aptitude. Such batteries are generally administered in high school and are used primarily for educational and vocational planning.

3. *Achievement.* Assessment of the various skill areas and of

183

general educational development should be scheduled at regular intervals. In the elementary grades, achievement batteries typically measure performance in reading, language arts, arithmetic, and study skills (use of graphs, maps, reference materials, and the like). These areas are also measured at the secondary level, but often here the battery is expanded to include tests in science, social science, and foreign languages.

4. *Interest.* Special inventories attempt to point up various interest patterns and to identify those areas which are strongest. Some instruments yield scores in broad interest areas, such as the scientific, social service, and artistic. Other instruments relate interests to specific occupations, such as that of engineer, teacher, or salesman. Interest inventories are usually programed at the secondary level. The results are often used to relate interests to aptitudes.

5. *Personality.* The use of personality tests with all students in system-wide testing programs has decreased considerably in recent years. Some schools, however, still find personality tests helpful for use in special situations or with certain students. It is usually best for schools not employing professionally trained psychologists or counselors to omit such instruments from their programs. The use of certain "adjustment" or "problem" inventories does not require such highly trained personnel, but even here interpretations must be made with caution.

## IDENTIFICATION OF SUPERIOR AND TALENTED STUDENTS

A school testing program provides several different kinds of information which can be helpful in identifying superior and talented students. However, information from other sources must not be overlooked. To yield a more complete picture of a student, test data should be combined with information from other sources. Information in the following important areas is among the most useful for identifying superior and talented students:

1. *Over-all ability.* Students vary in their capacity to achieve in the academic aspects of a school program: reading, mathematics, history, science, and so on. The capacity for general academic achievement (scholastic aptitude) is best measured by a test of general intelligence.

There is no particular IQ or percentile rank above which one finds only superior students and below which one finds no superior students. However, if one defines the top quarter of students in scholastic aptitude as superior, one may say that in the general population a percentile rank of 75 or an IQ of 110 will separate the top quarter from the rest of the population. It is important to remember that a cutoff score should not be interpreted so rigidly that every student with an IQ of 109 is automatically considered academically average, while every student with an IQ of 111 is automatically considered academically superior. It is more realistic to consider those students whose IQ's are at or above 115 on repeated measurement as almost certainly academically superior, and those students whose IQ's are between 105 and 115 as possibly superior. Additional evidence such as grades and achievement test scores should be used to help make judgments about this latter group.

It is important to keep in mind that some students with special talents (such as artistic, musical, mechanical) may not fall in the superior group as defined above. If an educational program for the development of a special talent is at least in part built around a core of academic work, a student pursuing such a program must have enough over-all ability to succeed in the academic aspects of the program.

2. *Special abilities.* Talent does not always distribute itself evenly, either among individuals or within individuals. Some students are especially proficient in mathematics and only average in English. Some students have special artistic or musical talents, which may or may not be associated with above-average scholastic aptitude. In general, though, the student with marked abilities in one area is likely to be highly able in other areas as well. The best school testing programs assess different intellectual abilities within the total area of scholastic aptitude by using differential aptitude tests. They also make provision for assessing special talents whenever such talents can be measured by objective tests. The assessment of such special abilities as artistic talent, however, will more often be based upon samples of work produced by the student than upon a paper-and-pencil test.

3. *Achievement.* Students' achievement is most commonly assessed through the use of teachers' grades. There is considerable evidence that past performance is the best predictor of future performance. A student with a C average in high school is a poorer

college risk than one with an A average. However, some high achievers would not be identified if grades were the only criterion of school achievement. For this reason there is a trend toward placing increasing reliance on the results of standardized achievement tests, especially as criteria for admission to college. Standardized achievement tests can objectively assess over-all achievement. In identifying superior students, reading and vocabulary test scores are of particular importance, although there are some scholastically superior students with reading deficiencies that require special remedial attention.

The talented student who is not academically superior will not be identified by achievement tests designed to measure general educational development. Talents such as musical ability are best identified through actual performance.

4. *Interests.* Superior and talented students who are most apt to make good use of their academic superiority or special talents usually pursue their interests with considerable fervor. They seek answers to questions of all sorts; they choose hobbies related to their talents; and often they pursue a particular problem or project with a curiosity and devotion far greater than that of the average student.

Interest inventory scores should be examined for high and low areas, and interests should be related to aptitudes and talents in an effort to spot consistencies and inconsistencies. There is no evidence that all superior students—or even a large number of them—have the same interest patterns. It is reasonable to expect, however, that talented students will have high interest scores in the area of their talent. A music student with a low musical interest score, or an art student with a low artistic interest score, may not be interested enough to succeed in his field of study. It may be that with the breadth and intensity of interests many superior students have, a forced-choice interest inventory puts them in a spot where it is almost impossible for certain strong interests to score high.

## GUIDANCE AND INSTRUCTION OF SUPERIOR AND TALENTED STUDENTS

A school testing program can provide information of value in the guidance and instruction of superior and talented students. It can help students understand themselves; it can help parents understand their sons and daughters; and it can help teachers and counselors understand their students. Test results can be used in the following ways:

1. *Tests measure potential achievement.* Tests help determine the level of achievement we should expect from students. Not all academically superior students are superior in the same degree. A student who scores in the 75th percentile on a test of mental ability may be far different, as far as potential is concerned, from one who scores in the 99th percentile. The first student is expected to do above-average elementary and high school work, although in many colleges he would probably do only average work. In fact, we might be cautious about recommending that such a student seek admission to a highly selective college or university. The second student is a good prospect for any institution of higher learning, provided that his study habits and other important attributes also indicate academic success.

A student with some special talent who ranks in the 55th percentile on a test of mental ability may be well advised to seek further training at some nonacademic institution having a program oriented toward development of that talent.

2. *Tests help determine individual strengths and weaknesses.* A superior student does not necessarily achieve at the same level in all areas. John may achieve at a high level in reading, vocabulary, and social studies, and be average in mathematics and science. Mary may be at the 75th percentile in science, but at the 90th percentile in mathematics. Such variations in achievement-test patterns have implications both for counseling students and for meeting individual differences in the classroom. A teacher who is aware of a student's areas of low achievement can plan special educational experiences in the appropriate areas. Also, the teacher can provide stimulating individual work in students' areas of special competence. Students with special nonacademic talents may be stimulated to their best possible performance in school if we capitalize on their talents in order to maintain interest in areas where success does not come easily.

3. *Tests spot underachievement.* They help evaluate discrepancies between potential and achievement. A student with an IQ of 130 may be expected to maintain better than a B average in high school. He has the ability to achieve at a very high level, and if he

is not doing so, teachers and counselors ought to seek the reasons why. Of course, high grades are not the only goals of a school education, but to the extent that they reflect achievement in and understanding of important educational content, we have a right to expect superior students to get good grades.

4. *Tests give direction to educational and vocational planning.* Not all superior students should be nuclear physicists. Not all talented students should be working toward a Carnegie Hall concert. Superior and talented students should and do seek vocational careers in almost all possible areas and at various skill levels. Superior students are fortunate in that, in general, they have the ability to succeed in some area in which they are interested. It may be necessary, however, to decide whether a particular pattern of abilities and achievements indicates success in a particular college with a program of preparation for a particular vocation. Statistical data which relate specific test scores to success in a specific school can be of great help in making such decisions. Counselors who assist students in their educational and vocational planning must consider scores from general intelligence tests, achievement tests, aptitude tests, and interest inventories, as well as other information.

5. *Tests facilitate grouping.* The education of some groups of superior students in certain areas may best be accomplished by segregating them—either from students in general, or from other superior students. If special grouping is to be successful, it must reduce the variability of the group with respect to the particular area in which the group is to receive instruction. As bases for grouping, achievement, intelligence, and aptitude-test scores may be useful either individually or in various combinations.

## CAUTIONS TO BE OBSERVED IN EVALUATING TEST RESULTS

A multitude of suggestions or cautions for using test results could be listed. Four important ones are:

1. *Look for patterns.* It is not wise to base decisions about an individual student on a single test score. Test scores are most reliable as data if there is more than one test, and if the scores fall into a pattern. Several estimates of IQ, the results of a good aptitude battery, achievement test scores from various years, and one or more interest inventory profiles all together provide a wealth of valuable information. If a consistent pattern of test scores also fits

into the total picture of a student—a picture derived from many sources, for example, teacher reports and interview data—one may place considerable faith in that pattern. If a pattern does not appear, it may be necessary to seek additional data—both objective and subjective.

2. *Evaluate various alternatives.* In seeking a pattern of test scores, one must not lose sight of data that do not fall into the pattern. It is important to let the test scores speak for themselves, even if they do not agree with other data or are not immediately comprehensible. Data which seem out of line must be evaluated and either dismissed as inconsequential or inaccurate (some test scores are), included in an alternate pattern, or kept on the shelf, so to speak, until further data are collected.

3. *Know tests.* Test scores cannot be meaningfully evaluated unless one knows something about the test instruments used and how they work. Suppose that Test A, a general intelligence test, has a standard deviation of 12, while Test B, another general intelligence test, has a standard deviation of 16. This means that an IQ of 112 on Test A corresponds to an IQ of 116 on Test B, and that 124 on Test A corresponds to 132 on Test B. A difference of 8 IQ points might be interpreted as significant if one did not understand the statistical bases of the tests. In the example above, only 4 per cent of all students would be expected to receive an IQ score of 120 or above on Test A, while 10 per cent would be expected to score 120 or above on Test B.

4. *Know the meaning of derived scores.* Anyone dealing with standardized tests will be confronted with IQ's, percentiles, standard scores, grade equivalents, and the like. If one hopes to use test scores in looking for a pattern, he must be able—either mentally or statistically—to convert all such scores to a common scale. It is also necessary to know the characteristics of different types of derived scores.

## CONCLUSION

Two generalizations should be kept in mind when considering the use of test results in the guidance of all students, including superior and talented students: (1) Test scores provide valuable information which can be helpful in guiding individual students. (2) Test scores are not infallible measures of individual student characteristics.

# 18 COLLEGE INFORMATION FOR SUPERIOR AND TALENTED STUDENTS

CALVIN J. DAANE
*Assistant Professor of Education, Division of Counseling and Guidance, Iowa State Teachers College*

College information is factual, easily understood, and readily available, but at the same time it is voluminous and ever changing. The program for disseminating college information must include features that allow full coverage and must have built-in methods for keeping materials up to date. For all students, but especially for the superior and talented, the program must involve the school's entire guidance department and all the counseling tools available. The organization of college material will provide the focus of communications between parent, talented student, counselor, and college admissions officer. In this chapter, three important questions will be considered in the attempt to define a pattern of organization for college information: (1) What information is needed by superior students who are college bound? (2) How can a secondary school organize the available information on colleges for its most efficient use? (3) What is the counselor's role in such a program?

## COLLEGE SELECTION

College admission is a two-sided story: proper selection within long-range plans for the high school student and counselor; and, for the college, recruitment of a good student body. The objective is the same for both: education that satisfies personal and national needs, and maximum efficiency of the process.

In attaining this objective, however, the goals of the college and of the high school counselor are not, on the surface, identical. The reputation of a college depends on the kinds of students it attracts, as well as on its endowment and current revenue. Each college seeks prospective students who will uphold or enhance the institution's prestige. The selection and admission of students have become very specialized parts of the college personnel program. Admissions officers distribute informative pamphlets and catalogues, make public speeches, and conduct direct interviewing. There has been an attempt in recent years to make college catalogues more realistically informative, but many of them still glamorize the details of college life. For years, colleges have been concerned with differences in quality among high schools as well as with differences in patterns of student preparation. High school counselors, on the other hand, are often reluctant to make value judgments about colleges. This judgmental restraint more often benefits the college than the individual student.

Actually, in the area of human and institutional evaluation, much of the needed information is hidden beneath the surface and thus unknown; much of what is known is often left unsaid. Could the admissions officer be expected to stress the limitations of his college, or spend much time pointing out its weaknesses? Could the counselor be expected to relate information surrounding attitude and motivation revealed to him in confidence? Even objective tests measure only achievement and maturity, and their results are subject to all the limitations of statistical estimates.

Most parents are well aware of the economic as well as the aesthetic advantages of a college education. Figures such as those quoted from the 1950 census, which show more college graduates than nongraduates with lifetime earnings over $100,000, are well publicized. Earnings of graduates of prestige schools are reported to be even higher, and parents often succumb to the lure of these schools without considering whether their qualities actually suit a particular youngster's needs. The prestige schools and those which border that description are expected to become still more selective in the future. Large numbers of other colleges are broadening their curriculums to include programs of technical training, and are striving to improve their faculties. Parents as well as students need and want access to more college information and a competent counselor's help in reviewing the possibilities of college selection.

*Lovejoy's College Guide* lists 2266 institutions of higher education. Most of these confer baccalaureate degrees. Some have very impressive faculties, beautiful campuses, and large enrollments, and some do not. There are obvious differences in size, location, and

customs. There are variations in tuition fee and in affiliation—
state, community, church, or private. There are men's colleges, two-
year colleges, and technical schools, as well as teachers colleges and
specialized graduate and professional schools. Recent reports predict that these colleges will accommodate more than six million
students in 1970.

## Accreditation

Regional accrediting associations, all major professions, and most
state departments of education provide approval ratings for colleges
which adhere to specific, established standards. Representatives of
the associations inspect the colleges for curriculum, quality of instruction, and available facilities. These endorsements are highly
prized by colleges and are always listed in college catalogues. Published listings are also available and they should influence the student in making value judgments. A degree from a nonaccredited
college may cause difficulties if application is made to a graduate
school. It is generally agreed that the most valued accreditation
comes from the six regional associations: the Middle States Association, the New England Association, the North Central Association,
the Northwest Association, the Southern Association, and the Western Association.

## Admissions Requirements

There are five major factors which colleges use in evaluating candidates: scholastic records from high school; test scores of achievement and ability; personal data about personality traits and motivation; recommendations from high school teachers, counselors, and
administrators; and the reputation of the recommending school.

Standardized tests of achievement and ability have been used
widely. Despite the previous absence of high correlation with actual
college success, more recent refinements in tests show encouraging
results and colleges rely upon them heavily.

Personal data gathered from autobiographies or from written
statements, either structured or unstructured, indicate general ability in written expression, as well as knowledge of communications

skills and active vocabulary. Application forms often include questions in the areas of current events, books, and plays. Some of the queries are designed so that the applicant will reveal his general health, emotional stability, and extracurricular and community participation. Often applicants are asked why they want a college education, or even why they chose a particular college. Unlike the other types of data assembled, these open-ended questions have some elements of the essay examination. Answers to these questions often indirectly reveal such things as level of aspiration, level of tolerance, patterns of defensive behaviors, and areas of active problems.

Recommendations from school officials are also important. Structured rating scales, as well as informal statements of opinion and objective observation, are frequently requested by colleges. Admissions officers rely heavily on these, especially as they learn the predictive value of certain school officials' recommendations.

## ORGANIZING A COLLEGE INFORMATION PROGRAM

There are three sources of information which will assist college-bound students: (1) information from tours and visits to college campuses; (2) information from speeches, group discussions, and audio-visual aids in the high school; and (3) information from published literature.

Some colleges invite high school seniors to visit the campus and even attend some classes if they desire to do so. The visit may include time for informal discussions with college officials and students, and a period when questions may be asked. Regardless of whether a college has set aside a special day, all admissions officers welcome visiting students and do what they can to make visits comfortable and informative. Whenever possible, students should plan to visit campuses before making application and after narrowing their choice to four or five colleges.

Admissions officers travel extensively and spend much of their time visiting high schools and speaking to faculty, parents, and students. College days, with representatives of several colleges visiting the same school, usually achieve most when assemblies or group discussions have been held as orientation for the day, and when students have done some thinking about tentative college choices. Some schools schedule several days, one per week, in order to make it more convenient for students to talk with representatives of various colleges. Sometimes the programs are held in the evening to avoid disruption of regular classes and to make it convenient for parents to attend. Often the college day is scheduled as the main event in a special week devoted to college information—with films, posters, after-school discussion groups, and special units presented in some classrooms. In other cases, admissions officers are invited to meet with students in small groups throughout the week.

Published descriptions and listings of colleges—including descriptions of courses of study—will supply most of the material needed on a college information shelf. The organization of this material will determine its usefulness to the students. All catalogues and publications meant for the student should be easily accessible in the library or in a separate room near the counselor's office. The information center should contain college directories and catalogues as well as books and pamphlets giving information on scholarships, loans, work-study opportunities, and financial aid in general.

The catalogues can be organized in several ways, each with advantages for efficient use. One good plan is to arrange the catalogues (alphabetically) in groups according to geographical location, with subgroups for junior colleges, technical schools, four-year degree-granting institutions, and graduate and professional schools. This will help many kinds of students including the student who is most interested in location, the student who can afford only two years of advanced education, and the student who has planned a long-range graduate program.

A loose-leaf folder providing a key to efficient use of the catalogues should be established. Whenever composite listings are available, such as *Lovejoy's College Guide*, which lists the schools granting degrees in various majors, the folder should refer to both this listing and the alphabetical list for each subgroup. Schools with ROTC units, seminaries, and other special facilities, listed in publications such as Brownstein's *College Bound*, can be similarly keyed. The loose-leaf folder, then, will afford maximum student use by anticipating questions and organizing information for ease in finding answers. The catalogue shelf itself should have attractive labels, and the sheets in the loose-leaf folder should be typed and carefully bound.

## Materials Available

There are several good directories of colleges which include brief descriptions of the institutions and specific information on tuition costs, entrance requirements, degrees conferred, facilities, and where to write for further information. Some list colleges by geographical location, major subject fields, membership in the College Entrance Examination Board, and other classifications. Volumes listing scholarships and how to apply for them are also available, along with many good publications on college preparation and planning. These materials are invaluable to the college-bound student, and a representative selection of them should be available in every high school. The following are suggested:

### General

Bogue, Jesse P. *American Junior Colleges* (4th ed. 1956; rev. Spring 1960). American Council on Education, 1785 Massachusetts Ave., N.W., Washington 6, D.C.

Brownstein, Samuel C. *College Bound* (1957). Barron's Educational Series, 343 Great Neck Rd., Great Neck, N.Y.

Burckel, Christian E. *College Blue Book* (1959). Christian E. Burckel, Publisher, Yonkers, N.Y.

Bunting, James E. *Private Independent Schools* (12th ed.) 12 N. Main St., Wallington, Conn.

Cohn, Nathan. *Vocational Training Directory of the United States* (1958). Potomac Press, 2607 Arlington Blvd., Arlington 1, Va.

Fine, Benjamin. *Fine's American College Counselor and Guide* (1958–59 edition). Prentice-Hall, Englewood Cliffs, N.J.

Hill, Alfred T. *A Directory of Small Colleges* (1958). Council for the Advancement of Small Colleges, 726 Jackson Pl., N.W., Washington 6, D.C.

Irwin, Mary (ed.), *American Universities and Colleges* (1956; rev. Spring 1960). American Council on Education, 1785 Massachusetts Ave., N.W., Washington 6, D.C.

Karl, S. Donald (ed.). *The College Handbook* (1959). College Entrance Examination Board, P.O. Box 592, Princeton, N.J., or Box 27896, Los Angeles, Calif.

Lovejoy, Clarence E. *Lovejoy's College Guide* (rev. ed. 1959). Simon & Schuster, 630 Fifth Ave., New York 20, N.Y.

*The Official Guide to Catholic Educational Institutions in the United States* (1959). Catholic Institutional Directory Co., Grand Central Terminal Building, New York 17, N.Y.

## Scholarships

American Legion National Child Welfare Division. *Need a Lift?: Educational Opportunities* (6th ed. 1956). Scholarship Information Service, National Child Welfare Division, American Legion, Indianapolis, Ind.
Brownstein, Samuel C., Weiner, Mitchel, and Kaplan, Stanley. *You Can Win a Scholarship* (1956). Barron's Educational Series, 343 Great Neck Rd., Great Neck, N.Y.
Feingold, Norman. *Scholarships, Fellowships and Loans* (3 vol. 1949). Bellman Publishing Co., P.O. Box 172, Cambridge 38, Mass. Vol. III is recommended.
Lovejoy, Clarence E., and Jones, Theodore S. *Lovejoy-Jones College Scholarship Guide* (1957). Simon & Schuster, 630 Fifth Ave., New York 20, N.Y.
Potter, Virginia Bosch. *Fellowships in the Arts and Sciences* (1959). Association of American Colleges, Publications Division, American Council on Education, 1785 Massachusetts Ave., N.W., Washington 6, D.C.
Welkins, Theresa. *Financial Aid for College Students: Undergraduate.* U.S. Office of Education Bulletin No. 18, (1957). Government Printing Office, Washington, D.C.

## College Preparation and Planning

Adams, George. *How To Afford That College Education and Where To Study* (1956). Harian Publications, Greenlawn, N.Y.
Bowles, Frank. *How To Get Into College* (1958). E. P. Dutton & Co., 300 Fourth Ave., New York 10, N.Y.
Brownstein, Samuel C. *How To Prepare for College Entrance Examinations* (1955). Barron's Educational Series, 343 Great Neck Rd., Great Neck, N.Y.
Daane, Calvin J., VanderLinden, Peters, and others. *Introduction To College* (1958). Allyn & Bacon, 150 Tremont St., Boston 11, Mass.
Fine, Benjamin. *How To Be Accepted by the College of Your Choice* (1957). Channel Press, Great Neck, N.Y.
Landis, Paul H. *So This Is College* (1954). McGraw-Hill Book Co., N.Y.
McReynolds, John W. *How To Plan for College and What To Do When You Get There* (1956). Simon & Schuster, 630 Fifth Ave., New York 20, N.Y.
National Vocational Guidance Association. *How To Visit Colleges* (1954). Public Information and Professional Relations Committee, National Vocational Guidance Association, 1605 New Hampshire Ave., N.W., Washington 9, D.C.
Science Research Associates. *How To Get into College and Stay There* (1958). Science Research Associates, 259 E. Erie St., Chicago 11, Ill.
Wilson, Eugene S., and Bucher, Charles A. *College Ahead* (1958). Harcourt, Brace & Co., 750 Third Ave., New York, N.Y.

## Advanced Placement and Early Admissions

Some high schools are now offering college-level courses during the senior year through the Advanced Placement Program. Other acceleration programs provide for summer sessions. In some of these courses, college credit can be earned on a college campus prior to high school graduation, usually following the junior year. Through the Early Admissions Plan, some colleges enroll freshmen after only three years of high school on the basis of a suitable record and high test results.

The College Entrance Examination Board's Advanced Placement Program now includes more than 400 high schools offering some college-level courses and 339 colleges that indicate a willingness to accept students in an accelerated program. A passing score on the Board's advanced placement examination and a good high school record are the criteria for acceptance of credit.

There are many of these experimental programs, and they vary in offerings and procedures. The counselor will need to scan publications and keep in touch with colleges in order to keep informed in a rapidly changing and experimental field. New programs open continually, and it is difficult to find descriptions that are current and accurate. One of the best sources of information is the education page in the News of the Week section of the *New York Times* Sunday edition.

## Scholarships, Aids, and Loans

There are many scholarships available to today's student. Perhaps the largest and most carefully organized of such programs is the National Merit Scholarship Program. Colleges themselves offer a variety of grants ranging from $100 a year to full tuition for four years. Various industries grant thousands of dollars each year, with one company alone awarding over 285 individual grants yearly. Added to these are funds supplied by private foundations, church groups, fraternal organizations, and individuals.

Scholarships are generally awarded on the basis of achievement, good character, and financial need. Often candidates take competitive tests, but more and more the criterion of financial need is recognized as the basic consideration. Many donors of financial assistance discourage financially able students from applying. The Association of College Admissions Counselors has publicly asked the co-operation of parents and counselors in this effort.

## Work Programs

Work programs designed to aid the talented and ambitious are also numerous. Almost every college offers some part-time employment. Summer jobs are available for student trainees in professional and technical careers: in the U. S. Department of Agriculture for food inspection and forest service; in the Department of the Air Force for scientific and engineering fields; and in the Department of Commerce for coast and geodetic surveys and highway road repair. Other government agencies, as well as private organizations, offer employment opportunities for able students.

## The Counseling Process

Keeping information about many colleges up to date is a large organizational project. The major concern of a college information program, however, is to help students toward true self-appraisal and evaluation. When college choice is put in the perspective of life experience, it must involve the individual's motivation, interests, social development, physical development, intellectual capacity, and various personality characteristics.

Choice of college as well as of specific majors is based on emotional exploration as well as on intellectual assessment, and making a choice involves giving up the lesser in order to pursue and gain the greater goal. Before students can really establish their greater goals they must understand themselves—their aspirations and their abilities.

The student will invariably pick up information relative to these factors in his daily contact with others. Some of it will be accurate and some of it will be inaccurate, but all of it will be relevant and eagerly appraised by the student. The absence of self-understanding is not so much due to incorrect information as it is to inadequate and unorganized information. A young person must organize the data he has gathered about himself before he can arrive at decisions.

How can counselors structure a program in the secondary schools which will help students organize information about themselves? The time-proven method, of course, is the individual counseling process. Through structured observations, the counselor can collect objective and subjective data about a student and assist the student in making an educated interpretation of the data.

An interpretation of data, as well as the student's understanding and acceptance of the interpretation, must be checked for its validity by means of the verbal clarification techniques used in counseling interviews. A counselee may examine his interpretation as the counselor uses techniques of reflection, clarification, and support. The counseling process provides the counselee with a relatively safe atmosphere in which to consider facts about himself. Counseling also allows a counselee to clarify, verbally, the important elements of his motives and primary objectives.

If a student is to make a mature decision about college, he must be aware of the social and psychological structure of occupations that require college training or other types of formal learning. He must have the information and tools he needs to discover a suitable vocational goal for himself. Motivation for college depends upon seeing college as a continuing link in preparation for productive life.

In the days of Ben Franklin, a father could take his son by the hand, walk down the street, stopping at various shops and factories, and answer the boy's questions as he observed firsthand the duties performed and the abilities required in each job. In one afternoon, the son could learn something about all the occupations being practiced. Today, it is not so simple: some twenty-two thousand occupations are listed in the *Dictionary of Occupational Titles*.

Counselors can no longer think in terms of a single appropriate job for a counselee; they must consider job groups or families. It has been known for some time that one individual, especially a superior one, might have the potential for any one of several vocational or educational choices. Only recently, however, have Tyler (241), and others developed this concept.

## SUMMARY

The college information program is not a library, but an integral part of the school's total guidance program. Both counselor and student must make a concerted effort to uncover information that will lead to the student's mature self-direction. All facts, materials, and efforts must support this end. The usefulness of the materials gathered depends on the relationship that exists between counselor and counselee. A Chinese proverb which says, "A load of books does not equal one good teacher" might be altered to say, "An armful of college materials does not equal one good counselor."

# 19 COUNSELING SERVICES FOR TALENTED HIGH SCHOOL STUDENTS

HERMAN J. PETERS
*Professor of Education,*
*The Ohio State University*

The purpose of this paper is to explore the counseling service for talented students in junior and senior high school. Most of the ideas reported here, however, are applicable to the counseling service for all students.

Counseling is a private, one-to-one psychological interaction in which the counselor assists the counselee to adjust to some concern or concerns. The heart of the counseling process is the interview. The counseling process consists of preparation for the interview through study of the student's records and the gathering of educational or vocational information pertaining to the student, interaction during the interview, study of what happens after the interview, and arrangements for another interview if necessary.

Process and interaction are the two key words in the analysis of counseling. Both terms connote an ongoing, evolving, dynamic stream of experiences as contrasted to one or more unrelated or distinct events that a student may experience in conferences. It is in the counseling service that the real meaning of all guidance activities finds expression. Other guidance activities may have an important and beneficial influence on students. Group guidance activities, for example, may make important contributions to some students' optimum development. Only individual counseling, however, can really be adapted to the unique needs of a particular student. Correll states:

> The counseling process may be construed as a learning process, instituted and maintained in an atmosphere removed from daily pressures of work, study, grades, and compelling social demands. It differs from the usual classroom learning situation, in that the understandings to be derived are usually more closely associated with the learner's own personal needs, his happiness, and his sense of security and well being. This being the case, it might be expected that the learner usually experiences a consid-

erable amount of emotional reaction to the subject under discussion. Equally important, is the fact that the learner also experiences some degree of emotional reaction to the learning process itself. The various attitudes and feelings of the learner manifest themselves in many diverse ways within the context of the learning situation. The learner's manifestations, together with the reactions and behaviors of the counselor, constitute the climate in which client-learning will develop. The formulation of the problem, the level and method of attack upon it, and the final specific and generalized solutions are all thus influenced by the characteristics of this learning climate that is established within the counseling setting (45).

Counseling, as well as other guidance services, is an integral part of a school's educational program and, as such, should facilitate a student's learning of subject matter so that he will reach maximum productivity and full personality development. This is important not only in terms of individual satisfaction, but also in terms of society's needs and goals. Guidance services seek to help students develop in a positive manner throughout their school careers. Guidance services are intended to assist students to progress toward educational, vocational, and personal fulfillment.

Before discussing the process of counseling in detail, it is appropriate to consider briefly the kind of person who should become a school counselor.

## WHO DOES THE COUNSELING?

The effectiveness of counseling depends on the kind of person the school counselor is. He should have completed at least a minimum of advanced graduate work, and should hold a master's degree in counseling and guidance. The school counselor should be an active member of the American School Counselors Association, a division of the American Personnel and Guidance Association. He should have demonstrated a high degree of scholarship in his academic studies, especially if he works with talented students. He should have developed a sensitivity to the affective development of adolescents. He should feel at ease with and understand both boys and girls, since relatively few schools now assign counselors to boys only or girls only. He should be a student of developmental psychology, and his warmth and interest in boys and girls should be matched by the dignity of having a purposeful direction in life. Finally, he should not impose his philosophy on others, but should himself exemplify the importance of having worthwhile goals.

## WHAT ARE THE FACILITIES NEEDED FOR THE COUNSELING SERVICE?

To be effective and in keeping with the principles of guidance, counseling should be conducted in an atmosphere of privacy. Therefore, the school counselor should have a private office that is easily accessible to students. Provision should be made so that some guidance reading material will be readily available to the students and most guidance records easily reached by the counselor. Decentralization of guidance records and reading materials often inhibits rather than facilitates their use.

In order that the counselor may have sufficient time to counsel with students, his full-time job should be counseling and other guidance duties. Responsibility for students should be assigned at the ratio of one counselor for each three hundred students.

## WHAT STUDENTS HAVE COUNSELING PRIORITY?

The writer recommends that the counselor assign the following counseling priorities for students: (1) bright motivated students, (2) normal motivated students, (3) bright minimally motivated students, (4) normal minimally motivated students, (5) slow-learning motivated students, (6) slow-learning minimally motivated students, and (7) behavioral incorrigibles.

Too often the school counselor wastes time working with dull or slow-learning students in the hope that the counseling service may assist them to more effective school achievement. Counseling is based in large measure on a student's ability to perceive new relationships in life as a result of insightful thinking prompted by the interactive process between himself and the counselor. To perceive these relationships, average or above-average intelligence is required. Slow-learning students may profit from individualized help of a highly directive nature. This kind of directive help, however, is not the real purpose of the counseling process.

In this latter half of the twentieth century it is imperative for national and individual welfare that considerable counseling service be provided for the able and outstanding student. This is well documented in the following statements by Russell and Cronbach, Witty, Terman and Oden, and Bray, respectively:

Individual counseling is an essential step in encouraging the talented. The interpretation of tests to students, parents, and school staffs must be done by specially trained counselors who know the meaning and limitations of tests and understand student motivation. Counseling is a difficult and specialized task which cannot be performed adequately even by good teachers if they lack this training. . . . (205)

The academically talented youth has many choices to make, and he needs help in understanding the alternatives, in estimating his own potentialities and in seeing the possible consequences of decisions. Indeed, guidance must be comprehensive, continually available and realistic in terms of desirable educational objectives. (43)

Counseling at the high school level is not only necessary to insure that more of the brighter students will get the amount of training they should have, but also to insure that each will get the kind of training best adapted to prepare him for later specialization. . . . (235)

A young person's occupational goal can strongly influence his motivation in school. The opposite is also true; intrinsic motivation to perform in school can influence his occupational choice. The youngster who enjoys school, does well, and is rewarded for his efforts generally wants to continue in school. He is, therefore, more likely to attain the educational qualifications that will permit him to choose an occupation which carries status. (28)

The above quotations illustrate the urgent need for counseling for the talented. In a very real sense the counseling service is the epitome of a democratic educational philosophy. The concern of counseling, in the case of each individual capable of participating in the counseling process, is that individual's unique personal progress toward maturity. Every other educational endeavor, excellent teaching included, is in some way related to a group process or group procedure.

## HOW MAY PRONENESS FOR COUNSELING BE DEVELOPED IN THE TALENTED STUDENT?

Talented youth can profit most from the counseling service if a proneness for counseling has been developed in them. Among the things that counselors may do to build this proneness are:

1. Administer an adjustment inventory such as the SRA Youth Inventory, the Minnesota Counseling Inventory, or the Mooney Problem Check List to classes that include talented youth. Students may wish to discuss their inventory profiles with the counselor.

2. Announce opportunities to discuss planning of high school courses with a counselor.

3. Call in students to encourage them to continue their outstanding performance. This may stimulate them to request further interviews.

4. Provide opportunities to analyze interest profiles with a counselor.

5. Provide the instructional staff with occupational information in their subject areas. Encourage the staff to disseminate this information and to discuss long-term educational planning with their students.

6. Use various communications media such as the public address system, bulletin board, and school newspaper to announce scholarships and scholarship testing. Encourage students to seek counseling interviews to discuss scholarship aid.

7. Schedule parent interviews. They may stimulate students to use the counseling service.

There are several general practices which the counselor should follow that may encourage superior students to use the counseling service. The following activities are recommended:

1. Emphasize a positive, developmental approach to the concerns of youth. Students should realize that the counseling service is equipped to help with the problems faced by *normal* students.

2. Follow through on decisions reached in a counseling interview. Thus, other students will soon hear that the counseling service is helpful.

3. Work with the school staff so that they will be aware of the activity in the counseling office. This does not mean the violation of confidences. Rather, it means that the counselor, student, and teacher should work as a team to help the student achieve maximum educational progress.

4. Send periodic reports to the parents on counseling service activities. Again, confidences should not be violated. However, parents are more apt to support the total guidance program if they know of the counseling as well as the other guidance activities.

5. Take into consideration that students, talented and otherwise, will readily discuss some concerns but not others. An emotionally disturbed adolescent, for example, may discuss course selection much more freely than he will his emotional problems.

## WHAT IS INVOLVED IN THE COUNSELING PROCESS?

The three factors which enable the counseling process to modify or change behavior are (1) the counselor, (2) the counselee, and (3) the interaction between the counselor and counselee. Volumes have been written on the counseling process—its theory and approaches. Only a few pertinent points relating to this process will be discussed here.

The counseling process may have immediate, short-term, and long-range effects. It is particularly important that the counselor give some kind of immediate help to the student—help which the student himself can perceive. Because adolescents live in the *now*, they are seldom consoled by learning that "things will work out in the long run." Superior students have a greater time perspective. This is one of the differences between superior and average students: superior students are more *future*-oriented, average students more *now*-oriented (60). Consequently, immediately perceptible help is not of such great importance in counseling superior students as in counseling other students. In any counseling situation, the counselor must keep in mind that he is professionally obligated to provide learning and emotional experiences that will have positive impact on long-range student concerns.

For an adolescent, the counseling interview probably affords the first opportunity in his school career to take a deep look at his inner self in an atmosphere of acceptance, permissiveness, and privacy. His inner and outer worlds are strange topics of conversation, and even stranger is discussing them with an adult—the counselor. Therefore, the counselor has the tremendous responsibility of assisting the adolescent to examine his attitudes toward life. Through this counseling process the talented adolescent has an unusual opportunity to use his intellectual ability in arriving at conclusions about himself and his future.

The counseling process is not advice giving. Counseling emphasizes helping the student to "see for himself." If a student arrives at his own decision, he is more likely to take positive action to implement that decision. Talented youth usually rise to the confidence adults demonstrate in their thinking. They reject paternalistic or maternalistic advice, regardless of its merit.

The nature of the guidance process, including the counseling service, is succinctly outlined in a U.S. Office of Education publication. The writer quotes at length from it because he agrees with the philosophy it incorporates.

The selection of curricular sequences at the eighth- and ninth-grade level is predicated on the following principles:

1. The voluntary selection of a curricular sequence is the privilege of each student.

2. Selection by the student of a curricular sequence and of vocational goals should be made only after all information pertinent to general *intellectual level* and specific aptitudes has been made available to him by his counselor. It follows that the procedures for getting information must apply to the entire student body and not just to those who are expected to enter a particular curriculum.

3. *After the curricular sequence has been selected* other factors such as vocational interests, personality characteristics, emotional maturity, and socio-economic status, should be identified and analyzed with respect to their positive and negative influences on the full development of curricular plan.

4. Guidance in the selection of curricular sequences consists of more than counseling. A systematic program of measurement should be carried on to get the information referred to in principle 2. Counseling is but one aspect of the guidance program and is dependent upon other procedures.

5. After a student has enrolled in one curricular sequence, there should be provisions in school regulations and guidance procedures to permit periodic reassessment of (1) the original curricular choice or decision, and (2) other personal and environmental factors, to determine the validity of the chosen sequence and to determine whether a revision of plans is indicated, such as, a transfer to other curricular sequence.

6. Effective guidance procedures at the junior and senior high school levels and appropriate articulation between high schools and colleges, should reduce the need for college entrance examinations.

These six principles which were determined by a reanalysis of youth characteristics are not entirely consistent with current thinking. Yet neither can they be considered as a radical departure. The approach generally accepted might be stated as follows:

The selection by the student of a curricular sequence should be accomplished after he and the counselor have as complete information as possible regarding his aptitudes, achievements, personality traits, and interests, the parents' desires, the economic status of the family, the curricular sequences, occupational fields, and the general summary of the situation as the counselor or other guidance official sees it. (211)

What does research tell us about counseling the talented? Although there are countless articles on the talented, few of them deal particularly with counseling the talented. This in itself reflects a need. Gowan reports a few research studies in the guidance area, but these are not specifically related to the counseling service. He says: "Evidence accumulates that lack of stimulation of gifted children is one of the important factors in underachievement and drop-out problems. Further research on the effects of early vocational stimulation of gifted children is needed" (91). Research is needed to determine the efficiency of counseling for the talented in relation to their specific concerns.

## CONCLUSION

The services of counseling for the talented student may be summarized as follows:

1. Counseling gives empathic personal recognition to the talented student's abilities.

2. The counseling process enables the talented student to explore fully the implications of his abilities, including the responsibility that goes with them.

3. The counseling interview provides encouragement for the talented youth who needs to re-energize his drive or reconfirm or reappraise his progress toward responsible adulthood.

To paraphrase Linnaeus, eighteenth century Swedish scientist and teacher: A counselor can never better distinguish himself in his work than by encouraging a clever pupil, for the true discoverers are among them, as comets among the stars.

# SECTION VI

## MOTIVATION

Educators now realize that they need to know more about a superior student than his ability level in order to challenge him in the educative process. They need to know and understand such operative factors as his self-concept, his school attitudes, his out-of-school pursuits, his perception of his family, his models, and his peer relationships. Many studies have documented the fact that certain personality and character traits, when combined with above-average intelligence, produce significant achievement. Because we are not yet able to understand the basis of some of these personality and character traits or to measure them objectively, many talented students go unchallenged.

With a knowledge of the motives that operate in the life of a superior student, a sensitive teacher is in a better position to help the student overcome any maladjustments that may be preventing achievement commensurate with his ability. Motives have a definite effect on a student's achievement, since learning is an individual process. Only the student himself can learn; no one can do it for him. Since instruction must be experienced by the individual, it is difficult to supply forms of motivation for an entire class.

Some teachers assume that if a student recognizes the value of education he will be sufficiently motivated. They reason that students will rise to the demands of school work by dint of sheer loyalty to abstract duty. Other teachers take the view that motivation originates from, and is sustained by, the physical (or biological) and social drives of the human organism. They feel that students achieve not because of loyalty to abstract duty, but because of intensity of commitment to a larger, more remote, more inclusive end.

Unexplained variations in academic achievement seem to account for much of the present concern with motivation. While curriculum can be thought of as external to the student, motivation cannot be. Motivation is particularly personal to the student. Just what it is and how it can be induced, however, remains unknown. Many people look upon school work as a means toward personal profit; more often than not, parents' main interest in having their children go to school is that the children "get ahead."

Motivation has been described as a kind of tension, a tension which involves something more than ordinary attention. Motivation has also been characterized as an emotional attachment or a propulsive fascination; that is, the learner derives a feeling of worth and approval from behavior or activity which his environment invites and approves. When a student accedes to the wishes of a teacher, to think that his purpose and the purpose in the mind of the teacher are necessarily similar may be a delusion.

An examination of motivation poses several questions. What goals do students strive for? How can teachers influence students to select desirable or appropriate goals? Does recognition of the need to motivate superior students constitute tacit admission that genuine motivation is lacking? Do such external inducements and artificial stimuli as grades, examinations, rewards, and punishments imply motivational bankruptcy?

Motivation of a superior student involves helping him develop purposes and expectations that will direct his activities and behavior toward the fulfillment of long-term aspirations and ambitions. All academic performance takes place in a framework of expectation. If teachers do not demand and expect achievement commensurate with a student's ability, they will not get it. This is true for parents and society as a whole, as well as for the school. At every level there must be a framework of high expectations within which talented students will assume that high achievement is a natural and desirable means.

It should be recognized that in the school's efforts to supply motivation for superior students, or for students in general, specifying that intellectual development and going to college are desirable goals sometimes creates conflicting value problems for such students. Educators assume that intellectual achievement and going to college are unquestionably desirable and necessary. But are they always clearly so? The value systems of some superior students may say it is more important for them to assume the responsibilities of marriage. Are all bright students to live by the values held by school officials?

Teachers are aware of the importance of motivation. They know that motivational factors help to account for the large number of talented youth who fail to complete high school or post-high-school education. It was estimated in 1957 that annually up to two hundred thousand American youths capable of college work failed either to enter or to complete college (43). Girls account for a large proportion of this loss of talent. In 1959 Indiana University studied the upper 10 per cent of Indiana high school graduates for 1955. It was found that a high percentage of bright high school girls failed to go on to college. There were twice as many girls as boys in the upper 10 per cent of the 1955 Indiana graduating class, yet only about 64 per cent of them went on to college (269). This educational loss of able women is increasing despite the fact that more women are working over a longer span of years than ever before. For example, although at all ages between five and eighteen there is a slightly larger per cent of the total population of girls in school than boys; and although American women, generally speaking, have about one-half year more of schooling than do American men; at the college level the men outnumber the women. At the postgraduate level, the disparity increases further. In 1956-57 women earned about one-third of the bachelor's and master's degrees, and about one-tenth of the doctorates. Women earned 16 per cent of the total number of doctorates granted in 1920; today they earn about 9 per cent.

In addition, the women who earned bachelor's degrees in 1956-57 for the most part studied subjects customarily popular with women —majoring in education, the fine and applied arts, English, journalism, and foreign languages. Relatively few had majored in the biological sciences, physical sciences, mathematics, law, or medicine. That same year, 70 per cent of the women receiving master's degrees and 31 per cent of those receiving doctorates received their degrees in education. Slightly over one-tenth of the relatively few women receiving doctorates had specialized in the biological sciences, about one-tenth in the social sciences, and almost one-tenth in English or journalism. The three most popular undergraduate majors for men that year were commerce, engineering, and the social sciences. In 1930 women constituted 32.5 per cent of the total number of college presidents, professors, and instructors, as opposed to 23.2 per cent in 1950.

Why are talented girls failing to develop their potential? Many authorities say it is because of an immature attitude on the part of society which makes it unattractive for a woman to be as intelligent as a man. Elizabeth Drews (60) believes many girls renounce intellectuality so that they will be sure to attract boys and find husbands. The attitudes in the school and home toward job discrimination and toward combining a career with marriage and motherhood need re-examination. Bright girls, as well as bright boys, must be encouraged to attend college. This encouragement is necessary because (1) bright girls need self-realization in the area of intellectual achievement, (2) an educated mother can be a powerful influence on her children's attitudes toward academic achievement, (3) society needs the products and services of these able women, and (4) more and more large corporations weigh the value of the wife (both her educational background and social acceptance) when considering her husband for an executive position. These "executive wives" carry far more weight than young girls want to believe; and when the truth is finally brought home, it is too late.

One of the most important things a school can do to increase motivation of superior students is to provide an adequate counseling staff. Counselors can assist the superior student to understand his own potentialities and can give him a sense of the opportunities and challenges that lie before him as a result of those potentialities. Some talented students are completely unaware of their abilities, and many are unaware of the opportunities open to them. If schools really want to help *every* superior student develop his potentialities to the fullest extent, they must provide counseling for those students who are underachieving or not attaining their aspirations.

Gwyn Lile discusses the psychiatric considerations of motivation in Chapter 20. He feels that in each case personnel workers should discover the impediments to achievement and what form the disturbances take. He describes and illustrates six types of emotional disturbance which may cause underachievement. He urges an individual approach to the bright student whose achievement is not commensurate with his ability.

In Chapter 21, Robert J. Havighurst considers the school and motivation, listing four factors which influence motivation toward good school work. In seven cases, he illustrates the differences between superior students with high educational motivation and those with low educational motivation. He lists some methods for motivating students and points out that the school's strategy for girls must be different from that for boys.

Robert S. Daniel, in Chapter 22, deals directly with the problem of underachievement. He gives a general description of the underachiever, and warns educators of the limitations of available research studies and the danger of using "word magic" for factors not well understood. He summarizes four contributions of psychological research which might well be applicable to motivation in the classroom.

In Chapter 23, Nicholas Hobbs analyzes the current social concern for motivation to high achievement. He believes a cultural revolution has been sparked in America which will assist the school in motivating bright students. From his own study of fifteen bright, high-achieving students and fifteen bright, low-achieving students, he reports that home environment, the origin of motivation, and relationships between high achievers and parents are factors that facilitate or impede motivation to high achievement. His study implies that parents can be influential in helping superior students understand their abilities and opportunities, and that both parents and teachers provide the framework in which children decide what is worth striving for.

# 20 PSYCHIATRIC CONSIDERATIONS OF MOTIVATION

GWYN H. LILE

*Assistant Professor of Psychiatry, University of Chicago, and Consultant in Psychiatry, Tinley Park State Medical Hospital, Chicago*

Modern psychiatry has extended its area of interest from the study of the peculiar, twisted mind of the mental patient to include the study of the many emotional currents and conflicts that affect and shape us all. Such action has resulted in better understanding of abnormal individuals and has led to some interesting and startling discoveries of principles that govern human behavior in general. The body of knowledge thus gained (although still incomplete) enables a psychiatrist to make some observations about motivation of the superior and talented.

There has been a great deal of study of sociological factors in the motivation of students. Miriam Goldberg summarizes this research in Chapter 4. As she says, "Social and cultural factors . . . alone cannot explain why a particular individual does or does not translate his ability into performance." This writer has seen the daughter of the town drunk graduate *summa cum laude* from college, and the near-genius son of a college professor flunk out. Surely there were other than sociological factors in operation in these cases. Psychiatry has not found the answer to what makes a person of superior intellect into a creative genius, and such an answer will not be possible for a long time (142, 118). Psychiatry, however, does offer a few insights for the teacher who is trying to understand the underachieving student.

## WHAT CAUSES UNDERACHIEVEMENT?

Let us begin by shifting the emphasis a little. It is a biological fact that all young organisms enjoy mastering things. This is one of the reasons for play. In the rough-and-tumble of playing, the young animal learns to use his muscles to master the mysterious forces of gravity, inertia, momentum, and balance, and this learning is a pleasant experience. A baby, for example, is delighted with his first faltering steps, and later will jump from higher and higher objects just for the pleasure of discovering that he can do it. There is a natural tendency for all growing animals to seek out tasks to master and to derive pleasure from mastering them. This pleasure in mastery continues throughout childhood well into adulthood, except under unusual circumstances—which leads to the following shift in emphasis: It is not that an underachieving child is unmotivated but rather that something has interfered with his natural tendency to want to learn. This shift in emphasis is especially important in the case of the underachieving superior student. The psychiatrist will not ask why he is unmotivated, but rather will seek to discover what it is that is interfering with this child's desire to learn.

Too frequently, teachers refer to a student who is not achieving as having a "low achievement drive." There is no objection to this term as a sort of shorthand expression, but it is disconcerting that some investigators think of it as an explanation. To use a rather ridiculous example to illustrate the point, we might also say that a man who likes to eat noodles has a "high noodle-eating drive" and feel that we have explained the situation completely. The real explanation for this man's fondness for noodles might lie in the fact that his mother always served noodles on Thanksgiving and Christmas, and that whenever he eats noodles he has pleasant memories.

The only case in which the term "low achievement drive" is really useful is that of a child who has some debilitating physical disease. This child, however, would be low in all types of drive, not just achievement. In most other cases of low achievement, trained scrutiny will reveal that a much more complex combination of factors is the cause.

Then, excluding physical disease and cultural factors for the moment, what are the things which interfere with a child's desire to master and achieve? Most learning takes place in a certain kind of emotional atmosphere—one in which there is an absence of other, more pressing concerns, relative freedom from fear, some confidence of success, and a feeling of trust in the surroundings. A horse crazed with fear and hatred of his master cannot be expected to perform well; nor can a student who is distrustful of all authority or overwhelmed with anxious sexual thoughts be expected to absorb knowledge. All the things which interfere with students' desire for mastery can be classified as *emotional disturbances*. The focus should be on the individual and his internal state of emotional well-being. Also, one should attempt *to discover what is causing the disturbance and what form the disturbance is taking*.

This paper will outline some of the signs and symptoms by which a person who is not highly trained can recognize the presence of an emotional disturbance. Also, some comments will be made as to what types of disturbance should be treated by a person with psychological training. Most of these remarks concern the period of adolescence, since this is the time in life when emotional disturbances are most common.

First, it should be recognized that any child under ten years of age whose achievement is seriously below his ability, and in whom social, cultural, or physical factors do not explain the incongruity, could probably benefit from a consultation with a psychiatrist, psychologist, or other person with professional psychological training. With adolescents, however, the situation is even more complex. An adolescent may fail to achieve for all the reasons a child fails to do so, and for others as well; and the underachievement may be either temporary or permanent. Many such learning difficulties can be better understood by closer examination of the psychology of the adolescent, which is discussed in more detail later in this chapter.

Most cases of emotional disturbance fall into six categories that have been delineated by clinicians. A discussion of each follows.

## Specific Learning Blocks

There are some children who seem unable to learn one particular subject (19, 127, 176, 186). Although they do well in other fields, they seem blocked on one particular kind of learning. The following case study illustrates a specific learning block:

> A boy of thirteen with the uncomfortable name of Napoleon was referred to a psychiatric clinic because he seemed to be having extreme difficulty with the subject of mathematics. School officials said he was doing well in all his other subjects. He was, in fact, an honor student

in everything but mathematics, where his performance was quite poor. The boy (in spite of his unusual name) was popular with his classmates, and had even been elected to a class office the very year of the referral.

The boy came to the interview willingly and was quite co-operative. He was a handsome, likable lad who related to the male interviewer in a surprisingly adult fashion, discussing his difficulty with much interest. It was of considerable concern to him, since he planned a career in law and knew that he would at least have to pass high school mathematics courses to be able to enter college. He himself had no idea why he had difficulty with the subject, since he liked his teachers and had always found school interesting, even a little too easy. He confessed to the interviewer that he had always been able to understand his lessons without much effort and had "flubbed off" a little so as not to be known as a "brain." Mathematics, however, was a mystery to him, and his achievement in mathematics tested at three years behind his grade level. He thought, as did school officials, that he was just stupid in mathematics.

At this point in the study the parents were called in for an interview, in keeping with the usual practice in cases involving children. The reason for the specific learning block was not long in emerging. The father was a rather mousy little man who worked as an accountant. In general, there was a good relationship between father and son, each having sincere affection and respect for the other. The father, however, was troubled by feelings of inferiority, and he felt that his one achievement in life had been his rather superior ability in mathematics as a boy. Under the guise of giving his son special tutoring, he had started the boy on multiplication tables even before the boy entered school. Sometimes the father drilled the son unmercifully until the youngster cried and ran away from his father.

Clinicians recognized the father's unconscious fear that his son would excel in the father's one area of achievement. His drilling of the boy, an overcompensation for this fear, inadvertently achieved its unconscious aim: it convinced the boy that, at least in mathematics, he had better not achieve or he would bring down the wrath of his father. The boy and the father were seen in psychotherapy for a brief time, and both showed remarkable ability to comprehend what had happened between them. Gradually Napoleon overcame his fear of mathematics and now he is doing well in law school.

In this example the student was conditioned by early experience to fear a particular subject. Repeated failure at an early age interfered with his desire to learn in this area. Also, the boy's unconscious fear of doing better than his father held him back.

In other cases the specific difficulty may be due to the connotation a subject has for a student. Several subjects have masculine or feminine connotations. For example, mechanical arts, mathematics, physical sciences, and athletics are associated with masculinity in our culture. Girls who are concerned about and need to exaggerate their femininity will have trouble with these subjects and will seem to find them hard. Some girls with the so-called "masculine protest" reaction, who feel the need to compete with boys, will try to excel at these subjects. Similarly, art, music, and, of course, such subjects as home economics will be hard for the boy who is trying to assert his masculinity. In each case the superior student who has fewer problems in accepting his or her sex will not be troubled by a subject's associations with masculinity or femininity; he will feel sufficiently secure in his sex role not to have to bolster his feelings by accepting or rejecting a subject because it is considered "masculine" or "feminine."

There are countless other examples of learning blocks. Those interested should consult a book by Gerald H. J. Pearson (186), which treats this subject extensively.

Cases of superior students with specific learning blocks, where it is suspected that early conditioning experiences are involved— such as the example given—require treatment by a professionally trained person. Sometimes learning blocks can be so discouraging to a superior student that he gives up plans for a challenging career which he might well be able to achieve (3, 74). Failure to recognize such interferences leads to considerable waste of talent.

### Revolt Against Authority

Students who revolt against authority are very disturbing problems for most teachers. The teacher must be an authority figure for the student, since part of the teacher's responsibility is to instruct the student in what to do and to limit the student's behavior in one way or another. For some children, school becomes a kind of unwelcome conscience against which they revolt, often in ways that are very difficult for the teacher and the school to handle. When this happens in students of superior ability, it is particularly troublesome.

Reactions against authority are especially pronounced in the years of adolescence. In fact, a few periods of defiance and a few antisocial acts are almost universal in normal adolescence. In some children this kind of behavior becomes extreme; or—and this is worse for the child—his few necessary acts of defiance are misinterpreted by the authorities, and he is branded a troublemaker. Some of these children are fixed in a pattern of defiance by the reasoning "have the name, have the game." Such occurrence is tragic.

The reason for the period of defiance in adolescence is not difficult to understand if one considers the psychological tasks the adolescent in our society has before him (or her). In a few short years he must go from the relative security of being a child (which is all he has ever known) to being an adult and taking care of himself. He experiences strange physical sensations, all of which are new to him. He feels urges that he cannot fulfill normally for many years, or until he becomes economically able to marry and take on the responsibility of rearing a family. Psychologically he is in limbo— neither child nor adult. In addition, he changes from day to day as he progresses toward adulthood. One day he is a rowdy boy playing baseball; the next he is a Hamlet involved in a philosophical muddle about the nature of things. One day he speaks with the voice of a child; the next he suddenly sounds like a frog. His legs grow alarmingly, and what he has learned about the manipulation of his feet no longer holds true and he trips over things. He can neither depend upon nor understand himself and, since he is changeable, he cannot depend on other people to understand him.

In a way, the adolescent is like a caterpillar becoming a butterfly, except that he cannot crawl into a cocoon to wait for the metamorphosis. In spite of his desire for wings, the temptation is strong to return to the untroubled years of childhood; some do return, remaining children all their lives. Most persons complete the metamorphosis, however, and one of the necessities of assuming a new shape is that the old shape must be thrown off. Until now the adolescent has accepted what his parents said without much real question. He may sometimes have thought they were unfair, but few children really consider their parents wrong in the final analysis. The child has been shaped by his parents and the parent surrogates in the school, and to assume the shape of an adult he must throw off this old shape. Thus he defies, but in his defiance he *is trying to change himself and his inner feelings* more than he is trying to defy specific people.

Two kinds of difficulty derive from this defiance in adolescents, and in clinical practice adolescents are divided into two groups on the basis of their behavior. One group of children does not accept authority and rebels against it. The second group accepts the authority of teachers, but rebels against it still, for reasons that will be explained. Since these two groups of children differ considerably —since not only the reasons behind their behavior, but also the proper methods of handling the difficulty, are different—they will be discussed separately.

In the first group are children who come from homes where discipline is poorly handled. The parents are often self-centered people who punish the child when they feel like it, not when he needs it. Often the parents themselves tend not to accept authority. The child identifies with his parents' lack of respect for authority. He feels that ordinary behavior controls are unnecessary and designed only to show power over him. He takes a "big guy" attitude with peers and is frequently known as a bully. His conduct is simply an attempt on his part to identify with parents and teachers.

Reasoning usually has little effect on this kind of boy (or girl), because he sees reasoning as a clever attempt to trick him and to rationalize the restrictions that are being placed on him. He feels that the real reason for restrictions is that teachers want to show how powerful they are, and it is hard to convince him otherwise. The only persons this kind of boy will really listen to are other members of his peer group, particularly peer group idols, to whom he is often quite dedicated and for whom he will do anything. Only a gifted teacher can reach such a boy and motivate him. Practically the only consistently successful method is for the teacher to become a hero figure whom the boy idolizes. This often requires considerable knowledge of adolescent jargon and thought patterns, some of which can be quite devious.

The other problem found in this group of adolescents is that subtly or overtly some parents foster a child's antisocial behavior, as illustrated by the following case history:

> A seven-year-old boy was brought to a clinic because he set fires. According to his mother, the boy was "incorrigible" in this behavior, setting fire to many things around the house. He had been doing this for several months. When asked how she handled such behavior, the mother was somewhat reticent at first, but then revealed in a self-justificatory way that she had tried to get the boy to set his fires in the sink instead of in the middle of the floor. This hardly seemed an adequate or normal parental reaction. Further investigation revealed that the mother was very unhappy with the father and that she had often thought she would like the house to burn down so that she could go back to live with her mother, from whom she had never freed herself psychologically.

This type of situation is often the explanation for adolescent antisocial acts. Some parents derive a vicarious gratification from their child's misbehavior and transmit this gratification to the child under a veneer of disapproval.

Obviously, problems of this sort are very difficult to solve. The child's behavior is a result of training and is not at all inconsistent with his background. Some psychiatrists feel that the most fruitful treatment of such situations is directed at family attitudes rather than at the child, who is simply doing what he feels he is supposed to do. Other psychiatrists feel that the problem is a social rather than a psychiatric one.

The children who do not rebel openly may also have psychological problems. These children seem to accept authority, but periodically they misbehave in some way. After misbehaving, they feel quite guilty, apologize, and promise to do better. This type of rebellion is illustrated in the following case study:

A seventeen-year-old girl was seen in therapy after she had attempted to take her life by means of sleeping pills. She had tried this several times before since she had been about thirteen years old. She had also exhibited other types of antisocial behavior, including periodic stealing and lying, and episodes in which she would go to a distant city for several days. She had been dismissed from high school because of "promiscuous sexual behavior," which consisted of having intercourse with one boy whom she intended to marry and, in fact, to whom she was married at the time of the suicide attempt referred to above. This fascinating patient was quite brilliant and on her own had completed a course of study equivalent to two years of college. Her taste in literature was excellent, and she wrote short stories, expressing some of her neurotic feelings in such an engrossing way that she had sold several stories to leading national magazines.

The girl's home background was one of extreme severity. Her mother was a harsh person who, because of sexual frigidity, had never felt gratified in her marriage and had strictly forbidden any kind of sexual behavior in her daughter. Sex was a forbidden subject in the house.

In therapy the girl was very contrite and seemed to feel guilty about what she had done and the trouble she had caused. She said she sincerely regretted it, but she warned the therapist that she did not know when such a thing might happen again. As she predicted, she did have new escapades to describe each time she reported for therapy. As the therapist showed her how she could have avoided each one by releasing some emotion a little earlier, she began to improve. She remarked one day after considerable progress, "I couldn't understand your attitude when you first started seeing me. You didn't think I was a terrible person as my mother always has. Poor Mother—she has missed so much, and she almost ruined my life. I guess I either had to give in to her or act like an untamed animal."

After a long and difficult course of therapy, the patient was able to return to college with her husband and she received a degree with honors.

This girl was typical of children who are exposed to severe restrictions in early life and to whose adolescent problems the only solution is to rebel or give in. Either way, they feel very unhappy and guilty. Such students should be given psychological help, and will fortunately usually benefit from it.

## Passivity

In contrast to the rebellious students are some students who are so passive that they are unable to achieve up to their ability. These students, as a rule, have always been quiet and obeyed the rules. Before the advent of intelligence tests and more discerning approaches to the measurement of personality, they were seldom recognized. Many of them do not get into trouble and are not considered problem children. Teachers are often surprised when such a child has a high IQ, and they may find that even concerted efforts to motivate the child produce no results. In fact, they may discover that increased pressure often results in decreased effort, and that at times the child will withdraw from such pressure with some flimsy excuse such as minor illness or fatigue. The following case study is illustrative:

A seventeen-year-old boy was referred to a clinic because of what the school referred to as "increasing entropy." His schoolwork showed less and less effort and his attendance had fallen off sharply. At times his papers were smudged and soiled, and the answers scrawled illegibly. A mysterious "allergy" which he was supposed to have had since childhood was bothering him, he said. When asked how this bothered him, he gave vague, evasive answers such as that it made him feel "bad" or "tired."

The boy had always been a mediocre student, backward in class participation in spite of a superior IQ. When interviewed, he seemed very anxious. He was an awkward six-footer, who looked furtively about the room and pasted a large grin on his face as he slouched in a chair. He answered questions in monosyllables, and the pasted-on smile never left his face.

The parents were seen together. At the time of the appointment the mother came charging into the room, greeted the interviewer with a hearty handshake, and then ushered in the father and showed him where to sit. The father sat silently while the mother told a long story of how the school didn't recognize the ability of "her little Ronnie" and didn't handle him correctly. When asked about their marital adjustment, the mother was quick to say that her husband was a "complete loss." He was a man of "limited education," she said, who had never made her happy. Through all this the father fingered his hat and looked at the floor.

Separate interviews were scheduled for the parents, and it soon became evident that the father was a typical "nice guy." He was a rather successful salesman for a large firm. He admitted that his wife dominated him and that he sometimes got angry, but he rarely said anything because he "figured she was always right anyway." He had previously been dominated by his own mother.

The boy's mother was able to shed some light on the recent deterioration of the boy's behavior. The father had within the past few months been offered a promotion which he turned down because it required "too much responsibility." The mother was furious with him for his attitude and had actually made the statement that her only hope for social progress lay in "little Ronnie" and his education. Thus, she had been putting considerable pressure on "little Ronnie."

This case illustrates several aspects of this type of problem. First, the mother, by her misplaced and excessive interest in the boy, had squelched any attempt on his part to be independent. He was her "little Ronnie" and not a personality in his own right. Schoolwork required too much initiative, and the allergy was his way of saving face. Also, clinicians discovered that the boy was unconsciously very frightened of his father. This situation is quite common in cases in which the mother has begun early to foster a boy's naturally strong fantasy that he will someday take over the father's place with her. When a boy is four or five years old, his father seems like a giant to him, regardless of what type of person the father really is. Ronnie had inhibited all evidences of competition or aggressiveness in himself at an early age for fear his father would discover these and take some kind of terrible retribution on him. This patient's case was complicated by the fact that his father's extreme passivity was all the boy had with which to identify.

Family therapy was attempted here, but was unsuccessful because after a brief time the mother developed negative feelings toward the clinic when both Ronnie and the father began to show signs of independence.

There are, of course, several reasons why a child will inhibit his competitiveness and become so passive that his schoolwork will be considerably below his ability. Quite frequently, however, the child is a "mama's boy" who is frightened by any kind of competitive feelings. This problem can be quite severe, and is often difficult to treat. Treatment should attempt to instill a normal amount of aggression, since this is necessary for a child's adequate, healthy functioning. Too often, children are allowed to remain mediocre and unchallenged. As one boy said, "As long as I don't stand out in any way, no one notices me—and no one bothers me."

## Withdrawal

Somewhat allied to passivity, but more severe, is withdrawal into fantasy (18). All children learn to use this mechanism when they are denied something they want, and many popular songs and myths encourage it. "Wishing will make it so" is a common theme in children's stories. Fantasy is quite prominent in adolescence because this is a time when children want many things they cannot have. Some children, however, overuse fantasy *to the point of interference with their everyday functioning*. The following case study is an example of such overuse of fantasy:

A fourteen-year-old girl was brought to a clinic because she had been found wandering on the road several miles from town. Although her parents were unaware of it, she had been absent from school for several days and had been making marginal grades for several weeks. Previously she had done well in school, although she had never achieved up to the level of her IQ. One of her teachers wrote, "She is like a ghost in class lately—she is there, but she is not there. I never know whether she is paying attention or not. I have tried to talk to her, but it is like talking to someone who is in another world."

The girl's history revealed severe infantile deprivation. Her mother told with surprising candor that she didn't want a baby at the time the patient was born, and so had paid little attention to her. Often the patient, as a baby, had been left alone on a screened-in porch for hours.

The mother read books while she fed the patient; she complained to the interviewer, "It took over a half hour for her to eat, she was such a slow eater." As an infant, the patient had suffered from eczema and had been placed in a hospital for several months because the mother felt it was too much work to take care of her at home.

An interview with the girl revealed alarming pathology. She said she had been out on the road following voices that told her to "run and run to there." Where "there" was, she didn't know. This in itself was enough to make a diagnosis of schizophrenia, a severe condition (not the popular mistranslation of split personality). She was hospitalized immediately and, in spite of vigorous attempts at therapy, she continued to regress and is still institutionalized with delusions and hallucinations.

This case illustrates the severity of this kind of difficulty. In

PSYCHIATRIC CONSIDERATIONS OF MOTIVATION 225

many cases the situation does not progress this far, but the individual remains in an isolated world although he continues to appear to
function. This kind of person is called a schizoid personality, and
psychiatric treatment is required.

## Obsessive-Compulsive Traits

Since schools teach and prize neatness and orderliness, obsessive-
compulsive traits often go unnoticed. A child may, however, be so
intent on preciseness that he loses all spontaneity. This child's
productivity will be limited, and the work he does produce is likely
to be without originality and at the price of great internal struggle.
Obsessive-compulsive traits are illustrated by this case study:

A twenty-year-old college student requested treatment because she
found that her grades were declining. In school she had always been
considered a bright student. Although her work had been superior,
she felt, as did the school, that she was not working up to her extremely
high ability. She explained her difficulty as follows:

"I am never satisfied with anything. If I read something once, I think
I ought to read it again; and, if I do read it again, I think I ought to go
over it again and underline the important parts. When I have done that,
I decide that I should make a synopsis in longhand. If I don't stop myself, I am up working half the night, and I never seem to get anything
accomplished. If I stop myself from doing these things, I can't sleep
because I am tortured with doubts about them, and I sometimes have to
get up several times to check something that I have been worrying about.
I can't finish one subject and put it down and go on to another, because
I worry all night about not having finished the first subject. In high
school I could get away with this, but in college it is harder—there are
more subjects, and I can't keep up. I never seem to get enough sleep,
and I never seem to have time for extracurricular activities like the other
girls."

The psychology in this case was complex, and it was found that this
girl had been trained never to allow herself any pleasure. She had had
very strict moral training at home and had been taught to feel that any
laxity on her part might lead to abuses. Particularly, she had been
severely criticized for the normal adolescent practice of masturbation
and, evenings when she was alone in her room, she had struggled with
this impulse.

In her schoolwork the girl applied the same rigid rules to herself.
She would never allow herself any pleasure in learning. This was particularly noticeable when she tried to produce themes and essays expressing her feelings or describing her experiences. Her papers were stilted
and lifeless, as she had been taught she herself should be. Psychotherapy
improved the situation considerably.

When obsessive-compulsive traits interfere with a student's functioning, there is a need for psychotherapy. Sometimes the teacher can help by gently and gradually encouraging the student to be himself. The student's work may become more careless for a while, but he will be happier and more productive in the long run.

This brings us to some remarks about handling neurotic problems. Since few teachers have had time for training in psychiatric principles, they should neither expect nor be expected to treat neuroses. This is a job requiring specialized education, and a well-meaning teacher without this education may harm the adolescent he is attempting to treat. This does not mean, however, that the teacher cannot help greatly by being warmly accepting of the student. The point is that the teacher should not be giving advice; giving understanding is quite another matter. The following case study illustrates this point:

A fifteen-year-old girl came to a clinic one evening, asking to see a psychiatrist. She said she had been discussing some of her problems about boys with her history teacher, a man in his forties, who had some interest in Freudian principles and had read a great deal of psychology.

The girl was in what psychiatrists call a panic reaction. She complained of feeling vaguely frightened of something, but she could not pin down what it was. She feared that she was abnormal in some way, and she felt funny tingling sensations. These frightened her and made her feel restless. She could not sit still. She said she was afraid to be alone in the room with the young psychiatrist who was interviewing her, but she realized this was foolish.

From this information the young psychiatrist began to piece together what had happened. The girl had had an adolescent crush on the male teacher and had been upset by him in some way. Careful questioning about what had been discussed that evening revealed that the teacher had told the girl about Freud's theory of the Oedipus complex, hoping that this would help her overcome her attachment to him, of which he was becoming uncomfortably aware. This had the opposite effect, since the girl interpreted what the teacher said to mean that it was natural for her to be "in love" with an older man, so that she felt unconsciously that the teacher was trying to seduce her. This, of course, was the farthest thing from the teacher's mind.

Discussion of her situation with the psychiatrist, with some clarification of the real meaning of the teacher's actions, as well as clarification of her own feelings in the matter, eventually cleared up the girl's problem.

Correctly applied to the job of teaching, psychological understanding can be an invaluable aid to the student as well as to the teacher. Understanding why a child needs to act the way he does is sometimes all that is necessary to relieve a difficult problem.

One basic principle of psychiatry is that all behavior, no matter how bizarre on the surface, has meaning if one examines it in terms of the subject's emotions. All behavior has some kind of emotional explanation.

## Distraction by Family Problems

Most of the emotional difficulties mentioned above are brought about and controlled by unconscious mechanisms. Therefore it is useless to ask a child why he is not doing well; the reason is as great a mystery to him as it is to everyone else. Sometimes, however, students can cite some home problem that is causing the difficulty with their schoolwork. Alcoholism or violence in the home can be so upsetting to a child that his work will suffer for days. This is well illustrated in the following case:

> In the course of psychotherapy with an adult patient, it became evident that her frequent violent arguments with her husband were causing severe emotional upset to her twelve-year-old son. The therapist asked her to keep a diary of everything that concerned her son. She listed everything, including his grades in school, and it was discovered that his frequent periods of low grades corresponded exactly with the times when she had had arguments with her husband. She was able to improve the situation by the simple maneuver of keeping the arguments away from the boy, but the tension generated in the family still caused the child some upset.

In such cases a teacher or counselor should be available to listen with understanding to the disturbed child.

## SEEING THE CHILD AS AN INDIVIDUAL

We have explored six of the possible reasons why a child does not match his ability with achievement. Some of these causes are amenable to treatment and some are not, but all may be understood if the child is considered as an individual with thoughts and feelings similar to those of the rest of humanity. The individual approach to the child is an essential ingredient in an insightful and complete understanding of the problems of motivation.

# 21  THE SCHOOL AND MOTIVATION

ROBERT J. HAVIGHURST
*Professor of Education and Member,*
*Institute of Community Development,*
*University of Chicago*

In the past decade there has been a remarkable increase in the proportion of youth from lower-income families who have gone to college. Table I gives the percentages of youth from the various social class groups who have entered college since 1920. Whereas the proportion of upper class and upper middle class boys entering college has doubled since 1920, the proportion of lower middle class

TABLE I

PERCENTAGES OF SOCIAL CLASS GROUPS ENTERING COLLEGE*

| Social Class | Percentage of Total Youth Population | 1920 (est.) | 1940 (est.) | 1948 Boston† Males | 1958 River City‡ | | 1960 (est.) | |
|---|---|---|---|---|---|---|---|---|
| | | | | | Males | Females | Males | Females |
| Upper and upper middle | 10 | 40 | 80 | 80 | 75 | 70 | 85 | 70 |
| Lower middle | 30 | 10 | 20 | 50 | 45 | 32 | 55 | 35 |
| Upper lower | 40 | 2 | 5 | 15 | 20 | 17 | 25 | 18 |
| Lower lower | 20 | 0 | 0 | 6 | 6 | 0 | 10 | 5 |

*Sources: Figures for 1920, 1940, and 1960 are the author's estimates for the United States

†Adapted from Joseph A. Kahl, "Educational and Occupational Aspirations of 'Common Man' Boys," *Harvard Educational Review,* XXIII (1953), 186–203.

‡From data gathered by the writer and his colleagues for a forthcoming book entitled *Growing Up in River City.*

228

boys has quintupled, and the proportion of upper lower class boys has been multiplied by twelve.

At present, about 40 per cent of boys and about 27 per cent of girls enter college. In the case of boys, we are clearly getting close to the limit if we think of the upper half (in terms of intelligence) as good material for college. As Table II shows, only about 16 per cent of boys in the upper half of the group in intelligence are not in college. Most of these boys come from working class homes or from homes in which the fathers have lesser white-collar jobs. These students lack personal incentive for higher education, and generally do not have enough money for further schooling.

TABLE II

INTELLECTUAL ABILITY AND COLLEGE ENTRANCE—1960§

| Quartile of Scholastic Aptitude | Percentages | | | |
|---|---|---|---|---|
| | Enter College | | Do Not Enter College | |
| | Male | Female | Male | Female |
| I (high) | 19 | 14 | 6 | 11 |
| II | 15 | 9 | 10 | 16 |
| III | 4 | 3 | 21 | 22 |
| IV | 2 | 1 | 23 | 24 |

§Source: *American Higher Education in the 1960's,* Ohio State University Press, Columbus, Ohio, 1960

The writer and his colleagues studied a group of 53 boys in the top quarter in terms of intelligence from the time they were in sixth grade until some of them went to college. Of these, 34 went to college. The 19 who did not go to college came mainly from working class homes, had average or below-average school grades, had lower achievement drives than the college-going boys, and lower personality adjustment scores than the college-goers. Five of them did not graduate from high school. The central problem related to these findings is: Why do some able boys not go to college?

A broader phrasing of this problem might be: Why do some able boys and more than half of the able girls not go to college?

One might pose a similar question about the high school achievement of able boys and girls. Why do some boys and girls with high intellectual ability do very well in school, whereas others with equal ability do only average or even poor work?

## FOUR FACTORS IN MOTIVATION

Motivation, or incentive to do good work, depends on four major factors (146, 147, 204, 220, 221). These four factors were explored in a study by Stivers (220, 221) of motivation for college in the ablest quarter of a high school class. James Pierce of the Quincy (Ill.) Youth Development Commission also studied motivation for high school achievement in the ablest quarter of a similar high school class. Pierce reported his study, "The Educational Motivation Patterns of Superior Students Who Do and Who Do Not Achieve in High School," in a paper to the Quincy Youth Development Commission in 1959.

### Need for Achievement

To measure basic need for achievement, Stivers (220, 221) used a test developed by McClelland (146). In this test, students looked at pictures showing young men who might be undertaking some task, and then wrote brief stories on what they thought the men were doing. For instance, in a picture showing a young man in a white coat standing before a desk and holding a small object up before him, a student might see a chemist analyzing a substance, a young man studying to be a doctor, or many other things. The students' stories were scored according to the kinds of ideas they included and the number that dealt with achievement of a goal, striving to succeed, or getting ahead in the world. The need for achievement is a deep and possibly an unconscious drive. Consequently, it must be measured by some indirect method, such as the McClelland test.

Stivers (220) found that the boys who were well motivated for college had a higher need for achievement than did those who were not motivated for college.

Pierce, in the study mentioned, found that able boys who achieved well in high school had a higher need for achievement than did those who did not achieve so well.

## Identification with Persons Who Have Gone to College

In Pierce's study students were asked which adults had been most influential in their lives. It was found that those students who were most anxious to go to college had more parents or close relatives who had gone to college and more teachers and other people who had urged them to go to college. Pierce also found that more of the mothers of high-achieving students had gone to college than was the case with mothers of low-achieving students.

## Social Pressure

Stivers (220, 221) interviewed students to find out which people and what agencies set college as a desirable goal—family, schoolteachers, age-mates, community leaders, books, and the like. The interviews were scored according to the number of influences that steered a child toward college, how intensively and how frequently they operated on him, and how close he felt to the people who advised him. Stivers found that those who were strongly motivated to attend college had a significantly greater set of social pressures that set college as a goal for them. That is, their parents, teachers, friends, and others tended to encourage them strongly to go to college.

## Intrinsic Pleasure in Learning

Intrinsic pleasure in learning has not been so thoroughly investigated as the other factors influencing decisions about college—perhaps because it is obvious that a person who enjoys studying will do well in school and go to college if possible. The author's study of 53 boys of high ability did reveal, however, that the able boys with good school records had more academic interests and hobbies than did the able boys who were doing only average or poor work in school.

## MOTIVATION FOR ACHIEVEMENT AND COLLEGE EDUCATION AMONG ABLE BOYS

The following case studies illustrate the differences between boys with high ability and high educational motivation and those with equally high ability but low educational motivation.

Paul, a lower lower class boy whose $n$-achievement‡ score was very high, said: "My father and mother never went to college. I thought I'd like to go, and do better in life than they did." As a child, Paul was placed in a boys' boarding school sponsored by a Protestant denomination. The superintendent and the teachers there were demanding, but encouraging. When Paul first went to the city high school, however, he did not do so well as he had in the boarding school. "English was about my worst subject. The teacher helped me, though, and I improved a lot. I consider her an important person in my life," he said. Paul considered farming as an occupation until a careers unit in civics class dissuaded him, and he turned to engineering and mathematics, which he enjoyed. Neither of his divorced parents had ever suggested college to Paul, but two of his closest friends had college plans, and the superintendent of the boarding school urged him to go. "He told me to go to college. He said I did good in school, and I ought to go," Paul remarked.

Ralph, an upper lower class boy with a high $n$-achievement score, planned to "attend the university and study to be a musician and a music teacher." In elementary school he had little competition and did well with scarcely any effort. His divorced mother had high hopes for him; both she and his older brother were proud of Ralph's success. In high school, except for some difficulty with geometry, Ralph continued to do well, especially in music. His mother and brother occasionally suggested college to him, and several of his best friends planned to go, but his greatest sources of encouragement were his music teacher and his own accomplishments in music.

"I once wanted to be a farmer. Father was one, as were two uncles of mine. But when we moved into town, my grandfather, a musician, predicted that I'd be one too. My mother also plays and sings a lot. I didn't get interested, though, until seventh grade, when I started my private music lessons. My present teacher, especially, has had a tremendous effect on me. With him, I built up my interest in music, and it's never dropped down. He has talked to me many times about going into music, and he told me that I'd have to choose between professional music and teaching. He built me up, maybe too much. After all, I'm no child prodigy; nor am I an idiot. To sum up, my teachers have influenced me to become as good as they are. Dick [Ralph's best friend, who is also a good student and a musician] is an influence, because

‡Refers to the basic need for achievement discussed earlier in connection with McClelland's work.

whatever is good for him is good for me. And my ability to play and strive for perfect music and my understanding of music are influences on me."

Tom, an upper lower class boy whose *n*-achievement score is below average, plans "to help Dad on the farm for a while and then probably get a job in town. I'm not sure what kind of job. I'll try for something better, though, and advance as much as I can." Tom's elementary school years were spent in a rural school, where he achieved well academically. In high school he did fairly well, although his teachers thought he should do better. "I usually don't do as well in English as in other subjects," he said. His mother used to talk about college, but has not mentioned the subject for several years. No other adult ever suggested that he should attend college, and none of his close friends were going.

"We've lived on a farm since I was five, so I got kind of interested in farming. Barry [Tom's best friend] belonged to the Future Farmers last year and told me about it, so I got interested in it. When I first came to high school, I took industrial arts, and down in electric shop I kind of got interested in that. So I joined the 4-H Club and went to electricity training school. Dad thinks I should get a job in town after high school; I don't know exactly what kind. Mother thinks so too: maybe some kind of carpentry work, because my father does a lot of that."

Alex, a lower middle class boy with a very low *n*-achievement score, said: "I haven't really got an idea of what I'd like to do, but probably something that has to do with math. I don't know. If I decided to be a doctor or a lawyer, I could be a success, but I don't believe I want to go into it. I don't like stuff like that. I wouldn't want to be a lawyer or a doctor."

In elementary school Alex's grades, especially in mathematics, were fairly good, and several teachers encouraged him to continue in this field. At the time of the study, however, his grades were dropping, though occasionally he received good grades in his favorite subject. His teachers and his parents thought he ought to do better, and Alex himself said, "I haven't lived up to my own standards, either. I think I play around quite a bit in class." None of his close friends planned to attend college, and no adult except his father ever encouraged him to go. "He [his father] would like for me to go to college and be a lawyer or doctor, but he doesn't talk about it too much."

## METHODS FOR INCREASING BOYS' MOTIVATION

It appears that the basic drive for achievement is "built into" a child early in his life and probably cannot be easily changed after these early years. Hence, school programs cannot do a great deal toward improving this factor. There is evidence, however, that some boys with a high $n$-achievement drive do not do particularly well in school and college because they lack some of the other factors that increase educational motivation. The following methods may be used to assist these boys:

1. Through an expanded counseling program in the junior and senior high school, identify the able boys who are not well motivated for college and inform them and their parents of the possibilities of college and the advantages that might ensue from a college education. Also, inform the teachers that the boys in this group are good college material but not likely to go to college unless the school influences them to do so.

2. Through the skillful use of honor awards, assembly programs, clubs, and other extracurricular activities, and through collaboration with service clubs and other community organizations, increase the social desirability and the social prestige in the community attached to going to college.

3. Through the academic program of the school, and through the selecting and training of teachers, make schoolwork more interesting and more rewarding to these boys. This is the most crucial but the least tangible method for motivating able boys. Some school programs are more interesting and challenging than others to able boys (and girls), and some teachers make their subjects so interesting that they win students and encourage them to continue a life of study.

## MOTIVATION FOR ACHIEVEMENT AND COLLEGE EDUCATION AMONG ABLE GIRLS

The motivation of girls for higher education is considerably different from that of boys. Girls' drive for achievement may take two directions in our society: (1) getting married and becoming a successful wife and mother; and (2) having a business or professional career which usually involves a college education. Girls with superior intellectual ability are likely to feel considerable conflict at this point, and to be uncertain about the steps they should take after high school graduation. In his interviews with able girls in the tenth grade, Stivers (221) found 25 who were "nonmotivated for college." Only 3 of this group actually entered college. Of the 38 girls whom Stivers did pronounce well motivated for college, however, 12 or almost one-third did not enter college. These girls probably felt some desire to go to college, but during their last two years of high school they decided that marriage and a family were more important. Six of these 12 girls were married by the end of the year following their high school graduation.

The motivation of able girls for high school achievement and college education is a more complex matter than that of boys. It is well known that up to the last year or two of high school girls achieve better in relation to their ability than do boys. At this point, however, the bright girl begins to face what seems to her a choice between becoming a wife and mother or a career woman. Even though increasing numbers of girls do not see pursuing the two roles simultaneously as an impossibility, and go ahead to achieve both goals, the majority of bright girls still experience the choice as a conflict. Consequently, while more girls than boys graduate from high school, more boys than girls enter college.

The following case studies, taken from Stivers's work, illustrate the motivational conflicts of girls:

Susan, a blonde, lower middle class girl with an extremely high *n*-achievement score, planned to get a secretarial job after graduation from high school. "I will work through the summer until around November. Then I plan to get married," she told the interviewer. During her earliest years in elementary school she received only above-average grades, although some of her teachers felt that she could get top grades in all subjects if she tried. Until she entered junior high school, however, no one else set high standards for her. "In the seventh grade I started to run around with Judy. She liked to get good grades, and she was jealous of mine. I didn't care at first, but in the end I tried to beat her, and I did," said Susan.

Through grade school and into high school, Susan's parents' attitude towards her grades did not change a great deal. "They're like me. They want me to get A's and B's, but if I get a C it doesn't bother them much." Other personal influences in her life did change, though. In high school her best friend made only average grades. Of the boy to whom Susan became engaged she said with a laugh, "Well, he gets average and sometimes maybe a little lower grades. He doesn't hate school or anything, but he enjoys himself while he's here." During this period Susan was also influenced by her sister, who was taking a correspondence course in art but planned early marriage.

Regarding her own plans, Susan explained: "I used to want to be an airline hostess, but no more. It's too dangerous, and I want to live. Now I want to be a secretary. Mother was a secretary for a lawyer, and the work sounds interesting to me. I like courts. I *do* know for sure that I will be married in November of the year I graduate. Whether I continue to work after that will depend on many things."

Nona, a tall, attractive, brunette, upper lower class girl with an extremely high $n$-achievement score, planned to "get a secretarial job here in the city. The money I earn is going to be put in the bank for a trip to Hollywood or New York, where I'll try my luck at acting," she told the interviewer.

When she was a child, mixed standards were set for her schoolwork. Her parents expected her to do well but said very little about the matter. Her oldest sister was a good student, but the next-older sister was not and quit school before she finished. Most of Nona's friends got average grades, and she remembered only one teacher who encouraged her. In those early years no one influenced her to go to college. When she was about eleven years old, her life goals began to take shape.

"Near the end of grade school I don't know what happened, but mother let me go places more, and I went to the show a lot. My hobby is collecting pictures of movie stars. I don't know what impressed me, but I guess it was seeing other people acting on the screen. When I saw them acting, I liked it. And I thought I could do it, since I've been in plays."

After she entered high school, Nona's parents were more vocal about how well she should do in her schoolwork.

"My father, especially, is always telling me he wants me to finish school, and he wants to make sure I do. When I bring cards home and there's something I've fallen down in, he usually gets kind of mad and tells me to work harder at it because he knows I can do better."

Regarding plans for the future, Nona's parents offered little specific advice. "Dad never says much, but he always tells me that when I get out of high school I should try to get a good job. He doesn't say what kind." One of the sisters worked as a telephone operator; the other worked in a supermarket. Among her friends, some had plans to get secretarial jobs; some planned to get married; some did not know what they would do. Of her own plans she said:

"There are really two things in my mind: movies and secretarial work. You see, when I started high school, I took typing. I had always liked that sort of thing, so I made good grades and really loved it. I decided then that since I got along so well in typing, I should be a secretary. Then in ninth grade I took speech and dramatics because it had so much to do with acting. Ever since I was old enough to go to the movies alone, I've wanted to be an actress. I'm now taking radio workshop and plan to take it in my next two years of school. But I'm keeping up on both my acting and secretarial work. I keep the latter to fall back on if acting doesn't work out. I know acting is a difficult field. I've always thought that I'd like to work in a big office. I like to be with people and maybe with important people. I think it would help me get over my shyness. So I suppose I'll start with secretarial work and keep working and save money, then travel some and go to Hollywood to see what I can find there—something to do with acting."

Louise, a lower middle class girl with an average $n$-achievement score, planned to go to college—a teachers college. "I want to get my master's degree and teach English," she told the interviewer. When she was a child, two of the most important people in her life were teachers. "They were sweet, wonderful persons. They expected good things of me—excellent grades—and they put me in the limelight frequently." Her parents—both had been teachers—also expected her to get excellent grades. "They placed a high value on study and mentioned it often. I think my grandmother mentioned it often, too. She didn't have the opportunity to go to college or even to finish high school, and she was always sorry." This atmosphere of great expectations agreed with Louise. She worked hard and did well, pleasing her elders a great deal and getting much personal satisfaction in the process.

In high school she found another teacher with whom to identify.

"My English teacher is a wonderful person and teacher, and does what I want to do. I see my old English teacher occasionally, too, and I would like to be a teacher just like her. I know they both expect good things from me. I made almost straight A's in their classes, but I think I should. English is a natural for me. I've told them of my ambition, and they've encouraged me."

Besides this support, there was encouragement from other quarters. In her circle of best friends—all very good students—two wanted to be English teachers. Her father was very pleased with his daughter's choice, as was her mother.

"Naturally they place a high value on education. They are proud that I have never missed the honor roll, and they hope that I make National Honor Society. Mom and Dad have influenced me a great deal, as have my English teachers all along the way. I admire them and hope to do the work they are doing. I know of no reason why I can't be an English teacher. Many others have made it."

## METHODS FOR INCREASING GIRLS' MOTIVATION

We need to understand why able girls who achieve well in high school sometimes fail to enter or complete college or to continue to work toward high-level academic performance. The following methods might be used to increase these girls' motivation:

1. Establish parent-counselor conferences to teach parents how they may encourage the academic aspirations of their daughters.

2. Provide contacts and conferences between able girl students and professional women selected to serve as intellectual models. As models, these women should embody high-level academic or intellectual attainment as well as femininity.

3. Provide counselors trained to assist bright girl students to examine and understand the roles of career woman and wife and mother, and how both may be pursued.

## SUMMARY

Values and motives may be so firmly fixed early in the student's life that the school's subsequent indirect experiences may have little effect in modifying them. In every case such experiences must be well selected and planned. The real problem facing the school is to develop—on a differential basis—interests, values, and motives that will facilitate academic achievement for boys and girls. To resolve this problem, improvements must be made in the school's counseling services. Counseling services must be extended to parents and to students early in students' school careers, where decisions affecting career choices and other decision-making points are critical.

# 22 UNDERACHIEVEMENT OF SUPERIOR AND TALENTED STUDENTS

ROBERT S. DANIEL
*Professor of Psychology, University of Missouri*

Although teachers have long been aware of discrepancies between certain students' ability and their performance, the term *underachiever*, spelled as one word and spoken as if it were capitalized, has come into wide use only recently. Just in the last few years has it appeared in the indexes of such guides as the *Psychological Abstracts* and the *Education Index*. We have become particularly concerned about underachievement in the post-Sputnik excitement over the need for developing more intellectual resources. A great deal has been said and written about underachievement; indeed, a whole issue (December 1958) of the *High School Journal* was entitled "Providing for the Underachiever." As the lead article in this publication states the problem, the underachiever is anyone "who sits on his potential, resisting various (devices) to get him off his potential, and possibly needing an adroitly directed kick in that same potential." The nine short essays in this issue of the journal are provocative and well worth reading.

## INVESTIGATIONS OF UNDERACHIEVEMENT

We are not without research on this problem. In fact there is abundant literature reporting investigations in which comparisons are made between underachievers and normal achievers. Many studies have been made across the country from New Hampshire to Portland, Oregon. Underachievement is a favorite topic for the doctorate dissertation in education, at least eight appearing in 1957 alone—some embarrassingly alike. In the typical study, two groups from a particular grade level are identified. The experimental group, usually called underachievers, is defined as those with a marked discrepancy between potential (as shown by ability tests) and performance (as shown by grades or achievement test scores). The control group consists of students with the same IQ level as the experimental group, but whose grades are superior and who exhibit little or no discrepancy between their potential and performance.

The two groups are usually examined for historical antecedents, socioeconomic variables, personality and interest differences, study habits, personal and social adjustment problems, or whatever other pertinent factors the investigator believes he can measure. Statistical tests are applied to eliminate chance differences. We shall summarize these studies by describing the underachiever as generalized from such research.

In respect to school behavior, the underachiever is unhappy and disinterested. He is frequently absent from school and he dislikes his teachers and his studies. He is a poor reader and does not read for pleasure. He is likely to be a source of disturbance in a social group, although he is strongly swayed by what the crowd does. His classroom behavior is undesirable, if not actually disruptive. He participates in extracurricular activities to the same degree as achievers, but not with the same devotion and loyalty.

Researchers do not agree on the personality characteristics investigated. Some claim that the underachiever is hostile and suspicious, whereas others disagree. He has been described both as an introvert and an extrovert. Some say he is seriously maladjusted, but others do not feel that he is. He does seem to be unrealistic in his self-appraisal, and to lack self-confidence and self-acceptance. He has a narrow range of strong interest and his occupational goals are lower and less well defined than those of the achievers. He has been labeled an "intellectual delinquent" by at least one writer (87).

There is good evidence of marked differences between the home atmospheres of the underachiever and the normal achiever. In the homes of underachievers, cultural advantages are absent, reduced, or perhaps even actively opposed by the parents—not necessarily for economic reasons. Fewer musical instruments, fewer outside lessons of any kind, and fewer books are characteristic of underachievers' homes. In the Hobbs study achievers read an average of three books a month outside of assignments; the underachievers read none. (Incidentally, Hobbs was also struck by the fact that *teachers*, in a poll of 100 of them, revealed that they themselves read less than two books a year.)

The interpersonal climate in underachievers' home was found by some researchers to be undesirable. It ranges from broken homes through open hostility to uncommunicativeness; but rarely, if ever, does it approach the strong family ties, the close give and take, and the confidences and loyalties which are found in the families of achievers. The self-confidence which wise parents build in their child by setting realistic goals, rewarding achievement, and maintaining close emotional and intellectual contact with him carries over into the child's behavior away from home and provides a mature self-directedness not found in the underachiever.

Two additional findings have been verified in several studies. First, underachievers are predominantly boys. Although nearly every study shows this sex factor, few researchers have followed it up experimentally. Boys have a wider range of activities and more freedom in choosing them than girls do. This means that there is more competition for a boy's time. The male is customarily the wage earner in our society. Since there are many avenues open to him that are neither academic nor scholarly, his interests may turn away from school pursuits at a relatively early age. It is therefore not surprising that underachievers are predominantly male. The implications of these observations should be followed up in a controlled investigation.

The second additional finding is that underachievement is not an emergent trait. This means that typically underachievement does not appear suddenly. In Robert Dowd's (70) study of freshmen at the University of New Hampshire, there was no evidence that underachievement had developed in the college situation. "It was present in our subjects when they were in high school," he says. In his review of the literature on this subject, Gowan (88) shows that the high school achievement pattern is established in grade school. Barrett (14) states that discrepancy between ability and achievement shows up as early as the fifth grade. There seem to be no studies of underachievers in kindergarten, but we do know that a child's personality patterns are partially formed by the time he enters the school system.

One research study of this problem which has not yet been published shows a unique, fresh approach. Joseph Kunce, under the direction of Robert Callis of the University of Missouri college of education, has just completed a study working in reverse, so to speak, of a group of adult mental patients—working back to their high school records of ability and achievement. Each of his subjects was matched in intelligence with a same-sex member of his own high school class. Kunce found a statistically greater discrepancy between intelligence test scores and grade-point averages for the hospitalized group than for the matched peers. The discrepancy was especially marked in those patients who exhibited severe withdrawal symptoms, whereas those persons who become paranoiac hospital patients were actually strong overachievers, at least in terms of scores. Kunce interprets his results as indicating that marked discrepancy between ability and achievement in either direction is a sign of potentially serious maladjustment and not merely a personality trait.

Although the psychological implications of underachievement have been explored in many research studies, each of these studies shares a common limitation. These studies are all correlative; that is, they explore and reveal variables that are *concomitant* with underachievement. Although this does not minimize the value of the research studies, it does make it necessary that we carefully avoid separating cause from effect. Some of the factors mentioned above, like home environment, can be *inferred* as causes rather than consequences, because of their historical priority. The studies, however, *do not demonstrate* this. Other factors, like personality characteristics or maladjustment, could just as easily be effects as causes. There is no reason why research people should apologize for correlational studies, especially in the early stages of a research area. Correlational studies are of immense value in *describing* phenomena and in pointing up reasonable hypotheses for later investigations.

Although we do know something about the dynamics of underachievement, specific conclusions about the exact causes of this phenomenon will not be reached until after several years of controlled research. It would seem, however, that the underachieving high school boy does not work as successfully at his formal studies as he can simply because he does not want to. He may prefer to devote his efforts to achievement in some competing endeavor—sports, a part-time job, delinquency, or automobiles. In some cases, he may have no systematic goal at all, but just be drifting from one vague goal to another. No human being who is healthy emotionally and physically is without some kind of arousal potential. The writer remembers an experience in an educational exhibit at a state fair. He was demonstrating the psychogalvanometer—an instrument which shows arousal by the deflection of a needle on a dial. One volunteer subject, a wizened little man who looked at least eighty, demonstrated no emotion and the psychogalvanometer's needle didn't move. The machine seemed to be broken until the old man was guided to a discussion of his hobby—raising prize tomatoes. The power of tomatoes in arousing this man was remarkable. Was he an underachiever? Certainly not, if tomato growing were the criterion for success.

## INGREDIENTS OF ACHIEVEMENT

The ingredients of achievement may be summarized under the heading AIM. This does not mean that one has merely to aim in order to achieve, but rather signifies that the letters in the word AIM are the initials of three important ingredients of achievement: ability, interests, and motivation. These three factors are relatively independent of each other. An accurate prediction of one cannot be made on the basis of another. We know a lot about abilities: Terman, the Thurstones, and many others have explored factors of intelligence, and special abilities. From the works of Strong, Kuder, Darley, and others we are learning about interests and how they form patterns and mature (like intelligence) throughout the growth period. Motivation, on the other hand, is not so well understood.

Motivation has been studied a great deal in recent years. Most of these studies, however, have been conducted with subhuman species, or with human beings under very restricted conditions. Now, the results of these studies should be verified with human underachievers. We know what kinds of hypotheses to test and how to design the experiments. We should use this information to make discoveries about underachievers.

We must guard against the use of nonprecise words when we are dealing with human dynamics. For example, we cannot say that a person underachieves because he isn't motivated, and feel that we have explained the underachievement. Rather, we should think of underachievement as the *evidence* of lack of motivation. Neither can we say that underachievement is entirely due to an individual's biological needs. Now, we realize that motivations are behavior operations attributable to rather specific events in an individual's past. We do not overlook the fact that these events (stimuli) play upon an intricate biological mechanism with established behavioral traits. In other words, within the limitations of its present behavior patterns, the organism is capable of some change as a result of stimulation.

The particular output which concerns us in motivation—a construct used to refer to a theoretical structure of what is expected—is either approach or withdrawal. The problem of underachievement, reduced to its simplest terms, is that certain students withdraw from activities their teachers think important, and they approach certain activities which teachers deem to be less important. Are not the teachers who fail to alter these tendencies also underachievers? The answer is yes, if the tendencies are alterable at the age the teacher comes in contact with the child. The answer is no if, like intelligence and interests, motivation patterns are firmly fixed before the teacher meets the child.

In college, most underachievers go unchallenged unless the cause of their underachievement is environmental or situational (that is, friction or distraction). These causes may be corrected and such cases reclaimed. On the other hand, every college dean can name several notorious intellectual delinquents. These are students whose habits of failure or marginal success (the "just get by" attitude) are so firmly fixed by the age of twenty that reclamation is impossible. At least, we have not yet learned how to erase the past for such persons.

At the high school age there are more opportunities for reclamation, but difficulties still exist. Patterns of underachievement are in the process of being fixed, and emotional development and the final stages of socialization are taking place. The teacher may assist in the reclamation of underachievers at this level, but the time and skills of the counselor or school psychologist will be required for most cases. The best efforts for reclamation involve all personnel and facilities available. G. O. Johnson, of Syracuse University, reports in the *High School Journal* (December 1958) that local reclamation programs have been tried sporadically with varying degrees of success. Most attempts were abandoned after a brief trial, he says, because of only partial understanding of the problem and unwillingness to modify existing programs.

The earlier teachers direct their attention to motivation, the more likely they will be to correct underachievement. Teachers must give the same attention to motivational growth that they give to intellectual growth, socialization, and adjustment. Motivation has long been in our vocabularies as part of these other functions. Perhaps we will soon understand motivational growth well enough to give it equal status.

Anne Roe's studies of men of unusual achievement in science emphasize the role of motivation in creative behavior. Although these accomplished men differed somewhat from the general population in personality traits and intelligence, they differed among themselves almost as much. The one outstanding characteristic which both set them apart and consistently identified them was devotion to work. Roe says, "The most distinctive thing about a first-class scientist is that he is completely wrapped up in . . . (his work): he eats and sleeps it" (202). She goes on to say, "Scientists, above all, are people who have retained a childlike curiosity which many of us lose as we grow up." Attention to the motivational growth of our students might help more of them retain and nurture this curiosity.

## PLANNING A PROGRAM

What would a program to prevent underachievement be like in its finer details? It would require a great deal of planning by many specialists in both psychology and education. Contributions from psychology would develop largely from what we have learned about motivating behavior. Although we need much more research to determine the applicability of laboratory findings to classroom problems, there are a number of well-established research conclusions that are useful. Four of these are summarized below:

1. *Approach behavior is engendered in a social atmosphere that is richly infused with the desired pursuit.* In the best circumstances, scholarly activities are present in both the home and the school. Hobbs (see Chapter 23) emphasizes the role of the teacher as a model. Unless intellectual activities are attractive for him, they are unlikely to be so for his students. Sidney Pressey (193), writing

on the nature and nurture of genius, suggests frequent contact between the promising youngster and adults who have already achieved in the area of promise. He outlines many other detailed suggestions for a program of reclamation of intellectual resources.

2. *Reinforcement is the key to the continuation of approach behavior in scholarly pursuits.* Application of this principle means rewarding *every* child for approaches to intellectual productivity—not just the high-ability achievers. We know that the first rewards must be immediate in order to reinforce the behavior which earned them. Also, they must be frequent at first in order to sustain effort. Later, schedules of reinforcement of less than 100 per cent are more effective in sustaining effort. We know, too, that rewards are more effective than punishments, and that very simple rewards—like receiving a high test score—can be quite successful.

3. *Approach behavior is more firmly established if the learner's activities are intrinsically rewarding.* Children will be more effectively motivated to acquire the basic skills in reading, writing, arithmetic and, above all, creative thinking, if they are shown that these skills are valuable in and of themselves. Children are curious by nature. The suspense and discovery which are inherent in the learning process provide built-in rewards that are more powerful than all the gold stars and good grades combined. External rewards are necessary, however, especially at first, but they should be less important than the rewards the child gives himself.

4. *A program of planned motivational growth should be built around the realization that the human organism can learn to be motivated.* From the work of Harry F. Harlow, of the University of Wisconsin, we know that organisms can learn to learn. Learning to be motivated is not a very great extension of this notion, since learning and motivation are so closely interrelated. This suggests that responsibility rests very heavily upon the teacher in the early grades, then shifts gradually to the student himself as he matures.

Underachievement and motivation have been studied for many years, yet a great deal remains to be done. The problem of underachievement is ideally suited for close interdisciplinary research—research which would sift the laboratory findings and check their applicability to the development of approach behavior for intellectually creative achievement in our students.

# 23 MOTIVATION TO HIGH ACHIEVEMENT

NICHOLAS HOBBS
*Professor of Educational Psychology and Director,*
*Bureau of Human Development and Guidance,*
*George Peabody College for Teachers*

The 1950's were a decade of growing disaffection toward our schools, growing concern about the intellectual fiber of our society, and almost frantic demand for educational reform. Long before the launching of the Russian satellites there was evidence that people were interested in doing something about these concerns. There were portents, even, of a revival of learning in the United States. The critics of educational complacency have done their job well and the war manpower authorities have pressed for measures to provide trained brains to run complex industrial and military operations. Quite independently of critics and crises, however, a welling concern for things of the mind and the human spirit had developed not only among scholars, but also among other people. Educators today have increasing assurance of the support of citizens—people who are concerned with simple survival, but who more and more are also dedicated to learning for its own intrinsic rewards. We may be privileged to participate in and perhaps contribute to a renaissance of the mind in the United States.

In considering how we may get on with our work, we should realize that motivational variables have been neglected and that motivation toward high achievement must be given explicit attention if many of the current and proposed programs for the academically talented are to be fruitful. Concern for the academically talented has found expression in three main kinds of program proposals: identification of the talented, reform of the curriculum, and provision of scholarships. All three of these program proposals assume a high level of motivation: if the talented are identified they will blossom; if the curriculum is made harder students will study harder; and if scholarships are made available students will take full advantage of them. While all of these assumptions have some truth in them (since each of the proposals has some intrinsic motivational value), it is unwarranted to assume that these program efforts, and others that might be envisioned, will succeed without explicit and sustained attention to the problem of motivation. For example, an argument frequently heard in support of scholarships for the talented is that 40 per cent of the top quarter of high school graduates do not go to college. This estimate, with its implicit prediction of probable success in college, is based on various measures of intelligence; but tests at best can account for only about two-fifths of the variance in academic success. The remaining three-fifths of the variance is attributable to a number of factors, the most important of which is motivation. In much of our planning, we ignore three-fifths of the factors that will determine the success of the plans.

The writer has a broad conception of the nature of motivation. The motivation of learning is often conceived of as a minor technical problem to be left to the classroom teacher and to be solved by such devices as awarding gold stars, praising extra effort, and so on. Actually, motivation is much more encompassing, touching the whole fabric of American life, defined at one extreme by the national ethos and at the other by the child-rearing practices which shaped the first two years of a person's life. It is in this larger context that we shall cast the problem. We shall start at the national level and move to the community, the school, the classroom, the family, and finally to the interior and private world of the child himself, where all our efforts, both conscious and unconscious, will find their ultimate validation.

## OUR NATIONAL VALUES

We live in a world in which the educated mind has finally and dramatically gained ascendancy over native wit and boldness as minimum equipment for survival. The main thesis of this paper is: If we are to endure in such a world and make our contribution not only to its survival but also to a realization of its exciting promise, *we as a people must effect a new integration of our national character with appreciation of the value of learning*. Assessment of our prospects for achieving this new integration may well begin with an estimate of the extent to which we now value the creative fulfillment of human potential. When education can be related to financial or social success, there is little doubt of its acceptance. The way to get ahead is to go to college; getting ahead is patently desirable, and few societies are as mobile as ours. But what of learning itself, for its own sake?

One way of estimating what Americans value is to find out what we are willing to pay for. While the private enterprise of the mind has its own pure rewards, and money is sometimes corrupting, we might be better off in America if our scholars were exposed a bit more to this kind of corruption. We certainly do not reward our teachers and scholars as well as other countries do. The average teacher in America earns less than the average plumber, and the average college professor earns about the same as the average assistant engineer on a diesel train. The top 1 per cent of our professors, at such universities as Harvard, earn about $13,000 a year while the top 1 per cent of our physicians earn about $60,000 a year. The economic situation of the academic man has actually declined in the last two decades. Not only has his salary failed to keep up in dollar equivalence, but he has suffered an actual decline in purchasing power. Since 1939, the average citizen in the United States has enjoyed a 79 per cent gain in purchasing power. Physicians have had a 98 per cent gain, dentists a 54 per cent gain, lawyers a 34 per cent gain, professors in state universities a meager 5 per cent gain, and professors in privately controlled universities an 8.5 per cent loss.

Comparisons with other nations are timely, if not encouraging. The Russians spend approximately 5 to 6 per cent of their national income on education as compared with 3 per cent spent in the United States. Alvin C. Eurich (67), after a study of education in Russia, reports that the base pay of a professor is about $18,000 and that a "top-ranking professor and academician might make as much in Russian values as the head of General Motors does here." He continues: "At all levels the teacher occupies a position of great prestige. . . .The teacher symbolizes Russia's hopes for an improved economy, for position in the world, for a rise in the population's level of thinking and living. He is the instrument of change and progress and is treated accordingly." We might recall that in studies of occupational prestige in the United States, the elementary school teacher occupies a position just above a practical nurse and two ranks below a secretary.

Another index of our national values may be the people we honor. To whom do laurels and kudos go? Einstein has become a popular legend and a metaphor for things complex, and most high school graduates have probably heard of Hemingway. We honor Salk for his polio vaccine, and Von Braun is a space-age hero. But the list soon runs thin. Consider, for example, Willis E. Lamb, Polycarp Kush, John Bardeen, Walter H. Brattain, and William B. Shockley. Who are these people? All of them, of course, are American physicists who have been honored with Nobel prizes within the past six years. How many of their names would be recognized by the mythical man on the street, or even by the unmythical teacher in the classroom? In a public recognition poll, who would come out ahead: the managers of the Dodgers, Giants, and Yankees, or the presidents of Harvard, Minnesota, and California Tech? The point is clear. We will become a learning nation when we become a nation that honors learners.

We might remark that the monetary rewards go to the entrepreneur, the entertainer, and the service worker, and public acclaim to an even more limited group; that our society provides few models for the academically talented to emulate; and that much of the current concern over scholarship has fear of Russia as its driving force. Yet in spite of all these unpropitious circumstances, the people of America have for some time been becoming much more involved with matters of the mind. Since favorable opinions on the achievements of the American educational system are so rare these days, however, the following items are offered as evidence: The decency and good sense of the American people defeated McCarthyism even while many political leaders lacked the courage to denounce it; in a society with less intellectual vigor, bigotry might have won out. The *Wechsler-Bellevue Intelligence Scale,* administered some fifteen years after its initial standardization to a large group from a similar population, yielded higher scores, indicating the possibility that people are smarter now than they used to be. The people read. Even if the magazine *Life* can't spell *misspell,* it is a highbrow publication successfully bringing to the American people all kinds of ideas that were formerly chattels of the intelligentsia. Books on American history are at least as popular as books on peace of mind.

*American Heritage,* a substantial historical magazine, has three hundred thousand paid subscriptions and no advertising. American communities support, without tax monies, thirty major symphony orchestras. About thirty million Americans a year attend concerts of serious music, and 7,525,000 children are learning to play musical instruments. Americans spend about sixty million dollars a year for classical records. The amateur theater is flourishing. People paint —not always by following numbers—and they buy good pictures in sufficient quantities to make it profitable to sell them at incredibly low prices. The young American adult—who worries pundits like Whyte because he no longer knocks himself out competing in business—confounds the prophets by getting married younger, raising a big family, and enjoying his new-found freedom. This new $6000-a-year aristocrat, a potential patron of the arts and sciences, is now perhaps a bit overoccupied with various do-it-yourself projects, but he is a better bet as a participant in the quickening intellectual revolution than is his counterpart anywhere else in the world. At least he is well enough educated, free enough, and concerned enough to respond to intellectual challenge by leaders who exemplify in their own lives a clear commitment to learning.

We have much to work with in America. There are many people capable of creating a new American dream comparable in vitality to the former dreams of opportunity, equality, and freedom. This new dream will assert the common man's right to learning and his ability to obtain it. The making of this dream is everybody's business. We cannot expect our children to work hard at learning unless we commit ourselves to learning, become interested in it, become familiar with its frustrations, and enjoy its pleasures. *Commitment to learning must become a part of the American way of life, an integral facet of our national character.*

## THE COMMUNITY'S RESPONSIBILITY

National character is an elusive concept. It is hard to know how to go about changing a nation's values, from the top down, even though the necessity for doing so may be compellingly apparent. We need a smaller unit to work with—the community, for example. The values of the people of a community at least appear to be more manageable, and it is perhaps through community action that we can reach the national mind. Efforts to raise the level of general intelligence in America will be successful to the extent that communities mobilize their resources to motivate and sustain learning among all their citizens, adults and children alike. The problem of upgrading intelligence cannot be left to the schools alone; the schools must be sustained by a total community effort.

We may get at the heart of the motivational problem by asking what kinds of behavior our communities currently reinforce. What kinds of behavior are singled out for public recognition and support? Most American communities support good basketball playing, for example. Many towns elect a young businessman of the year, a waitress of the year, or a teacher of the year. While some young people do not need community reinforcement for their learning behavior because their family encouragement is sufficient, it seems clear that the community can increase students' motivation to high achievement in many ways.

There are communities, of course, which have reinforced intellectual, artistic, and scientific behavior. For example Springfield, Tennessee, has launched an exciting program for the encouragement of academic achievement by providing community recognition and college scholarships for high school students with outstanding records. This is especially exciting because it is a local effort and not part of a national scholarship plan. A few years ago Nashville had an out-of-school club with the exuberant title Science Unlimited; the club was instrumental in furthering the careers of several adolescent boys who have since gone on to become productive scientists. Other community endeavors have also become familiar to educators: the Quincy (Illinois) Youth Development Project, the Worcester Art Museum, the Brooklyn Children's Museum, the Dallas Poetry Writing Club, among others. These pioneering efforts provide good models for community programs in the interest of the talented.

Let us imagine that an American community deliberately set about developing the talents of its young people to the fullest. If the people took very seriously the idea that intellectual vigor is as important as industry, a clean water supply, or winning athletic teams, we could be confident that the job would be done, and done well.

## SCHOOLS AND MOTIVATION

The schools are next in the hierarchy of institutions that affect motivation to high achievement. In studying the schools' influence on motivation, we must consider the evolution of educational philosophies and practices as they reflect the events of a particular period, and as they reflect national values as well as specific educational planning.

The conception of motivation that has guided our educational efforts in the last three decades was shaped in a world quite different from the contemporary world of atomic energy, intercontinental missiles, and space travel. The 1920's and 1930's were delightful, improbable, incredible times. They were times of tree sitters, transatlantic flights, and bewildering economic collapse; they were times of both optimism and resignation, with optimism holding an edge. The technocrats were going to usher in the promised land of abundance for all. The vision of a world without struggle and conflict was in our eyes. One of the best expressions of this dream was the concept of motivation implicit in progressive education. Progressive education held that learning is fun; competition and conflict are harmful and should be avoided; adjustment is perhaps more important than mastery; discipline should come from within; the group is as important as the individual; and grades are an unworthy index of really important achievement. These are exciting and important ideas. Of course the general confidence and optimism of those times were marred by a couple of annoying and socially atavistic situations that would need to be cleared up: a depression and Hitler. These, however, could be looked after in the future.

Looking backward, what seems to have been miscalculated in this optimistic estimate of man's destiny was man's need to struggle, to pit himself against that which he thinks he can master but about which he might be wrong. We may have been wrong in assuming that struggle is an inconvenience reflecting certain temporary environmental dislocations. Even if struggle is an environmental inadvertence, it is clear now that, vis-à-vis Russia, we are in for a long stint of environmental inconvenience. We struggle or perish. It seems as simple as that. There is also the possibility that struggle is not an environmentally induced phenomenon but an expression of man's more enduring nature. It may be that Khrushchev is merely another way station from Job to eternity. One is reminded of William James's call for a moral equivalent of war, and of the answer the conqueror of Mt. Everest gave when he was asked why he climbed it: "Because it is there." Certainly, one of the most conspicuous characteristics of man is his tendency to precipitate himself into just-manageable conflict.

If these remarks seem to have a flavor as forbidding as the communist system itself, we can move quickly to consider why it is so important to reappraise the contingency that struggle will always be with us, as certainly it will be for some time to come. The point is this, and it is a point of particular concern to our schools: How can education incorporate a concept of struggle without losing all that has been gained in the past several decades of educational reform? How can we teach youngsters to struggle effectively and at the same time nurture gentleness, compassion, decency, fair play, respect for man, and reverence for life? The task of our schools is much greater than we have ever thought it to be.

Our schools have been building on what Abraham Maslow would call growth motivation—a kind of motivation that stems from abundance, assurance, and perceived competence even in the face of great threat. The molders of our educational objectives must hold out against clamorous pressures to operate on deficit motivation. It is distressing that so much of our current public interest in learning is motivated by fear. Political leaders and editors tell us we must improve our educational system if we are to survive the ongoing struggle with Russia. Undoubtedly they are right; but fear is a poor basis for a national educational philosophy, and it is not likely to help us achieve the goals we aspire to. Furthermore, the punitive flavor of much current commentary is not reassuring. For what is surely a shared responsibility, the public is urged to blame the schools, castigate the teachers, or pour it on the pupils. Those with fear-narrowed vision ask us to reduce the variability in our educational efforts, when all evidence indicates that variability heightens individuals' problem-solving ability and increases their chances for adaptive survival. It is heartening to read of Byron Hollinshead's recent defense of the American educational system as compared with its European counterpart, which seems so attractive to the schools' eager critics. We must continue to seek better ways of educating all young people. We must raise the ceiling for all kinds of achievement, and develop ways to offset the threatening mechanization of man in the nation's push toward scientific and technological adequacy. While scientists are essential to survival, we must have scholars, artists, musicians, social critics, playwrights, novelists, poets, philosophers, and other creative interpreters of man. Then we may be sure that our society has as much reason to survive as it has the technological competence to do so.

One final comment on the schools and public responsibility: American schools and colleges, which are now being severely criticized for having incorporated the national ideal of intellectual equalitarianism (an ideal which is fading fast), should at least be complimented for being responsive to public values. Our schools have invented the most elaborate system in history for the identification and development of the kind of talent that entertains the people— athletic talent. Early identification, special tutoring in small classes, highly paid professors of Saturday afternoon classics, acceleration, segregation, special scholarships, uniforms, weekly field trips, and even special diets are parts of our remarkable system for the discovery and development of public entertainers. As Professor Edward Teller, the eminent physicist, said recently, "Doubtlessly we are ahead of Russia in football." Before we criticize our schools, we should ask ourselves what we expected of them before the Sputnik scare.

## THE TEACHER'S ROLE

Let us now turn to the teacher and to the values which guide his efforts to communicate with children, influencing their motivation and helping them form judgments of what is good and worth working for.

The writer believes that the dramatic launching of the Russian satellites has sparked a cultural revolution in America and that in this cultural revolution no one will be as profoundly affected as the teacher. The launching of the man-made moons has clarified the fact that, in the sense of the military scientist Clausewitz, the United States is at war. War used to be the business of soldiers. During World War I, however, and then overwhelmingly in World War II, we realized that the industrial worker was as important as the soldier, if not more important. Our victory in World War II was in no small measure due to the incredible skill and rapidity with which our industrial enterprise and our workers produced the instruments of war. But what has changed now? Just this: the production of weapons is much less important than the production of ideas. Our victory in the present struggle (and it is recognized here that victory has taken on a much more complex meaning than the defeat of an adversary, which now seems impossible: no one wins wars any more), or our resolution of the present conflict, will depend on the skill and rapidity with which our educational enterprise and our teachers produce the new instruments of total war or of ultimate peace. These instruments, of course, are ideas. Just as the worker was propelled into ascendancy over the soldier, so now the teacher will be propelled into ascendancy over both. The main line of defense has moved from the trenches, to the factory, to the classroom. This is the major cultural change of our time. As teachers, we may not like the role this change thrusts upon us, yet we must accept it with all the courage and wisdom we can muster.

How well prepared are we to meet this kind of challenge?

In research with bright, high-achieving adolescents, teachers frequently emerge as having awakened or channelled a young person's interests in activities of substantial consequence. Teachers can be major influences in motivating youngsters to high achievement. An adolescent will often single out a particular teacher as having influenced him to work in some important direction, and it is very exciting to learn of a teacher who through the years has raised and helped focus the aspirations of young people. In many communities there are four or five teachers who have earned this reputation. Should they not be especially rewarded, these multipliers of talent? Should they not be studied to find out how they set young people on fire to learn?

Perhaps we really have not expected our teachers to be good models for our children, except in the spheres of morals and personality. Most teachers work hard and are eager to learn more about children. They seldom read books, however, just for the fun of learning. In a poll of one hundred teachers it was found that the median number of books read during the preceding year was under two, and the most frequently read book (the title appeared six times) was *How To Coach Winning Basketball*. Teachers should be expected to lead lives as intellectually vigorous as necessary to discharge their responsibilities to academically talented youngsters.

## THE CONTRIBUTIONS OF HOME ENVIRONMENT

When individuals rather than institutions are being studied, one must rely heavily upon research, a fact that will influence the tone of the remainder of this paper. We must therefore introduce a note of tentativeness in our observations. Most of the following tentative observations on motivation to high achievement—and the queries which grow from them—are based on a study that the author is conducting of bright high-achieving and bright low-achieving adolescents. The subjects have been studied intensively, and data have been collected on fifteen young people in each of the two groups who, with their parents, make a total of thirty families and ninety subjects. Since the study is only half completed, the tentative results must be interpreted cautiously.

We might first explore this question: *What kinds of homes motivate intelligent adolescents to high achievement?* Perhaps the most firmly established generalization is that high-achieving youngsters come from culturally rich and stimulating homes, while low-achieving youngsters come from homes providing less nourishment for intellectual interests. The high-achieving subjects in our study reported they personally owned about twice as many books as the low achievers, and the difference in family libraries was even greater. The average number of books read in three months was ten for the high group, considerably more than the numbers read by the low achievers. Children in the productive group had traveled somewhat more. There were twice as many musical instruments in the homes of the high group as in the homes of the low group; no high-group home was without at least one instrument, and three of the low-group homes reported no instruments. One of the most striking differences between the two groups was the number of different kinds of outside lessons taken and the amount of time devoted to this extra learning: the high group took more than twice as many outside lessons and devoted more than three times as much time to these studies. These differences reflect in part the way the groups were originally chosen, but they also indicate the extent to which the two sets of families made opportunities available to their children. Terman (234) reports comparable data on richness of home background of his 150 most successful and 150 least successful men. The home libraries of the parents of the successful subjects contained an average of 427 books, as compared with 290 for the unsuccessful.

Another characteristic of the home environment which appears to be differentially associated with productivity is the amount of communication among family members. While both groups in our study described their homes in predominantly favorable terms, the high achievers generally came from homes where ideas were shared, where group activities—such as playing music together—were common, and where there was careful planning for the development of members of the family. As we might have expected, values seem to be shared if they are talked about and if models are available for emulation.

Terman's study showed that the parents of gifted children are predominantly in professional and managerial occupations. It is probable that since Terman's initial study there has been an important change in American life favoring the development of talent. There has been a general extension upward of socioeconomic level and a general extension downward of opportunities for learning and for participation in talent-developing activities. A study by Elizabeth Drews (60) supports this observation.

A second question reflects a persistent notion about the origins of motivation to high achievement: *To what extent is productivity a neurotic phenomenon, a product of sublimation, or a mechanism for reducing anxiety?* In our data there was no evidence of differences in personal adjustment between the high- and low-achieving groups, nor were there consistent differences in the amount of conflict in the home. There were two subjects, one in each group, who appeared to be caught up in some neurotic conflict. One was achieving extremely well, but saw herself as often miserable and misunderstood. The other caused his family and teachers grave concern because he neglected his schoolwork and associated with older boys with bad reputations. Terman's successful and unsucessful adults could not be differentiated, as children, with reference to adjustment; but as adults there were highly significant differences, with serious maladjustment reported more frequently by the unsuccessful group. Anne Roe's (202) eminent scientists manifested some neurotic difficulties in feelings of isolation and, among the social scientists, in parental conflict and marital adjustment; but their urge to achievement was clearly a positive force yielding deep satisfactions, and not the ever defeating and always incomplete satisfactions arising from neurotic compensation.

While one can hardly say that productive people are free from neurotic conflict, it seems safe to say that high productivity motivated primarily by neurotic strivings is the exception rather than the rule, at least in the fields for which we have data. There is a possibility that the popular conception of high achievement as the product of inner conflict may gain support from studies of artists, poets, musicians, or writers, but we suspect that systematic inquiry will gradually reduce the tenability of the sublimation hypothesis as a generalized explanation of cultural achievement.

A still more perplexing question which is central to our study is: *In what ways is productivity differentially associated with the quality of the relationship between the child and his mother and father?* It seems likely that we will eventually find in this triadic relationship factors which will account for a substantial portion of the variance in need for achievement. We started on the hunch that mothers are more important than fathers in determining the level of life aspiration of children, both male and female. The idea came originally from some work by Stewart on the *Strong Vocational Interest Blank,* in which he found that the O. L. score on the *Strong,* which is supposed to be a measure of the subject's occupational aspiration level, was positively related to the actual occupational level of the maternal forebears but unrelated to the occupational level of the paternal forebears. Anecdotal evidence of the mother's influence on the child is abundantly available in our study: for example the mother who bought a piano before her child was born, started the child on music lessons at 3½ years, and for twelve years took her each week to her music lesson, without fail. Relative detachment of the father from the process of value development seemed also to be indicated in a study by Engel (66) of unselected high school children and their parents, using Q-sort methodology. She found a "father syndrome" of expectancies for their children, which most of the children did not share. Fathers agree with other fathers most, with their wives next, and their children least, in terms of expressed aspirations for their children.

The foregoing data are for unselected children. In our sample of bright high- and low-producing young people, the Q-sort correlations of mother and child were consistently higher than those of father and child. In terms of frequency, for the twenty-four families who completed the Q-sorts, the mother-child correlation was higher in eighteen instances and the father-child correlation was higher in six instances. A simple sign test for significance, even with this small number of cases, indicated that the difference is reliable. On the basis of the Q-sorts, it would seem that mothers and children are considerably more in accord with reference to life ambitions than are fathers and children. The *Incomplete Sentences Test* yielded similar and perhaps even more striking results. With equal invitation in the sentence stems to respond with reference to either the father or the mother, the mother was mentioned twice as frequently as the father. All but five of the references to the father were required by the test and elicited by the printed stem "My father . . . ." In sharp contrast was the number of references to the mother: There were thirty-eight such references beyond those elicited by the stem "My mother . . . ." In completing the stem "I am closest to . . . ," nine of the subjects said "my mother" and only one said "my father." In completing the stem "The person who has influenced me most is . . . ," fourteen of the subjects said "my mother" and none said "my father." There were no differences between the high- and low-producing groups.

Since these studies emphasized so heavily the congruence of attitudes of mother and child and the feelings of closeness of child to mother, we were beginning to develop some confidence in the interpretation that mothers are more influential than fathers in determining ambitions of children. More data, however, proved that the issue is certainly not as simple as we first thought it to be. Consider, for instance, Terman's findings. In his study of scientists and nonscientists in a group of 800 gifted men, Terman found no differential effect of the occupations of maternal and paternal forebears. Anne Roe found that fathers loomed large as positive influences in the lives of eminent physicists, but that eminent social scientists tended to be in conflict with both parents. The last two volumes of *The History of Psychology in Autobiography* were consulted for evidence on the relative influence of fathers and mothers on the lives of psychologists. Fathers were much more frequently perceived by these eminent psychologists as having had a predominating influence on their lives. Thus the issue remains important but unclear.

## TWO MORE VARIABLES

There are two other characteristics in which the high- and low-achieving groups in our study differed. For these two variables we have as yet no substantial quantitative data, but we feel confident that in time we shall be able to pin down specifically what are at present insistent general impressions.

First, our productive young people had an incredibly far-ranging and time-absorbing program of activities, and they vigorously resisted any intrusion upon it. This degree of commitment did not show up in quantitative tallying of activities, because the nonproductive subjects had many activities too: they were members of highly organized schools and churches in which clubs, hobby groups, choruses, orchestras, and so on abounded. There was, however, a great difference in intensity of commitment between the two groups. The nonproductive subjects seemed to accept the testing program as just another interesting activity in which they had been invited to engage. It was something of an honor, and they came readily. The productive subjects, on the other hand, had a hard time fitting visits to the laboratory into their well-ordered and demanding schedules. One practiced the clarinet four hours a day; another had rehearsals for three different musical groups; another regularly scheduled an afternoon a week at the city library; many had outside lessons. It was in their concentration of effort and intensity of purpose, rather than in sheer number of activities, that the groups differed most significantly.

The second variable concerned the extent to which members of the two groups regarded themselves as relatively autonomous, goal-directed people (at least with respect to the important aspects of their lives), which brought them to our attention originally. This variable involved self-concept and manifested itself most clearly in the tendency of the nonproductive subjects to depend on others— mostly their parents and teachers—for rewards and admonitions in the guidance of their activities. The productive subjects, however, tended to administer their own rewards and punishments. By adolescence, highly productive youngsters have their own built-in system of reinforcement, which certainly is not entirely independent of reinforcement from others, but which has an impressive ongoing autonomy.

## APPLYING OUR KNOWLEDGE OF MOTIVATION

We must ask ourselves: *How can we make personal sense out of the many observations about motivation to high achievement?* We can contribute to a redefinition of national character by valuing learning ourselves; and we can motivate the young people with whom we work by the motivations that we exhibit in our own lives. Motivation to high achievement thus becomes a very personal challenge.

Inherent in the kinds of transactions bright, high-achieving youngsters seem to make with their worlds, there are some manifest principles that will help us in observing and counseling them. These principles should provide guides for establishing school programs that allow fully for the implications of motivation. These principles should help us escape the temptation to believe that we are accomplishing enough when we simply provide for acceleration, ability grouping, enrichment, counsulting teachers, or any of the currently popular ways of adjusting school programs for the more able student. We need a finer sense of what is involved in self-fulfilling accomplishment. Here are six of the critical dimensions:

First, it seems that the gifted child experiences his most important learnings at a point of exquisite balance between safety and danger. The most impressive thing about a finely functioning, able child is his tendency to precipitate himself into just-manageable difficulties. He has a fine flair for getting himself into trouble— good trouble. He delights in upsetting conceptual equilibriums, and then working to re-establish conceptual order. The gifted child often seems determined not so much to master subject matter or a skill as to master a new image of himself. The school must provide the child with both a secure base to operate from and an array of opportunities for getting into self-redefining, intellectual, and developmental trouble.

Second, the able child who realizes his productive potential will need far more independence and autonomy than are ordinarily provided in school programs. Research has shown that the bright, high-achieving adolescent will tend to be inner-directed and process-oriented. He will often be disrupted in his learning by the bits and pieces of experience that we provide to engage children whose motivations are less constant.

On the other hand, the gifted child will not be able to achieve the fullest expression of his potential on his own. He needs to be provided with tools with which to work. There is a temptation for us to let an able child move ahead in areas of already achieved competence without mastering the other skills essential to later development. The teacher of the able child must be extremely flexible, sometimes giving freedom that almost seems to be license, and at other times imposing sanctions that seem, to the child at least, to be arbitrary irrelevancies.

The fourth principle is that substantial accomplishment in any endeavor requires the ability to delay rewards, to postpone gratification. While highly productive youngsters do get intrinsic rewards simply from doing what they believe to be important, we cannot expect that they will sustain their efforts indefinitely without some external recognition. On the other hand, they should not need the inventions (and indeed many will be harmed by them) that teachers provide as immediate and frequent rewards for children who must have constant external reinforcement. This does not mean that an able child should be a Madame Curie stirring a pot of hot pitch in a cold shack for twenty-five years with no intervening rewards, but rather that he should be helped to sustain deprivation and to reinforce himself over long periods without extrinsic gratification.

A fifth dimension is one we know little about, but one that is probably essential to sustained creative accomplishment. This is the ability to regress, to be intensely responsive to primary experiences, and to be fully aware of oneself and one's immediate world with a minimum of distortion. It seems that productive people who are also creative have the ability to let themselves go, to escape the binding demands of daily routines, and to cut free from the web of expectancies that gets woven about us by our families, friends, colleagues, teachers, professors, bosses, audiences, and people in general. Creative people can revert to simpler ways of experiencing, to fresher ways of perceiving. They can throw away the common templates that are used to order the world and confidently seek simpler, newer ones. Now this, of course, is intensely personal business, and we are not sure how such regression is fostered. We are fairly confident, however, that it can be stifled by the elaborate machinery we use to encourage learning in more stimulus-bound children.

Productivity in scholarship, science, writing, music, or similar endeavors usually means that the maturing youngster is setting off down a very lonesome road. We should sustain him in his choice and, if we can, help him prepare for its consequences. Studies of the lives of eminent men repeatedly reveal the theme of lonely struggle. Most of us are highly gregarious people, addicted to assemblies and committees and dedicated to cookouts, boating parties, bridge, bowling, and book clubs. Even the protesting beatnik needs to belong, although he may not be aware of it. As teachers, we were delighted and captivated a few years back by the invention of the sociogram, which enabled us to identify the "isolate" and bring him back from the library to have his hot chocolate with the group. We may not know how to nurture the necessity for aloneness, but at least we should not intrude on the engrossing occupations of a child. Recall the young and undistinguished university student who, some three hundred years ago, left Cambridge because of a plague, went home to his mother's cottage at Wolsthorpe, and there, with no professors to bother him, invented the calculus, formulated the principle of mutual attraction of bodies, and began his famous experiments on optics.

Now, the final dimension. There is considerable evidence that the character of a child is strongly influenced by the process of identification, by the adult models he chooses to emulate. We will be effective teachers of the gifted to the extent that we exemplify in our own lives a commitment to learning commensurate with our high expectations of them.

# SECTION VII

## THE TEACHER

Almost all studies of the problem have indicated the importance of the teacher's role in recognizing and developing superior and talented students. His daily association with superior students places him in a strategic position to implement the objectives of the talent development program. He acts as co-ordinator of all the forces, materials, and personnel being mobilized for the development of talent. It might be said that he holds the fate of the superior student in his hands.

There are, of course, many approaches to the teaching of superior students. Some people view it as a battle of wits and wills between the teacher and the student. They feel that the student has somewhere inside him the information the teacher wants regurgitated, and that teaching techniques should be designed to force, trick, or cajole the student into releasing the desired information. First-hand experiences of teachers indicate that such approaches and expectations are outside the range of probability. Experienced teachers know that instructing bright youngsters involves an interaction between the teacher and the student. If this interaction is improperly handled, the teacher may restrict and distort the superior student's flow of learning; if it is properly handled, the student's knowledge, skills, and insights will emerge and flourish.

The learning that takes place in this interaction process is an individual matter. Although a teacher may be responsible for a special class of twenty or more high-ability students, the learning is done by the individual. Due to differences in general capacity to learn and in specific aptitudes and attitudes, even the members of a relatively homogeneous class group have widely different proficiencies. This variability makes it necessary for teachers to have mastered a wide range of subject matter and teaching practices. Appropriate teaching of a group of bright students cannot consist merely of making a single assignment; it must supply each individual with appropriate and challenging tasks. Each student must be stimulated to strive for competency in basic learnings as well as to undertake imaginative and creative tasks.

The teacher of a class of high-ability students must understand the characteristics commonly found in bright and talented youngsters. The teacher must accept the fact that some of these students will tend to be eccentric, others will be nonconformists and skeptics, and still others may show intellectual arrogance or narrow-mindedness. Most of these characteristics are neither symptoms nor results of superior ability. Questioning, however, that sometimes borders on arrogance and is tinged with skepticism, is an essential ingredient of innovation and should be prized in the educative process.

Our knowledge of the nature and origin of giftedness is scant, but we do know that giftedness can be aborted and stifled. What the teacher must do is find some way to combine the freedom that stimulates creativity with the rules that make possible some measure of stability in a classroom. As Crawford Greenewalt (93) says:

> Conformity in behavior is a human necessity; conformity in patterns of thought is a human danger. Unfortunately, people have come in modern times to mistake one for the other. There is a strong body of opinion which assumes that the conformist is the boy who gets ahead. School boys are now given grades on their ability to co-operate, presumably on the theory that this will advance their fortunes once they launch their careers. "Co-operation" is, of course, a necessity at any time, but any premium is and always must be on original approaches.

The ability to teach superior students effectively is a personal skill which some teachers possess and some do not. Intellectual achievement cannot be stimulated by teachers who have not themselves experienced intellectual achievement. A student will not learn what is worth learning from teachers who are unaware of what is worth teaching. This knowledge of subject matter and ability to distinguish the central from the peripheral must be accompanied by knowledge of and skill in the teaching process. Brandwein (22) says that teaching:

> is the result of many years of work coupled with the interplay of factors of heredity, personality, and the larger forces of the environment—education, home, church, and community. Yet there is no doubt that some teachers have invented a better teaching method than have others —better in the sense that they affect the growth of youngsters in a wholesome and desirable way. Furthermore, these youngsters are aware of this stimulation and acknowledge it.

A major task facing the administrator of a talent development program is to identify those teachers who have mastered both subject matter and teaching practices and who can "affect the growth of youngsters in a wholesome and desirable way." The same approaches that are effective in seeking out and identifying superior students will be effective in identifying the teacher who is equipped to further their education.

The chapters in this section deal with the teachers of superior students. In Chapter 24, Glenn Snider discusses their pre-service and in-service education. He points out that the present teacher-education institutions seem unprepared to train teachers to instruct bright students and that teachers depend on in-service experiences provided by the local school system.

In Chapter 25, Clifford Williams suggests that administrators select teachers of superior students on the basis of the characteristics of the students themselves. He analyzes the functions and the many roles undertaken by the teacher. He describes briefly some problems faced by school administrators in selecting teachers for gifted students.

# 24 PRE-SERVICE AND IN-SERVICE EDUCATION FOR TEACHERS OF THE GIFTED

GLENN SNIDER
*Associate Professor of Education and Director of Teacher Education, Oklahoma University*

The success of any effort to change or improve significantly any aspect of the educational program is largely dependent upon the professional and personal competence of the classroom practitioner. This generalization applies particularly to the school's efforts to provide more challenging educational experiences for children and adolescents who are superior in an academic, creative, or social sense.

It is generally conceded that teaching is both an art and a craft and that a teacher's success is related to his unique skills, proficiencies, attitudes, general and specialized knowledges, and personal characteristics. Only a minimum of competencies are likely to be developed within the framework of a typical four-year pre-service teacher education program at the undergraduate level. The important elements of general education, specialized subject matter, and professional education must all be crowded into the program leading to standard certification of the teaching practitioner. An examination of pre-service teacher education programs throughout the country shows rather conclusively that the typical program is almost barren of specific provisions for preparing either elementary or secondary teachers to work effectively with gifted youngsters. The implications of this lack are significant. In general, it means that recently graduated teachers are not prepared to work effectively with gifted students unless they have been involved with challenging in-service experiences since graduation.

## CHARACTERISTICS OF THE TEACHER OF THE GIFTED

Before examining pre-service programs, we should consider the qualities and characteristics which seem to be related to effective

teaching of gifted students. French (70) states that the most frequently listed characteristics for the teacher of the gifted are: high
intelligence, special aptitudes, deep knowledge of his own field, broad
knowledge of related fields, knowledge of teaching techniques, flexibility, creativity, and acceptance of student ideas. Witty (259)
contends that the "education of gifted children requires teachers
who have the ability to recognize giftedness, to create an atmosphere and environment favorable to its development, to provide
conditions that give it a chance to emerge and blossom." Witty
(260) further suggests that the skilled teacher is friendly, has a
constructive attitude toward people, is eager to understand students,
possesses adequate knowledge of his subject and sources of information related to it, and has a genuine respect for and faith in each
individual.

Others have commented on the importance of the teacher's impact
on the student. For example, Davis (57) emphasizes that the
teacher's ability must be accompanied by a capacity to encourage
specific qualities of the gifted and channel them into worthwhile
learning experiences. The teacher of gifted students must understand
their characteristics and know how to encourage them to assume
responsibility and take initiative.

Like all teachers, the practitioner who works with the academically able should be familiar with child and adolescent behavior in
order to understand the emotional, social, physical, and intellectual
characteristics of students. Without such understanding, no teacher
will be able to identify or encourage students with unusual talent,
ability, or creativity.

Unimaginative, stereotyped approaches to teaching are not likely
to be successful in working with gifted students. These students are
no more challenged by such procedures than they are stimulated
by an individual whose background is narrow and whose insights
are limited.

The following six items (100) have been mentioned as important
characteristics of the teacher of academically gifted students: (1)
the ability to foster in gifted students social responsibility, a desire
to serve society, and a recognition of the worth of others; (2) the
ability to create a climate in which the gifted participate efficiently

in group discussions and in wholesome social relationships; (3) the ability to develop a classroom atmosphere conducive to good mental health; (4) the ability to teach the gifted to use the problem-solving approach to learning, to apply this to independent study and research, and to evaluate their own progress; (5) the ability to recognize the social and emotional problems which accelerated mental development causes some students; and (6) the ability to develop a flexible, individualized, enriching curriculum suited to the superior students' needs, avoiding stereotyped demands that are identical for each student.

## CURRENT CERTIFICATION PROGRAMS FOR TEACHERS OF THE GIFTED

Do states in general provide special certification for teachers of the gifted? How do current teacher education programs relate to the teaching of the gifted? What specific provisions for working with the gifted are generally incorporated into such programs?

Mackie and Dunn (148) reported in 1953 that Pennsylvania was the only state which had developed a special certificate for teachers of the gifted. At the same time, most states had special certification programs for other areas of special education, such as the slow learning, the physically handicapped, and the speech-handicapped. The philosophy that pervaded American society and education in the 1930's and 1940's encouraged the development of various special education programs devoted to improving the lot of the handicapped, and discouraged the development of programs for the intellectually able. Many states added specialists in the education of the handicapped to the staffs of their state departments of education and provided additional financial support to public schools establishing classes in special education. In 1954 the U. S. Office of Education (70) reported that no state department of education employed a staff member who devoted his major efforts to the provision of services related to the education of the gifted.

The lack of special certification for teachers of the gifted is probably due in large part to the lack of demand from the public schools for teachers in this area. Until quite recently most school systems provided for the major needs of superior students within regular, heterogeneous classrooms, and depended on the unselected teacher's skill in adapting his instruction to the varying needs, interests, and abilities of the students. The U. S. Office of Education reported in 1954 that the secondary school enrollment in special classes for the mentally gifted increased significantly between 1947 and 1953, while the enrollment in elementary schools decreased. However, since very few classes for academically able students existed at the time, these figures may not be too meaningful. The events of the past six years have prompted many schools to organize such classes, sometimes without thoughtful attention to the identification, curriculum, and teaching procedures so necessary for both initial and continued success.

Another reason for the dearth of certification programs in this area is the absence of planning and of general agreement concerning the elements which should be incorporated into such programs. The clash between the so-called subject-matter specialist and the professional educator has already been felt in this area, although steps are being taken to reconcile the two sides.

## THE PRE-SERVICE PROGRAM FOR PREPARING TEACHERS

The pre-service program for preparing secondary school teachers is typically a four-year undergraduate program including (1) general education designed to provide the student with a broad background of knowledge in the major intellectual disciplines; (2) specialization in at least one subject-matter area; and (3) an introduction to the basic elements of professional educational theory. The professional curriculum generally includes efforts to provide: an understanding of learning as related to child and adolescent behavior; an understanding of appropriate educational methods and materials; and direct experiences with boys and girls, culminating in an effective student- or apprentice-teaching experience. General education is typically provided through an assortment of offerings taught by the various academic departments, chiefly at the freshman and sophomore level, while subject-matter specialization is made available by a specific academic department or group of related departments. Other departments sometimes co-operate with the education department in introducing subjects helpful to professional educators, such as specialized methodology.

## Inadequacies of the Present Four-Year General Program for Teachers of the Gifted

Many faculty members in teacher-education institutions believe that the curriculum of the present four-year teacher-education program is already too heavily overburdened to be able to turn out young teachers who possess even a minimum of competence. The advocate of general education, which typically constitutes about 40 to 50 per cent of the teacher-education program, often insists that more background is needed in this area. The subject-matter specialist, too, often insists that special subject matter, now comprising about 25 to 30 per cent of the total program, is inadequate in depth. And the professional educator is rarely happy with the 15 to 20 per cent of the program allotted to his area, a significant portion of which is taken up by student teaching.

The current four-year teacher education program is not likely to be expanded to include important areas of learning related to the gifted. Nor is there any evidence that subject-matter specialization or basic general education will differ qualitatively or quantitatively for the prospective teacher of the gifted.

In many programs of professional education for prospective secondary school teachers, however, it may be possible to include some experiences relating to the education of gifted students. Such experiences may be provided through including selected units or problems of study within the framework of existing professional education courses. Such units or problems of study might involve the identification of gifted students, their special characteristics and needs, and techniques and procedures found to be promising in work with gifted students. In most cases this would mean a reorganization of course content. There is evidence that changes of this nature have occurred in some teacher-education programs. In a 1951 study conducted by Wilson (252), a little over half of the respondents reported that there was some attention to problems of the gifted student through instructional units or other approaches, chiefly in such courses as principles of education, child and adolescent psychology, educational psychology, and methods of teaching. A repetition of the same study on a smaller scale five years later found little change.

## Current Status of Pre-Service Preparation

In 1958 many institutions in the United States provided course offerings related to teaching the gifted, but Pennyslvania State University and Hunter College were the only schools offering a specific sequence of courses in this area, and these were partly at the graduate level. Abraham (1) states that a recent report reveals that out of 4601 persons majoring in the various areas of special education, only twenty-one persons specialized in the gifted child, and out of 1549 who were granted degrees in special education only two persons concentrated in gifted-child education. He also reports that of 897 higher education faculty members working in special education, only two were in the field of the gifted and none were devoting full time to this work. There are indications, though, that this situation is changing. Many dissertations are being written on the gifted, and most major universities now have at least one staff member with strong interests in the field.

In summary, the current major contributions of teacher-education institutions to the education of teachers of the gifted at the undergraduate level are: (1) providing occasional units or segments of work on the gifted student within the framework of established professional education courses; and (2) providing occasional opportunities for undergraduates to take a specific course devoted to the gifted.

## Programs and Methods for Training Teachers of the Gifted

What can teacher-education institutions do to prepare teachers of the gifted? The evidence indicates that (1) it should not be the responsibility of the four-year undergraduate teacher-education program to produce persons who are ready to begin work immediately with groups of gifted students; (2) it would not be wise to develop an extensive four-year undergraduate program leading to special certification in this field; and (3) undergraduate students should have the opportunity to explore education for the gifted through actual course work or through adequately developed instructional units within appropriately related courses.

The Fifty-Seventh Yearbook of the National Society for the Study of Education (100) lists seven practices which might be used by teacher-education institutions to improve the prospective teacher's capacity to serve the gifted. Some of these practices may be incorporated into the undergraduate professional sequence, but some are likely to be effective only as part of well-planned courses in this area.

Every teacher-education program can, however, attempt to locate the prospective elementary and secondary teachers who show unusual promise of success in working with the academically gifted student. These prospective teachers might then be guided into taking such courses as will help them develop an understanding of the able student. In their training program, these teachers can be encouraged to observe and participate in situations involving gifted individuals, perhaps as student teachers in classes that include intellectually able students. Since grouping is becoming more common, it is frequently possible to place student teachers with gifted groups.

Even if teacher-education programs provide such experiences, however, the new graduate is not likely to be highly effective in working with groups of the academically able. Actual experience in teaching will usually result in greater competencies and have the further advantage of demonstrating to the young teacher himself, as well as to his colleagues and his supervisors, whether or not he is likely to be successful in working with superior students.

At present there are only a limited number of positions available for teachers of the gifted, and the demand is likely to remain low in the immediate future. Except in the largest secondary schools, teachers in all the major subjects will be teaching only one or two classes of the academically superior. Perhaps this is as it should be, for it allows the teacher to maintain a proper perspective of the make-up of the entire student universe. This is particularly true if the teacher works with slow children as well as average groups.

## A Five-Year Education Program for Teachers of the Gifted

It is possible that a five-year program of pre-service preparation could be adapted to preparing teachers of the gifted. Forty-four per cent of secondary teachers and many elementary teachers throughout the country hold master's degrees. It would seem, then, that the better teacher-education institutions, particularly those providing graduate work, could quickly establish five-year programs of teacher education, especially for individuals showing significant promise as prospective teachers of the gifted. The program might well offer both a bachelor's and a master's degree (if the institution provides graduate work). Such a program could improve upon the basic four-year program by including elements that are difficult to work into the average four-year undergraduate program, such as: (1) additional depth in basic or specialized subjects; (2) a sequence of appropriate course work related to teaching the gifted; and (3) extensive opportunities for observation of the gifted, and actual student-teaching or internship experience—at the appropriate level of preparation—with special groups of superior boys and girls. Teachers completing such a program would certainly be welcome additions to the staff of any school system seeking competent persons for teaching the gifted. After working with heterogeneous classes, or classes consisting of average or below-average children or adolescents, these teachers could be moved into positions where they would work with superior students.

## IN-SERVICE PREPARATION OF THE TEACHER OF THE GIFTED

We know that professional pre-service programs provide the beginning practitioner with only a minimum of competence for teaching boys and girls. Master teachers are most often the product of profitable professional and personal growth on the job in a school where competent leadership and strong faculty provide high-level stimulation. In-service education may be undertaken through (1) organized attempts at program improvement and staff stimulation under the direction of the individual school or school system, chiefly utilizing local staff; (2) haphazard attempts at program improvement and staff stimulation in a school or school system, including what Abraham calls "the go-it-alone route of personal betterment"; or (3) in-service programs carefully planned by the school or school system, utilizing some professional personnel from nearby institutions of higher learning.

### In-Service Preparation by the School System

As school systems have approached the problem of developing and implementing arrangements for more adequate instruction of academically able youth, they have turned increasingly to the in-service institute, workshop, or conference for building the competence teachers need to operate such programs. Public schools often secure the consultative professional help of personnel already on the local staff or of specialists imported from the staffs of teacher-education institutions. Unfortunately, there are not enough such consultants, but their number is growing as the demand increases. These consultants generally serve as lecturers, professional advisers, or conference leaders. Wilson (252) suggests that their contribution has had a greater effect on school practice and theory than it has on the improvement of programs within the teacher-education institution.

In reporting on a questionnaire study investigating the in-service activities of school systems, Wilson says: (1) the majority of school systems make little use of special courses in their in-service preparation; (2) 70 per cent of the school systems use conferences for purposes of in-service stimulation of the education of the gifted; (3) many systems use workshops, held chiefly in the summer; (4) a few systems use field or laboratory experiences; and (5) a great many systems have various kinds of leadership activities by staff personnel.

## In-Service Preparation by the Graduate School or College

Contributions by teacher-education institutions to the preparation of teachers of the gifted are usually at the graduate rather than at the undergraduate level. This is true particularly of institution-sponsored workshops or conferences, which are generally available in the summer sessions. An increasingly common practice among institutions with staff personnel competent in the field of teaching the gifted is to develop specific courses or to institute workshops concerned with teaching superior students. A well-planned workshop, offered by the school system and utilizing the services of competent personnel from the system or from the staffs of colleges and universities, is perhaps the most effective in-service activity. The success of this particular activity may be due to the close relationship between the workshop offerings and the actual needs and characteristics of the school system.

Effective collaboration between the education faculty and the various academic faculties on the college campus will enhance the value of in-service summer programs for teachers. Most teacher-education institutions should have little difficulty in organizing such programs in collaboration with local school systems. Summer demonstration schools similar to the one functioning at Kent State University (Kent, Ohio) offer enrollees the opportunity to work with groups of superior boys and girls.

## CONCLUSION

The present inadequate supply of well-prepared teachers of the gifted accents the need for strong teacher-education institutions in America: institutions with the resources to provide the best in teacher education at both the pre-service and in-service levels. In general, these resources are now lacking.

# 25 SELECTION AND ROLE OF THE TEACHER OF SUPERIOR AND TALENTED STUDENTS

CLIFFORD WILLIAMS
*Supervisor, Gifted Child Program, Portland Public Schools, Portland, Oregon*

Before considering the selection of teachers of academically able and talented students it is necessary to examine the role of such teachers as contrasted with the role of teachers generally. The differences in these roles have implications for school administrators seeking to select appropriate teachers to instruct able students.

## THE ROLE OF SPECIAL CLASS TEACHERS

There is no reason to believe that the teaching and learning processes in classes for the superior and talented should be entirely different from those in classes for average students. The personal characteristics and professional qualifications of teachers of able students may be more like those desirable in all teachers than they are unlike them. We cannot say, however, that "a benevolent disposition, good health, pleasing appearance, and genuine interest and sympathy for the young" (260) are necessarily sufficient requisites for teachers of the able.

Although certain general qualities are desirable in all teachers, we need to look beyond these qualities to locate the specific characteristics that should be present in teachers of superior and talented students. We shall examine the role of such teachers in the day-to-day teaching situation, and we shall also consider the qualities which bright students expect them to have. This information about the personality characteristics needed by a teacher of gifted students should help school administrators choose these very important teachers.

279

## The Teacher Teaches the Subject

>    Knowledge of subject matter is the quality most valued in teachers
> by able students. This does not mean that students expect teachers to
> digest the contents and feed them like birds. It does imply that the
> teacher who knows his field is most likely to guide students along the
> correct route to learning (250).

The high school teacher of advanced or gifted students finds that
he is called upon to be a specialist. When he steps before a group of
bright young people he is likely to have to utilize his most complex
skills to satisfy the needs of individual students. He finds that in
such classes, more than in regular classes, he is teaching subject
matter. He is taking students through step-by-step developmental
experiences toward advanced levels of the subject being studied. He
may find it necessary to spend long teaching sessions helping students acquire facts out of books, a kind of teaching often deplored
by theorists. Like any other students, however, gifted students
must learn facts before they can go on to more advanced learning.
Able students in high school have the intellectual foresight to realize
that further ability to attack problems depends on the acquisition
of facts, skills, and knowledge. Moreover, contrary to popular belief, such students enjoy factual learning whether or not they are
aware of any future use for the knowledge.

A thorough knowledge of the subject matter is an essential for the
teacher of English literature, composition, or history, just as it is
for the teacher of mathematics or science. Teachers of the superior
and talented should be familiar with source material, original documents, parallel texts, related reading, relevant research, and counter
theories. Bright students often ask their teachers to suggest further
study in books and periodicals as their curiosity is aroused.

## The Teacher Teaches Learning Skills

The teacher of able students also spends considerable effort and
energy developing the learning skills of his students. Among these
skills are reading, creative and critical writing, techniques of elementary research, and methods of study. With superior students
much time will be spent on creative and evaluative reading. In
order to help students develop these skills, the teacher must
thoroughly understand the processes of reading, know the rules of

good writing (whether or not he is a teacher of composition), know what constitutes research, and be familiar with the best methods of acquiring learning through study. This means that the teacher will be responsible for assessing strengths, diagnosing difficulties, and prescribing correctional measures. Even a relatively homogeneous class of able students includes individuals who need help, and the teacher will find that he must be a specialist in the nature of learning as well as in the subject matter of his course.

Students with exceptional ability are often subject to obstructive deficiencies in skills and attitudes. They may have progressed through school, getting high grades for superficial, but relatively satisfactory, written work. Because they learn easily, many do not develop work habits which insure continued intellectual success. After years of excelling in normal classes, they may be shocked to find that other students are equally able or superior. Furthermore, it is not unusual to find an exceptionally able boy or girl whose varied and numerous interests spread his time and effort so thin that he is generally ineffective. The teacher must work to help students overcome these deficiencies in skills and attitudes and must sometimes encourage students to curtail their extracurricular activities in the interest of increased effectiveness.

In his teaching role the instructor of gifted students practices the art of education. With all students, but particularly with able students, the teacher must "supply the degree of dominance or withdrawal necessary to increase the ability of students to be self-directing" (248). Students should be encouraged to question and challenge. Perhaps the most important aspect of a student's development is a growing recognition of his own convictions and the willingness to abide by them. A high school teacher cannot simply lecture to a class, expect students to listen and believe, and assume that the exercise of good judgment will follow automatically. A teacher who expects nothing but tailor-made answers to his lectures actually prolongs the dependence of boys and girls and makes them prey to demagogues of the future. Good teaching involves a fine balance of lecture, reading, small group discussion, problem solving, and research. A good teacher is secure enough not to view questioning of his generalizations as a personal threat and flexible enough to be skillful in a variety of teaching methods.

## The Teacher Counsels Students

The teacher, whether or not he is officially part of a school guidance department, will be called upon to function as a counselor. "He has an unusual opportunity to know and understand each student in his own class, to stimulate those with special interests, and to discuss with all the pupils the broader meanings and personal implications of their studies and experiences" (64). With classes of gifted students, the teacher-counselor's guidance will be largely educational advice—how to prepare for college, which colleges are appropriate, how to apply for scholarships, what college courses to take, and how to set suitable vocational goals. Vocational counseling may not be as immediately job-oriented as it would be in classes of average students—although ultimate vocational goals, broad though they may be, are important considerations in educational planning. To carry on a complete guidance program, the teacher will of course need the help of experts—as is generally true of any guidance program. Nevertheless, students will seek the teacher's opinion and advice in direct proportion to the rapport which he establishes with them.

One necessary quality in the teacher of gifted students needs repeated emphasis. *He must be willing to work harder than ever before.* Many teachers who have accepted the responsibility of teaching such a class have naively expected that it would be ideal to have nothing but capable students. The first shock comes early, probably at the initial class meeting, when it becomes apparent that the avid reading common in such a group has placed their knowledge of the subject far beyond expectations. The teacher must then spend many hours replanning the material to be covered and examining more advanced source books and texts. The second shock usually occurs when the instructor becomes aware that some students know more about certain phases of his subject, and have sharper insight for problem solving, than he does. This certainly does not mean that the teacher has nothing to offer the student. Through his mature judgment and his ability to guide and counsel, the teacher can contribute significantly to a student's development. It is a long time before some teachers realize this fact.

In general, the teacher of the gifted will find that a sense of humor and a feeling of personal security are necessities.

## Student Characteristics Are Important

Some insight into the qualities desirable in a teacher of gifted students and into the tasks that such a teacher must perform can be gained by comparing the characteristics of gifted students with those of other youngsters. Experience with classes for gifted boys and girls in Portland, Oregon, suggests that "the two major characteristics which gifted children seem to have more than average children are (1) a capacity for learning more difficult and complex material; and (2) a more questioning attitude and interest in finding new approaches to problems" (190).

Teachers in the Portland program agree on only a limited number of characteristics that a teacher of gifted students should have, and these are related to the two student characteristics mentioned above. Most of the Portland teachers mentioned the following qualities:

1. Greater knowledge of the subject
2. Ability and willingness to encourage questions and independent study
3. Willingness to work harder
4. Respect for and interest in gifted students

Several studies have been made of able students' ideas about their teachers. One report lists the following qualities as preferred by able students: sense of humor, encouragement of responsibility, knowledge of subject, firmness and fairness, understanding of children, and enjoyment of teaching (57).

Parents of gifted students also mentioned qualifications they feel desirable in teachers of superior pupils. In one study parents suggested such characteristics as the avoidance of exploitation of students, the ability to develop critical thinking and ability to co-operate with parents (100).

In summary, the teacher of superior and talented students should be:

1. A specialist in his subject, abreast of developments in his field, and aware of trends and future possibilities
2. Scholarly enough to be acquainted with major written works, sources, and research in his field of teaching
3. Adept at diagnosing learning difficulties, and skillful at providing corrective measures
4. Aware of the value of various teaching procedures in providing opportunity for students to learn to think, to write, and to speak

5. Alert to opportunities to counsel and advise students with educational and vocational problems

## SELECTING SPECIAL CLASS TEACHERS

The administrator of any large high school (one thousand or more students) has several teachers in most of the subject departments of his school. If he plans classes for superior and talented students he must select teachers for these special classes. Some teachers will not want to teach special classes and should be eliminated on those grounds. For those who would agree to such an assignment, the administrator should consider these factors: personal ability and scholarship, ability to command respect and inspire students to enthusiastic work, personal security and sense of humor, general knowledge of many subjects, creative ability as shown by personal efforts, and capacity for hard work. The administrator should avoid selecting teachers who have difficulty handling normal classes, who have a reputation as complainers or school critics, who are in their first year of teaching, or who are not interested in opportunities for educational improvement.

Some schools are fortunate enough to have several teachers in each department who are able and willing to teach classes of superior and talented students. Such schools often rotate teachers for their gifted and regular classes, and the teachers usually find a three-year rotation plan fairly satisfactory. Because almost a year is required to gear oneself to the demands of a special group of students, an annual or biennial plan of rotation is unsatisfactory for both teachers and students.

There are several advantages to rotating teachers of special classes. If a department has several competent teachers, there may be a tendency toward some jealousy. The special class is looked upon as a highly desirable assignment, and giving several teachers a chance at it may help keep peace in the family. Also, rotation will give more teachers experience in teaching gifted students, increasing their understanding of such youngsters and improving their attitude toward special classes and appropriate learning experiences.

Justman and Wrightstone (120), in a study of teachers' attitudes toward special classes, report that two groups of teachers—younger teachers and teachers with experience in teaching bright youngsters—have more favorable attitudes than do any other groups. To summarize the differences: Younger teachers and teachers with class experience in teaching superior students tend to maintain that intellectually gifted children in special classes are *not* too competitive, get better leadership training, tend to be above average in social adjustment, get along well with children from other classes, and do *not* become conceited. These two groups also maintain that teachers of gifted classes spend more time in preparation than do regular teachers, get more co-operation and interest from parents, and get *no* more than a fair share of school supplies and equipment. Older teachers and teachers *without* gifted class experience tend to maintain that too many children are placed in special classes who do not belong there, that they would have made more progress in regular classes, that their personal problems are aggravated, that they tend to show off, and that they do not develop respect for adults. These teachers also feel that having small gifted classes is unfair to other teachers and that parents tend to interfere more with special classes.

We can conclude from the Justman and Wrightstone study that giving more teachers an opportunity to work with classes of gifted students is likely to create a more favorable climate for appropriate adjustments in the instructional program.

An obvious disadvantage of rotating the assignment of special classes is that for most teachers up to a year will elapse between the time they begin to teach a gifted class and the time their teaching becomes truly effective. Because they are not yet familiar with the potential of gifted students, beginning teachers often waste time in ineffective assignments, covering previously learned concepts, reading already familiar or too elementary material, and establishing inadequate standards of performance. Teachers also need time to become familiar with more advanced texts and supplementary literature, and to review concepts and relearn skills which normal classes do not require. Furthermore, recent developments in some academic fields—mathematics and science particularly—need to be studied, since gifted students will be somewhat familiar with them and will expect the instructor to be up to date. Each administrator will have to realize that developing a competent teacher of gifted students will require considerable time.

Administrators in smaller schools will have different problems, since it is unlikely that there will be several teachers to consider as potential instructors of gifted classes. Smaller schools need to determine the special strengths of individuals on the faculty and use them in establishing special classes of after-school seminars. One principal organized an excellent seminar using a teacher, two specialists from the community, and himself. The teacher, known to be a strong instructor in early American history, taught the first eight weeks of the seminar on the subject "The Development of the American Constitution." A local attorney came to the school three mornings each week for the second eight weeks to teach "The Constitution as a Basis for American Laws." The students spent the other two seminar periods each week in reading and study pertinent to the subject. The third eight-week seminar period was taught by a local contractor who had served in the state legislature and had been most interested in the state constitution. His unit was called "The Constitution of the State: An Enlargement of Article X." The final seminar period of the year, taught by the principal, was intended to instruct the students in the techniques of research; part of the time was spent studying examples of research projects made available by a nearby college. Each of the four instructors was assigned to act as an adviser to a group of students in the writing of term papers on topics suggested by the course.

A seminar like the one described above may be established even if a school's faculty does not permit offering a variety of advanced courses. Such a seminar may be the school's single effort for gifted students. High achievement is the result of appropriate developmental tasks provided by competent and sympathetic teachers. If schools do not search for ways to use the most qualified teachers to teach superior but underachieving students, they may expect to relinquish their task of education to others.

# SECTION VIII

## COMMUNITY PARTICIPATION IN
## TALENT DEVELOPMENT PROGRAMS

The size and nature of a community, its wealth and resources, and its values and leadership all affect the contributions which that community can make to talent development programs. Never before have communities been so receptive to talent development programs. Never have people been more anxious to participate in their talent development programs and to help improve them. Never before have so many towns and cities throughout the United States been involved in identifying and educating their superior students.

How can a school integrate the resources available in its community? First, school administrators may select a lay advisory committee to participate in the planning and policy recommendation phases of the talent development program. Second, efforts should be made to interpret the program to the community. Third, an inventory should be taken of the personnel, organizations, agencies, activities, materials, and opportunities in the community that might further the objectives of the program. Fourth, plans should be drawn up for relating such resources to the program. Fifth, the program should be evaluated periodically and a report made to the public. Experimental and pilot programs which are evaluated some time after their initiation can often be improved by redefinition or revision.

The purpose of using community resources for talented students is to help the students learn more thoroughly and efficiently what the school is trying to teach, and to enrich and expand their interests and experiences. Activities involving community resources should be oriented toward the personal growth of students; that is, they should be educative in nature.

The advantages of joint efforts on the part of both community and school to help gifted students are many. Using community resources in a school's talent development program may accomplish the following:

1. It may develop an increasing awareness of and sensitivity to the talent development program as an outgrowth of community needs and characteristics.

2. It may relate the personal interests of the bright student to those of resource people in his immediate environment, making learning more meaningful to the bright student, particularly if his experiences are followed up by an alert teacher.

3. It may vitalize, enrich, and extend the experiences of bright students.

4. It may result in improvement in the intellectual level of the community.

5. It may counteract isolation of the school from the realities of community life by fostering co-operation between individuals and agencies interested in elevating the intellectual and aspirational levels of bright boys and girls.

What an urban school system with a large number of superior and talented students can undertake may not be feasible in a small town or in a suburban or rural community. However, since evidence indicates that the greatest talent loss is in rural and small town areas, it is especially important that schools in such areas explore and utilize all possible community resources. Some smaller communities have pooled their resources. Smaller communities might also consider the following procedures: teacher-directed independent study in advanced areas; correspondence courses and self-teaching materials for bright students; opportunities for community specialists to share their skills, experiences, and resources with students in a variety of ways, including the teaching of Saturday or after-school seminars; and small classes to facilitate individual and personalized instruction.

Parents and school personnel should consider every resource the community has to offer. Some resources frequently overlooked are:

community recreational programs that offer craft opportunities; some educational television programs; carefully selected commercial television programs for children and adolescents; YMCA and YWCA programs in science, art, and physical education; museums, art galleries, and concerts; science exhibits; college-sponsored youth programs in the fine arts, languages, theater, and other areas; retired professional or business men and women who maintain an active interest in their fields and in children; and the various special-interest groups that are a part of every school, such as the PTA and the Dads Club. Utilizing these resources will require many hours of extra work on the part of the teacher, counselor, and administrator, but the rewards—intellectual, moral, and social— are more than worth it.

Community resources include people who can contribute to all phases of a school's talent development program. These people may act as visiting lecturers, part-time teachers, or consultants. They may provide specialized instruction in the classroom or confer individually with bright students. Community resources also include agencies and civic organizations which can assist talented students in solving their individual and group problems.

Lay advisory councils and committees can be important means of contact with parents and other individuals in the community. The school administrator is largely responsible for organizing these groups. Effective school-community relationships depend upon the school administrator's sensitivity to community values. The administrator must be skillful in communicating with the community and must participate in community-school undertakings and experiences. After fully assessing the characteristics of the superior and talented students with whom he is to work, the school administrator should inventory the interests, activities, personnel, and materials of the local community to determine which ones will contribute to the students' development.

Willard Abraham, in Chapter 26, discusses school and community resources. Among the resources available to a talent development program in any school in any community are people, places, books and publications, organizations, and the students in the school. The task, according to Abraham, is to become aware that resources exist in every community. Every community, large or small, urban or rural, contains the basic social processes of making a living, preserving health, and participating in public life. Good resources, then, are merely a matter of intelligent selection and utilization.

In Chapter 27, Jacob Shapiro discusses the Joe Berg Foundation's action program in science for gifted students. This program is an example of relating community resources to the development of talent. The strength of the program lies in the flexibility with which it solicits and uses the help of many people and agencies in the community. The young people who participate in it receive recognition, interest, understanding, and leadership. The program enables bright students interested in science to have personal contact with scientists on the job. The emphasis is on problem solving and on vivid and direct learning experiences that capitalize on student interests and thereby provide intrinsic motivation for participating students.

Claude Kelly, in Chapter 28, points out that educators must encourage community participation in and support of talent development programs. Such co-operation, he asserts, will be most likely to occur in a democratic setting, and will not only prevent misunderstandings, but will help to effect desirable changes and improvements in school programs. Kelly feels that the school and community can achieve a close relationship through this co-operative planning, participation, and accomplishment. Such a relationship is essential, since classes and curriculum for superior and talented students are not entirely classroom centered, but related to community mores and the problems of everyday living.

# 26 SCHOOL AND COMMUNITY RESOURCES FOR SUPERIOR AND TALENTED STUDENTS

WILLARD ABRAHAM

*Chairman, Department of Special Education, Arizona State University*

*Resources? In this neighborhood? With these parents and children? In the midst of all this poverty of ideas, people, and facilities? It's a miracle we can get any teaching done. We don't talk about implementing what doesn't even exist, and challenging the bright ones—that's expecting the impossible. With nothing to work with, and nothing to expect from an environment that's barren in every way, we have no resources to tap and none to implement. That's the problem at its worst, and that's the one we face here.*

Despite the barrenness and pessimism of this statement, let's see whether we can drain some little bit of hope from the place, the adults, and the children—from this least promising of all atmospheres. Let's see whether there aren't some resources in every community—in every neighborhood—that can be turned toward the development of superior and talented students and the betterment of education for all children.

## HUMAN AND INSTITUTIONAL RESOURCES

Our first hope lies in the fact that *people are resources*—such people as parents, community leaders, teachers, administrators, guidance personnel, and other professional persons. The pupils of Natalie Cole, a teacher in Los Angeles, found this out, for they had a skilled teacher who brought to the surface all the brightness of their buried talent. The communities touched by the Joe Berg Foundation* also found it out as they began to utilize the knowledge and abilities of chemists, doctors, dentists, ministers, and others.

---

*See Chapter 27 for an outline of the Foundation's activities.

Cities such as Cleveland, St. Louis, Portland, and Palo Alto learned that certain teachers and administrators had the ability to challenge and stimulate bright youngsters.

Our second hope lies in the fact that *places are resources*—places close by and far away, places that cannot very well be separated from the people in them. Some of these places are teacher preparation institutions whose courses are increasingly being directed toward providing prospective teachers with knowledge about individual differences and needs. Institutions such as these, emphasizing that teaching bright children can be fun but is never easy, have made important contributions to in-service programs related to superior and talented children. Teachers and students may take field trips to other resource places, including government and utility buildings, local industries and businesses, museums, zoos, and many others.

The people and places already mentioned are just a few of the resources schools may call upon. There are countless other aids available to teachers and administrators whose vision is not limited by the limited opportunities of their own childhood and education. Some schools have found that what were thought to be dreams of enrichment are realistic ideas after all. A school may find benefactors who are interested in bright youngsters and willing to provide expensive resources for their education. Even more important, it may discover valuable resources that cost nothing at all, as the following examples indicate:

> One young mother of four children in Phoenix, Arizona, is a skilled mathematician. She spends a few hours each week with six gifted upper-elementary youngsters. She is having a wonderful time working with these youngsters, and they, too, are enjoying the special opportunity.
>
> A graduate student on a college campus set up special Saturday morning classes for children gifted in art. The local schools have been inspired by this student's initiative and by the enthusiasm of the children participating in the classes.
>
> An elementary school principal who loves to teach has set up two special classes for bright older children. He has taken time out from his busy administrative schedule to work with them in certain areas of science, social studies, and foreign languages.

These three busy people have very little spare time. Because they are interested in children, however, each one has found time to serve superior and talented youth.

## BOOKS AND OTHER PUBLISHED MATERIAL

Current bibliographies on gifted children list many titles—books, pamphlets, and articles. We should make use of the wealth of material available to us by maintaining professional libraries in the schools and by reading current literature in the field. The professional magazines in subject-matter fields contain much valuable material.

We should not overlook published accounts of current experiments and studies concerned with the identification and education of gifted children—many of which appear in the educational and psychological journals.

We would never countenance a gap in the knowledge of the men who handle our legal, medical, or dental affairs; nor should we tolerate such a gap in the knowledge of our educators. Like almost everyone else, educators are rushed in this hectic world of ours, but such guides as the *Review of Educational Research* and the *Education Index* help us keep up to date on recent major research on such subjects as creativity, grouping, special classes, enrichment, identification, and motivation.

## ORGANIZATIONS

Many organizations have a direct or indirect interest in superior and talented youngsters. For example, the National Education Association (NEA) has devoted considerable energy and emphasis to the Academically Talented Pupil Project, and has already released several publications of specific value to subject-matter teachers on the high-school level. A division of the NEA, the Council for Exceptional Children, which publishes the journal *Exceptional Children,* has made extensive contributions to this field. Other organizations such as the Joe Berg Foundation, the National Merit Scholarship Corporation, and the National Scholarship Service and Fund for Negro Students are resources of value to communities and schools all over the country. Foundation assistance, such as the Carnegie Corporation's support of the North Central Association Superior and Talented Student Project, is also an important resource.

## THE MOST SIGNIFICANT RESOURCE

The most significant resource of all is one which we frequently neglect, because we do not think of it as a resource. This resource is the *children* themselves—their talents, abilities, and aspirations. It is in terms of this central resource that all the other resources mentioned must be employed.

The bright student who is handicapped physically or emotionally, the bright girl whose parents feel they cannot afford to further her education, and the minority group youngster whose talent may be hidden in a background of cultural deprivation—these are some of the resources of which our schools may be unaware. Another resource is the nonconformist, the child who often strains the teacher's patience. Still another resource is the unmotivated, the underachieving student, who may work up to the grade level for his age but not up to his capacity—and for whom we are constantly seeking an inspiration, a spark, or an approach that will activate his ability.

The combination of able and ambitious youngsters (or of those who are able and unambitious but whom we have discovered how to motivate) with a skilled teacher provides the school with its most important resource. All other resources only supplement this essential combination, the goals of which are: (1) the best teaching ever seen, heard about, read about, or performed; and (2) an excited, curious, questioning, critical, and doubting child who has the potential to achieve at a high level and has been guided to do just that.

All resources of every kind available should be discovered and used to accomplish these objectives. Those of us who are serious about educating our bright children—and all our children—to the fullest extent possible will never be satisfied with less.

# 27 AN ACTION PROGRAM IN SCIENCE FOR SUPERIOR AND TALENTED STUDENTS

JACOB W. SHAPIRO
*Co-ordinator, the Joe Berg Foundation,*
*Chicago, Illinois*

How would you like to teach a class of ninth-grade boys and girls with most or all of the following characteristics:

1. IQ of 135 or over
2. College sophomore reading comprehension and vocabulary level
3. Achievement test scores in the 95th percentile or above
4. School performance at the honor-roll level or above
5. Demonstrated high motivation in science and mathematics

Probably you would answer in the affirmative—that you would like to teach such a class. But since there are only 168 hours in a week, wouldn't you also hesitate to take on such a responsibility? So much more time seems to be required to stimulate and challenge a class of twenty-five such youngsters.

This is the problem: How can we provide adequate educational experiences for these superior and talented students when teachers are already overburdened and when most other citizens have more activities than they have time for? Here is a partial solution: Multiply time by vitalizing already existing community assets and harnessing them in a co-operative effort involving the gifted child, his parents, trained laymen, the school, industry, and industry's laboratories.

This solution is the basis of the Plan for the Advancement of Science sponsored by the Joe Berg Foundation.* The Joe Berg

---

*The Joe Berg Foundation, which sponsors action programs in more than 375 high schools in the United States and Canada, was initiated in November 1957 through the generosity of Mr. Joe Berg, a Chicago industrialist. The foundation is supported by Mr. Berg personally and by the Berg Manufacturing and Sales Company.

For free descriptive material, write to the Joe Berg Foundation, 1712 S. Michigan, Chicago 16, Ill., or see Albert Q. Maisel, "An Imaginative Program To Spark Science Students," *Parents' Magazine*, August 1958.

Foundation sponsors seminars which, at practically no cost to any-one, provide extracurricular educational experiences for gifted students. These seminars offer science instruction that is more advanced, rigorous, and individualized than that provided in the regular curriculum. The instruction is especially meaningful, because the seminar staffs are made up primarily of volunteer trained laymen employed by industry in the fields of research and technology.

## ESTABLISHING A SCIENCE SEMINAR

Here are the steps involved in the process of setting up a science seminar in a given community:

First, consult governing school authorities and obtain permission to start a seminar. Second, discuss the idea with school personnel, representatives of local industry, and interested laymen. Then form a planning committee to proceed with organization of a seminar.

The first order of business for the planning committee will be to select two co-ordinators, one from the school system and one from industry. Other working committees should then be established and placed under the general direction of the co-ordinators. All committees should include teachers, interested laymen, professional men and women in the community, and school administrators.

The Joe Berg Foundation has found the following committees helpful in establishing a science seminar:

1. Advisory or steering committee to establish policy and to give general direction to the program

2. Staff recruitment committee to locate sufficient personnel to form a staff with a student-teacher ratio of one to one

3. Admissions and standards committee to set up the requirements for admission of superior students to the program and for their retention in the program

4. Physical facilities committee to locate, at no cost to the school, places and equipment needed for students to work on their projects

5. Projects committee to counsel the youngsters in selecting their projects and to see that their experimental work is carried out under safe conditions

6. Public relations committee to handle communications with the general community and with other schools

7. Curriculum committee to develop a curriculum for the program

The science-mathematics seminar should not take up the material covered in a recognized science or mathematics course. Rather it should explore advanced areas of thought and stimulate the talented student's interest in specific areas of science and mathematics.

Topics frequently discussed in seminar programs include the Bohr atom, the periodic table, digital computers, living molecules, the structure of organic molecules, the theory of relativity, carbon dating, optics, statistics and probability, solid-state physics, and the basis for modern science.

## TYPICAL SEMINAR OUTLINES

The two outlines that follow are typical of the advance lesson plans that are made for seminars. Copies of these outlines are distributed to the members of the seminar far enough in advance for them to make adequate preparation.

SCHOOL DISTRICT OF ABINGTON TOWNSHIP
Abington, Pennsylvania

Date:     Thursday, May 7, 1959
Place:    Abington Senior High School
Topic:    *Solid-State Physics*
Program Chairman:     John E. Remick
                      Manager, Technical Division
                      Philco Corporation

Speaker:              John W. Tiley
                      Engineering Group Supervisor
                      G/I Division
                      Philco Corporation, Philadelphia

Outline of Program
  1. The structure of solids
  2. Insulators and conductors
  3. History of semiconductors
  4. Transistors
  5. Fifteen-minute film (color) on laboratory techniques
     in transistor technology
  6. Transistors under the microscope
  7. Discussion-question period

References

1. *Introduction to Solid State Physics*, Charles Killet
   (John Wiley & Sons).
2. *Proceedings of the Institute of Radio Engineers*, Vol. XLVI,
   No. 6, June 1958.
3. *Fundamental Principles of Physical Chemistry*, C. F. Prutton
   and S. H. Marron (MacMillan Co.).
4. *Procedures in Experimental Physics*, John Strong
   (Prentice-Hall Co.).
5. *Proceedings of the Institute of Radio Engineers*, December
   1953, pp. 1702-1720.
6. *Holes and Electrons*, William Shockley (Bell Laboratories
   Technical Series).

HORTON WATKINS SEMINAR
Ladue, Missouri

Title: The Basis for Modern Science
Seminar No.: 1                    Date: November 17, 1959
Leader:   Dr. R. S. Gordon

Assignments:

Required Reading:
A. *The Making of the Modern Mind*, John Herman Randall
   (Houghton Mifflin Co., rev. ed., 1940).
   Book I, Chapter I, "The Coming of Age of the
      Western Peoples," pp. 9-16.
   Book I, Chapter II, "The World as the Scene of
      the Drama of Salvation," pp. 17-37.
   Book I, Chapter III, "The Chief End of Man:
      The Enjoyment of Eternal Life," pp. 52-56.
   Book I, Chapter IV, "The Embodiment:—*The City
      of God*," pp. 58-73, 75-80.
   Book I, Chapter V, "The Embodiment:—Lay Society,"
      pp. 92-102.
   Book II, Chapter VI, "The New Interest of the
      Modern Age:—The Natural Man," pp. 111-24.
   Book II, Chapter IX, "The New Interest of the
      Modern Age:—The World of Nature," pp. 205-25.

Book II, Chapter X, "The New Scene of Human Life,"
  pp. 226-39.
B. *The Story of Philosophy*, Will Durant
  (Garden City Publishing Co., 1943).
    Chapter II, "Aristotle and Greek Science."
    Chapter III, "From Aristotle to the Renaissance."
C. *Ancient Science and Modern Civilization*, George Sarton
  (Harper & Bros., Torch Science Library, pp. 37-111).
D. *Essays in Science and Philosophy*, Alfred North Whitehead
  (Philosophical Library, Inc.).
    "The First Physical Synthesis," pp. 166-76.

Optional Reading:
A. *Science for the Citizen*, Lancelot Hogben (London:
  George Allen & Unwin, Ltd., 1940).
    Chapter I, Part I, pp. 1-17.

Essay Preparation:
  (choice of *one* of the following—200-250 words—to be done
    neatly in ink or preferably with typewriter)
1. Do you use logic?
    (Hint: Durant, Chapter II, Part 3)
2. How did medieval scholastics pervert Aristotle?
    (Hint: Randall, p. 98)
3. Do you think there should have been a conflict between
  Galileo and the pope?
    (Hint: Whitehead, p. 167)
4. Does *The City of God* conflict with experimental science?
    (Hint: Randall, pp. 58-81)
5. Why is humanism antiscientific?
    (Hint: Randall, p. 212)

## SOME TYPICAL PROJECTS

The following projects are typical of those undertaken by seminar
students:
- Construction of an electronic digital computer
- Gas chromatography
- Building a short-wave radio receiver
- Examination of the side effects of tranquilizers

- Design of an optimum automobile turn indicator
- Mechanics of corrosion
- Preparation and study of brass alloys
- Preparation and molding of plastics
- Measurement of an individual's information-processing ability
- Effects of stathmokinetic agents on planarian reconstitution: nitrogen mustard and maleic acid hydrazide

## VARIETY OF COMMUNITY PATTERNS

Whether the seminar plan operates in a rural or urban community, in a public, parochial, or private school, and whether it is initiated by a teacher, parent, civic leader, or industrial magnate—it works!

In Neodosha, Kansas, a one-industry rural community about 115 miles from Wichita, the program is now entering its second year. Fifteen boys and girls are working on special projects including such studies as: A Survey of Common Arthropods of Wilson County, The Effects of Chlorpromazine on Rats, and A Study of Gyroscopic Motion.

Lorain County, Ohio, has set up two seminar units for students selected from seventeen schools; and sixty instructors, both men and women, have been recruited from the county's fifteen major industries.

In Westmoreland County, Pennsylvania, five seminars serve more than twenty neighboring school districts.

In El Paso, Texas, and Louisville, Kentucky, the programs were introduced to the school authorities by the local Rotary Clubs. Similarly, Junior Chamber of Commerce units have been instrumental in the organization of many successful groups, notably those in Jeffersonville and Hammond, Indiana. A local businessman helped to bring the plan to Savannah, Georgia. In Gary, Indiana, a newspaper editor initiated the program.

Too numerous to mention are the communities in which alert science teachers and school administrators have taken the initiative not only in establishing programs in their own schools, but also in calling them to the attention of their colleagues in other communities.

In Flint, Michigan, all eight Catholic high schools joined forces to organize a seminar; the Catholic schools of Cleveland followed suit.

Evergreen Park, Illinois, and Annapolis, Maryland, were among the first to set up seminars that included students selected from adjacent public, private, and parochial schools. This pattern is now being followed in a number of places.

## THE FOUNDATION'S AIMS

In summary, the Joe Berg Foundation has four aims:

1. To publicize the concept of a co-operative community effort as developed by the Berg Plan for the Advancement of Science

2. To assist, without charge, in the organization of such programs when assistance is requested by the appropriate school authorities

3. To develop materials in this field and to distribute them without charge

4. To develop similar programs in fields of human endeavor other than science and mathematics

# 28 INSURING COMMUNITY SUPPORT FOR TALENT DEVELOPMENT PROGRAMS

CLAUDE KELLEY

*Associate Professor of Education, University of Oklahoma, Norman, Oklahoma*

Public education in the United States is based on certain basic principles, such as the principle of democracy, the principle of equal opportunities for education, and the principle that education is a function of the state. Each of these principles has implications for the development and implementation of a gifted student program. If such a program is initiated, these principles will be the bases upon which program efforts are both justified and evaluated.

Most teachers are already aware of the desirability of talent development programs in schools. Teachers have long been concerned about their inability to provide satisfactorily for the extremes found in groups of students, and have sometimes criticized the administration for not organizing groups of students who are more nearly alike in ability. For the most part, teachers realize that a program for the gifted will result in relatively homogeneous groups with a smaller range of individual differences. Although different criteria may be used to identify the talented, teachers usually welcome all efforts to make such identification as a beginning toward alleviating the problem of providing for individual differences.

The general public is also awakening to the need for talent development programs. Many citizens have become concerned about the problem after reading articles about wasted talent in popular journals, newspapers, and magazines. Critics of our schools have charged that we fail to provide an adequate education for those with high ability.

Because most teachers and many citizens are in favor of talent development programs, part of our public relations work has already been done. However, there will be no assurance of the community support that is needed as long as only a portion of each community is concerned about provisions for the able. Each community must be helped to realize the extent of what needs to be done for the gifted group. No talent development program will be successful unless public recognition of the need for such a program is well established.

Schools have developed a variety of programs to provide for the gifted. But no matter what program arrangements are made, all attempts to gain public support depend on the philosophy of the administration and faculty. Public relations efforts may be described in terms of the underlying beliefs that shape them.

## TYPES OF PHILOSOPHIES

What are the different types of philosophies that may prevail in different schools?

A school system may be characterized by a highly *authoritarian* philosophy. In such a system, school personnel would have little interest in gaining community support. Administrators and teachers would establish programs according to their own ideas, without considering community attitudes and wishes.

A second philosophy might be described as *semiautocratic*. If this philosophy prevailed, public relations efforts would consist largely of advertising—advertising designed to influence people to think well of the school. Mistakes, inadequacies, or lack of success would not be mentioned; the chief intent would be to keep the public satisfied so that support would be available when needed.

A third type of philosophy might be called the *interpretive* approach. A public relations program based on this philosophy would attempt to interpret to the community what the school is trying to do, why these efforts are being made, and how successful they are. The goal would be to keep the community informed, although the community's desires might not necessarily be taken into consideration.

The fourth type of philosophy may be referred to as *democratic*. This philosophy sees community relations as involving mutual interaction between the school people and the public. Those who subscribe to the mutual interaction position hold that there must be co-operation in arriving at decisions that affect the school. They feel that educators and laymen representing many different groups should work together to decide how the schools should be operated.

The aim of a public relations program is to secure community support for a specific venture. How an educator promotes his school's talent development program will be determined by the philosophy to which he subscribes, and his philosophy will be influenced by his perception of himself and of those with whom he deals. Let's examine the attitudes of educators who hold the four philosophies we have mentioned.

## The Authoritarian Philosophy

The authoritarian individual, or the "dictator," has a particular set of beliefs upon which he bases his approach to public relations. First, he believes that he knows what is best in education because he has had years of special training and years of experience in working with boys and girls. Second, he is not certain about other people's ability to plan intelligently for the education of their children. He believes that his background makes him the one best qualified to make decisions about what the school should do for children. He develops a program in isolation from other people and he imposes that program upon them. He doesn't need public relations. Sometimes he finds that he must look about for another administrative position.

## The Semiautocratic Philosophy

The semiautocratic educator, or the "benevolent autocrat," feels that although he is superior he has a responsibility to others and must persuade them to accept his decisions. He would like to describe himself as a great supporter of American democracy. He feels that the people are entitled to know what is going on, but he doesn't have much confidence in their ability to arrive at a good solution or decision for most problems. He, too, imposes his program on the community, but he wants to sugar-coat it by explaining it in such a manner that people will see it as he sees it. Since he developed it, he is sure that it is a good program. Therefore, he initiates the program and then advertises and explains it to the community.

## The Interpretive Philosophy

In the interpretive approach to public relations, the educator gives priority to methods of explaining and clarifying his program. He believes that school officials and patrons should sit down together periodically and discuss the progress and problems of the program. This type of administrator, however, relies primarily on himself and his teachers to conduct the planning and development of the program. He reports regularly to the community, but he seldom or never invites the community to participate in the decision-making processes.

## The Democratic Philosophy

The educator whose philosophy is democratic thinks people are basically honest and good and that they can make good decisions. He believes that "two heads are better than one" and that other people in the school and community should share in making decisions and carrying out policy.

The democratic administrator will first identify those individuals who feel that gifted children are of special concern, and who want to do something for our able and talented youth. He will survey the teaching staff as well as the people in the community. If only a few individuals in the community are deeply concerned about the gifted, the administrator will meet with the interested individuals in planning sessions designed to explore the possibilities of providing for the gifted. After these sessions he will have "missionaries" at work. These missionaries will have a definite plan for a gifted student program; they will be able to express their own ideas; they will have participated in developing something that is of importance to them. They, in turn, communicate their zeal to others.

The democratic school superintendent will employ a variety of media to encourage support for his program. He will prepare newspaper releases, make speeches to service clubs, give radio addresses, send letters to parents, assemble the student body and explain the program, talk at PTA meetings, and enlist school and community assistance in many other ways.

The democratic administrator realizes the limitations of the devices often used in community relations programs. He knows that these traditional communications media often only cement opinion that has already been formed—opinion that may be either favorable or unfavorable. They may do little to create new opinion. The democratic administrator therefore relies on people—people who become involved in the program and spread their interest to others, gaining the support of an increasing number of individuals.

## ANSWERING QUESTIONS

As efforts are exerted to develop public support for any new or different program in a school system, questions will surely arise if the public is at all concerned. Some of these questions may be anticipated, but the answers will be dependent on the kind of program developed by each school. The following are some of the questions likely to be asked.

*How are the gifted determined?* This question can be answered easily by explaining the school's system of identification, but there will be some corollary questions. "Why isn't my child one of those selected? I know those you have designated as gifted, and my child is just as able. How does the cutoff point happen to be just above him? He has an IQ of 129. Why did it have to be 130?" If the public relations program is to result in active community support, these questions must be answered.

*Who is going to teach these children?* The talented child should have an able teacher. Does this mean that less talented youngsters do not deserve an able teacher? If there are special classes for the gifted, assigning teachers for these classes is a serious problem. Some people believe that the less able need the best teachers and that the gifted will learn in spite of the teacher.

*Is this an additional program in the school?* People will want to know if new funds have been made available for the program, or if some other program is going to receive less financial support in the future. Even if there has been an increase in revenue, some people will claim that school offerings have been expanded until more has been added than can be accomplished.

*Is equality of opportunity provided in this program?* Some people feel that equal opportunity cannot be provided if youngsters are separated into homogeneous class groups. They will ask what special provisions are to be made for the children who do not engage in the special or extra activities of the gifted program. Many educators claim that our schools are able to provide for the individual differences of children without special provisions. They feel that it would be unfair to single out the gifted group for additional special attention.

*If this program is good for the gifted child, why isn't the same program good for all children?* For example, if gifted youngsters should have two years of higher mathematics, why shouldn't other children have the same experience?

If attempts to gain support for a talent development program are to be successful, satisfactory answers to all these questions will have to be provided.

## EDUCATION FOR MODERN LIVING

At one time the traditional subject-centered classroom may have met the demands that our society placed upon its educational system. But life and the times have changed, and our schools, too, are in a state of transition. If our schools did not change, the situation would be similar to that which Olsen (178) describes. He imagines a school on an island within a bay, with the community or city on the mainland. The island is close enough to the mainland for a drawbridge to provide for traffic to and from the island. This drawbridge, however, is lowered for only a few minutes twice each day. Each morning at almost eight o'clock there is a shrill ringing of bells; the drawbridge is lowered; and the teachers, closely pursued by the students, walk to the island. The drawbridge is then raised until three o'clock, when the harsh clamoring of the bells indicates that it will be lowered again. Then the students, closely pursued by the teachers, rush back to the mainland. While the school is in session on the island, nothing is emphasized that would be of interest or concern to the people on the mainland. The experiences provided by the island school are largely artificial as compared to the immediate and real-life situations on the mainland. It is difficult for the students to perceive any relationship between their experiences on the island and the life they lead away from the island.

We cannot afford for our educational system to be isolated from the society it serves. A program for gifted children must include opportunities for the public to see what the students are doing, learning, and accomplishing. The youngsters who participate in the program should have real experiences that will prepare them for the tasks they will face in the modern world. Sometimes it is difficult to perceive the relationship between required subjects and life. Children should be helped to see this relationship, and to realize that an education will enable them to function effectively in a changing world throughout their lives.

In order to achieve the goal of education for modern living, the school—including its students and its program—must become an integral part of community affairs and activities. Classroom learning must have a relationship—direct or indirect—to real life.

## CONCLUSION

The following points have been made about building community support for a talent development program:

First, people are influenced to a much higher degree by contact with other people than by indirect contacts. A public relations program will have greater success if it is based on personal contacts than if it is based on impersonal contacts. Nevertheless, impersonal contacts will make some contribution to such a program.

Second, a public relations program will achieve the best results if it emphasizes personal involvement and participation. People will be more apt to understand and accept what is going on if they feel they have a part in the program.

Insuring community support for a talent development program will enhance that program's chances for success and will result in better education for gifted boys and girls.

# SECTION IX

## FOUR SUPERIOR AND TALENTED
## STUDENT PROGRAMS

Any discussion of provisions for superior students must eventually include on-going programs. This section includes descriptions of four such on-going programs—all located in high schools participating in the one-hundred-school Superior and Talented Student Project sponsored by the North Central Association of Colleges and Secondary Schools. These programs have been selected not because they are the best of the one hundred efforts, but because they illustrate typical program situations. The information about each school helps us toward an understanding of the school's efforts in behalf of talented students. These schools have taken more than halting, cautious steps toward their objective of providing for superior students. The bridge between theory and practice in education is notoriously long, but these schools are taking strides to cross it.

In each of these schools the first step in building a program for superior students has been to establish teamwork among administrators, counselors, and teachers. Each shares in forming the program's objectives and each has a co-operative role in developing procedures to accomplish these objectives.

If a superior student program is to be a vital force in the school, teachers, counselors, and administrators must work to provide a rich variety of activities that will enable students to explore and develop their academic, personal, vocational, and cultural interests.

Any school can build a program for its superior students if it
identifies these students, establishes objectives for them, experiments with different practices, and makes imaginative use of its
resources. Regardless of the framework within which the program
operates, the emphasis must be on the development of each student
in terms of his needs, abilities, and aspirations.

The sociology of the neighborhood and the school climate must be
considered in determining the direction and approach of the school's
program for the talented child. A careful investigation of the cultural background from which the school's superior students come
should precede the establishment of any program. Close attention
to these factors will facilitate better understanding of the most
effective means of encouraging academic achievement.

Many public schools in the United States are engaging in some
type of program for superior students. Some of the procedures
they are following have long been the practice of better schools.
But to accomplish most within the framework of its organization a
program must be adapted to the needs of a particular school and
community. The descriptions in this section illustrate how particular schools have evolved programs that suit their situations. The
accounts make it clear that each of these high schools has increased
its effectiveness in educating superior students, although their
methods and procedures vary considerably.

In Chapter 29 John Waters discusses the first year of operation
of the STS Project in Phoenix (Arizona) Union High School. Chapter 30, by Edward Masonbrink, describes the efforts of McKinley
High School (Canton, Ohio) to serve its superior and talented
students. Henry Cunningham in Chapter 31 points out the practices used by Marshall (Michigan) High School to achieve development of its talented students. In Chapter 32 Ralph Hamilton describes the program launched by Central High School (Springfield,
Missouri) to provide for its superior students.

# 29 THE STS PROGRAM IN PHOENIX UNION HIGH SCHOOL

JOHN WATERS
*Assistant Principal*

Phoenix Union High School, Phoenix, Arizona, is a four-year institution with a student population of approximately 4600, including students of Anglo-American, Spanish-American, Negro, and oriental descent. It is one of seven high schools serving a community of approximately 300,000. The attendance area for Phoenix Union represents a socioeconomic cross-section of the community. Twelve elementary districts, each governed by a separate board of education and administration, are served by the Phoenix Union High School.

## ORGANIZING A PROGRAM

A program for the academically able student should be a logical and integral part of the total curriculum plan of the school, with clearly defined objectives. Phoenix Union decided to provide such a program for a relatively large group of children—the top 25 per cent as determined by national norms. The need for co-operation among the elementary, junior high, and high schools to insure continuity from one school level to the next was stressed. Leadership in the over-all plan was supplied by the superintendent and principal; identification and individual interviews were handled by the counseling staff; implementation of the program was carried out by department heads and the faculty; and advice and support came from resource people.

To identify the top 25 per cent on national norms, a thorough testing program (in addition to teacher identification) was initiated. Adjustments of curriculum were made, with provisions for accelerated classes in some areas and creation of special seminar classes in other areas. A final step was an evaluative study at the end of one year of operation to determine whether the program had produced the intended results.

## Program Objectives

The short-range objectives of the STS project at Phoenix Union High School were:
1. To identify all students in the school who rank above the 75th percentile in academic ability, based on national norms
2. To help each of these students form a realistic concept of his abilities
3. To inform the entire staff who the superior and talented students are and to encourage the staff to participate in the identification and especially in the motivation of these students
4. To devise and utilize the best possible motivational techniques for helping these students to do their best
5. To make curricular adjustments to meet the needs of the superior students

## Identification

A meeting of teachers and department heads was called to discuss the organization of special classes for the academically able and ambitious students. These teachers and department heads constituted the steering committee for the program. The objectives and provisions of the program were discussed, and a definite identification plan was outlined as follows:
1. Initial referral by teacher and counselors
2. Testing of all referrals with the *Iowa Tests of Educational Development* in order to identify those in the upper 25 per cent on national norms
3. Check of past school performance
4. Counselor recommendations
5. Student and parent approval

To assist the faculty in selecting academically able and ambitious students, a list of behavior characteristics indicative of intellectual ability was obtained from the NCA Superior and Talented Student Project brochure *Identification,* and mimeographed copies were given to each teacher. Four hundred fifty students were identified. This was not a final list, as the program was flexible enough to permit adding students not previously identified. Provision also was made to transfer students out of the classes if they were unable to cope successfully with the program. Of the 450 superior and talented students, less than 200 were actually assigned to special classes. However, the program at Phoenix Union has been concerned with all the students identified.

## Special Grouping

The term used to define superior and talented students at Phoenix Union is *able and ambitious*. Special classes of these students are designated by the symbol "AA." Areas of study covered in these classes are: English, foreign languages, mathematics, music, science, social studies, and industrial arts. Emphasis throughout the program has been on the student who not only has superior ability, but who also has the ambition to do the level of work of which he is capable.

Students in the able and ambitious classes were identified by teachers and assigned to special classes with the consent of themselves and their parents. The students were told at the outset that in order to remain in the able and ambitious classes, they would have to earn grades of 1 or 2 (A or B). Whenever a student's grade fell below the standard, the teacher notified his parents by letter, and a conference among the teacher, counselor and parents was held to ascertain and correct the causes of underachievement.

## Parents' Night

A meeting for parents of students who had been identified as superior and talented was called. The purposes of this meeting were:

1. To acquaint parents with the STS project, its philosophy, and general objectives
2. To explain the basis for selecting able and ambitious students
3. To inform parents of the level of performance expected of AA students and of the policy for transferring students who do not perform satisfactorily
4. To explain the policy on grading

5. To ask parents' co-operation for success of the program

This meeting provided an opportunity for parents to meet teachers and to visit classrooms where AA students were instructed. Previous contacts with parents had been limited to open house or to Parent-Teacher Association meetings. Although parents are free to visit the school to arrange conferences with teachers, students at this mental ability level seldom create the obvious problems, of a disciplinary or other nature, which require a conference.

## Counselor's Role

Counseling at Phoenix Union covers three areas: educational programing, vocational planning, and personal problems or emotional difficulties. A special program of counseling for all superior students includes three interviews by appointment. The interviews have the following purposes:

1. To explain the program to the student and to point out why he was selected

2. To evaluate the student's program

3. To continue evaluation and to plan the student's program for the next year

At Phoenix Union, the counselor is the liaison between the teachers and the administrators who are responsible for the program. Administering the various tests, interpreting and evaluating the results, selecting students for the program, and counseling these students are the responsibilities of the thirteen trained counselors.

The counselor conducts group testing. He contacts parents and may send them a profile of test results and an invitation to discuss their child's potential. When the evaluation of test results is completed, the counselor determines which students will be placed in AA classes. While teachers may recommend certain students for particular subject-matter classes, test results give an over-all picture of a student's capacity or ability to perform. Counseling students on the purpose of AA classes and helping them adjust to the accelerated program by practicing good study habits and planning their schedules are services rendered by the counselor on a continuous basis. Counselors also assist seniors in applying for scholarships, selecting colleges, electing suitable courses of study, and finding employment.

For those superior students not in AA classes, counseling services are provided to assist them with such problems as study habits, school achievement, career choices, and personal problems.

## MOTIVATING THE ABLE AND AMBITIOUS

Phoenix Union High School was interested in discovering techniques for giving significance or status to academic achievement. It was suggested that a school banquet—somewhat similar to those held in recognition of other kinds of ability—be planned to honor academic ability. A service club or some civic organization is usually willing to sponsor a banquet of this type. Since the Arizona AFL-CIO had an annual scholarship program the officers of this organization were contacted in regard to sponsoring a banquet. Not only did they agree to sponsor the affair, but they also indicated they would like to give the banquet for the next two to five years. After the banquet, the parents of the students being honored were invited to a meeting in the auditorium.

Other devices designed to motivate able and ambitious students at Phoenix Union include:

*Academic honors assembly.* This event honors students who receive straight A grades. A certificate is awarded to each honor student.

*Field trips.* Whenever students request them and arrangements can be made, field trips are approved. In 1960 a group of students traveled to Arizona State University, where they were guests of Willard Abraham. They toured the science department and the General Electric Computer Center.

*Honor assembly.* This assembly, held in May, gives recognition to students who have received scholarships, awards for shop achievements, awards for outstanding performance in subject-matter fields, and other civic and cultural prizes. Scholarships received by students at Phoenix Union High School totaled $63,016 in 1959.

*National honor society.* The top 25 per cent of graduating seniors are candidates for this honor, but only 15 per cent are elected to membership. Members are selected on the basis of grades and citizenship record.

*Parnassus club.* Members of this group are students who have maintained at least a B average during the preceding semester. Seniors who have been members for six semesters or more receive awards and special seals on their diplomas. Juniors with a five-semester membership and sophomores with a three-semester membership also receive awards. Each student must re-establish his membership at the beginning of each semester.

*Resource people.* Professional people from local industries have expressed their desire to work with able and ambitious students. One group of students interested in science and engineering met with engineers from Arizona Public Service and engineering personnel from the University of Arizona.

*Honors at graduation.* The following seals, signifying high academic performance, are issued to graduates and affixed to their diplomas:

A gold seal awarded to the top 5 per cent, indicating "With High Distinction"

A blue seal awarded to the second 5 per cent, indicating "With Distinction"

A second gold seal awarded to members of Parnassus for six-semester membership

## PUBLIC RELATIONS FOR THE PROGRAM

In addition to the public contacts established through meetings with parents of superior and talented students, the public relations campaign utilized press, radio, and television services. Several articles appeared in local papers, and a local television station offered Phoenix Union High School fifteen-minute blocks of time. Four television programs were presented, two of which were presented by AA students from the English and science departments. The assistant principal spoke about the accelerated student program at Phoenix Union on one of the local radio stations.

The principal and assistant principal discussed with the publicity director of the Phoenix Chamber of Commerce other methods of interpreting the NCA STS project to the community. One of the results of this meeting was a Saturday workshop in which students met with professional people from the electronics industry.

The program also received invaluable assistance from Willard

Abraham, of Arizona State University, who has gained national recognition for his contributions to educational theory in the area of the gifted child. Throughout the project's first year, Dr. Abraham participated in numerous programs at Phoenix Union High School.

## EVALUATION OF THE PROGRAM

At the end of the school year 1958-59, a questionnaire was prepared which offered students and parents an opportunity to evaluate the able and ambitious program at Phoenix Union High School. All of the general questions required a yes-or-no answer, except the one which asked the number of hours spent doing homework. Space was provided at the bottom of the sheet for comments from both groups.

The results of this questionnaire do not reflect a statistical evaluation of the STS program at this school. A true evaluation will not be possible until the program is completed. In preparing this questionnaire, suggestions were sought that might improve techniques and procedures for serving superior and talented students.

The following questions were included in the questionnaire:

1. Do you feel that you have been encouraged to do better school work?
2. Have you had to do more homework?
   a. Has there been too much homework?
   b. Has the amount of homework restricted your participation in other school activities?
   c. Approximately how much time at home do you spend each day on all homework?
3. Has the program stimulated you into taking a more active part in the total school program?
4. Do you feel that you have received more guidance and counseling as a result of being in the program?
5. Has the program increased your own contact with the school?
6. Do you think you are learning more as a direct result of being in the program?
7. Do you think this kind of program should be continued at P.U.H.S.?

The responses to the questionnaire have been summarized as follows:

1. Most students (89 per cent) and parents (93 per cent) felt that the program encouraged better work at school.

2. More than half the students (52 per cent) and parents (63 per cent) agreed that there was *more* homework.

    a. Most students (91 per cent) and parents (78 per cent) felt that the amount of homework was not excessive.

    b. Most students (85 per cent) and parents (82 per cent) believed that the heavier academic program did not restrict participation in other school activities.

    c. Slightly over half the students (56 per cent) and parents (54 per cent) indicated that participation in school activities was stimulated by the program.

3. A majority of parents (75 per cent) and students (65 per cent) felt that students had received more guidance and counseling as a result of the program.

4. Many parents (64 per cent) and students (54 per cent) believed that the program had increased parental contact with the school.

5. Both groups—students (87 per cent) and parents (92 per cent)—felt that the students were learning more as a result of the program.

6. Parents and students (99 per cent in each group) were overwhelmingly in favor of the continuance of the STS program at Phoenix Union.

## Summary of Comments

As indicated, most of the selected students, and the parents as well, were in favor of the program as it was conducted. Other informal comments indicated that the able students felt that special grouping according to intellectual ability improved the class atmosphere. They liked the idea of moving forward as a group, without waiting for slow students to catch up. They also believed that their chances for scholarships were improved as a result of accelerated classes.

Another aspect of evaluation was to ask for suggestions for program improvement. Some of the most frequently made student comments follow:

1. Teachers should be well informed in the subject they are teaching, and they should take a greater interest in their students.

2. Work in AA classes should be harder and more challenging.

3. Students should feel free to withdraw from AA classes if they are not completely satisfied.

4. Less time should be spent on homework with more stress on quality than on quantity.

5. More emphasis should be placed on learning a subject well than on making a good grade.

6. The importance of good study habits should be emphasized and help in developing them should be provided.

7. A program should be initiated to place able and ambitious students from grades 9 through 12 in accelerated classes.

Comments from parents were varied. Some indicated that there was a tendency to tag students in the AA classes as "brains." Many parents indicated that these students had to study harder and longer than average students. If students were in more than one or two AA classes, their parents felt that the homework was over-burdening. Parents agreed with students that teachers should be well informed and that they should take more interest in their students. Some parents expressed the hope that more emphasis would be placed on making good citizens of students.

# 30 THE STS PROGRAM IN McKINLEY HIGH SCHOOL

EDWARD MASONBRINK
*Principal*

Canton, Ohio, is a city of many industries. Its corporate population is approximately 126,000. McKinley High School, located in the downtown section of the city, has an enrollment of nearly two thousand students in grades 9 through 12. The school building is about forty years old; but it has been carefully maintained, with some modernization of the original structure. At one time the school's enrollment was over four thousand students in grades 10, 11, and 12, but other high schools have been opened in the city and new high schools have been built in the suburban areas.

McKinley High School's student population represents a number of different racial and religious groups. It is not a typical population, since most of the students come from the lower socioeconomic group. In forty years the school has built great traditions in scholarship, athletics, forensics, and music. About 35 per cent of its graduates go on to some form of higher education.

## GETTING STARTED ON A PROGRAM

The STS program at McKinley High School was preceded by several attempts to provide for the individual differences of students. During the 1956-57 school year, freshman noncredit sections in English and arithmetic were organized for those incoming students whose achievement was three or more years below their grade level as measured by standardized tests. This program was very successful and provided some background for later work with superior students.

In 1958, with the advent of the STS project, special English and algebra sections were organized for superior freshmen. Students

320

were selected for these sections on the basis of achievement and aptitude test scores, grades, and eighth-grade teacher recommendations. The aim was to provide an accelerated course in algebra for those who had the ability to profit from such acceleration, and an advanced English course for those who would profit from greater depth and who did not need to repeat fundamentals already learned. After two years of planning, research, and study, the program included not only these courses for freshmen but also English courses at the sophomore and junior levels. The 1959-60 program added advanced mathematics on the sophomore level.

The courses described above are certainly not the first instances of grouping at McKinley High School. Informal grouping has always been a part of the school's program. As in any comprehensive curriculum, certain subjects such as advanced mathematics and science will be selected only by those students who have been successful in their earlier experiences and whose objectives require these courses. In certain majors, such as foreign languages, the tendency is to group students in the advanced levels of their study. All schedules are approved by counselors who have full knowledge of the students' ambitions and capabilities. To some extent this factor also contributes to ability grouping.

## Mathematics and Science Seminar

Wide interest in mathematics and science spurred McKinley High School to offer a mathematics and science seminar for seniors. This seminar is taken concurrently with physics and fourth-year mathematics, and enables the students to experiment independently and to investigate and study beyond the areas covered in the regular courses. Students in the seminar meet daily with the teacher to plan and discuss their work. Credit is given, but no grades are recorded on the permanent record. This seminar introduces the students to many aspects of science and mathematics that they would ordinarily not encounter before college.

## Culture Seminar

The culture seminar provides superior seniors with an opportunity to learn more about the culture of their community, state, and nation. The group meets daily for one period. As with the mathematics and science seminar, credit is given but no grades are recorded on the permanent record. Some of the outstanding people of the community are invited to speak before the group. Men with interesting vocations and avocations which contribute to the cultural background of the community are weekly lecturers. Since the lecture topic is known in advance, the students make extensive preparation, take careful notes during the lecture, follow up the talk with a thorough evaluation of the speaker's remarks, and keep a comprehensive notebook covering the entire seminar. This seminar has provided experiences that are substantially different from those normally found in the high school curriculum. It has stimulated research and thinking in areas that are sometimes overlooked, and it has developed research and communication skills that will be highly valuable in education beyond high school.

## Guidance Procedures

The guidance program at McKinley High School begins with an early spring meeting with eighth-grade teachers and elementary school principals from the feeder schools. At this meeting the courses of study provided in the high school curriculum are described, including the levels or tracks of English and mathematics and the criteria for assignment to the upper levels. Later the high school counselors visit each elementary school and assist eighth-grade students in filling out their registration cards. The elementary school teachers examine these cards and recommend the track or level in which they feel students should be placed.

As soon as students are assigned to McKinley High School, a letter is sent informing them of an incoming freshman meeting prior to the opening of school in the fall. In August another letter is sent to them verifying the time, place, and date of the meeting. At this meeting the incoming freshmen learn the locations of their classes and homerooms. Student guides distribute maps of the school, a list of do's and dont's, and other valuable and informative material. An orientation program is planned and carried out by the student leaders of the school. The program ends with student-conducted tours of the building.

In March or April, when registration cards are received for incoming freshmen, the following information is collected: achievement test scores, aptitude test scores, grades, attendance records, and teacher recommendations regarding appropriate tracks or levels. From this information a list is made of the students with superior ability. The elementary school is again consulted about the accuracy of the list. Students are then assigned to sections commensurate with their abilities.

During the summer the students who have been selected for the STS program, as well as their parents, are notified by letter and invited to attend a meeting. At this meeting the STS project is explained and discussed. In addition, the methods used in selecting students are fully described and the limitations of these methods, as well as their strengths, are explained. Levels of achievement, problems in motivation, and areas of caution are presented to the parents. The parents and students are told what is expected of the students who are selected for the STS program, and the objectives of the program are explained.

Sometimes inadequate information on students who transfer from other districts causes them to be overlooked. After school opens, therefore, teachers are asked to be on the alert for students who are doing outstanding work but who may not have been identified for the program. Also, the STS sections are checked to determine whether all students who have been placed there are capable of carrying on the work. Students may be transferred in or out of the program if the move seems to be in their best interests. A transfer is always preceded by a thorough investigation. A request by student or parents for a transfer is always honored with thorough investigation and explanation.

## PROGRAM PROVISIONS

The STS program for freshmen offers select sections in English and algebra. In English the objective is to present a course that requires greater comprehension and offers more depth than the ordinary freshman English curriculum. No time is wasted on what has already been learned. In the sophomore year advanced English and plane geometry are included in the program. There are also special

groups for biology students. In the junior year, sections of STS
English are formed; but since only capable students enroll in advanced mathematics, there is no additional grouping in this subject.
Chemistry is taught on different levels, including academic, industrial, and household. For the senior year the seminars previously
described are offered to the superior students.

## IDENTIFICATION TOOLS

Listed below are the identification tools used in each grade level
to select students for the STS program:

Freshman:
*Iowa Tests of Basic Skills*
*Stanford Achievement Series*
*California Test of Mental Maturity*
Subject grades
Cumulative file records
Teacher recommendations

Sophomore:
*Iowa Tests of Educational Development*
*California Test of Mental Maturity*
Cumulative file records
Subject grades
Teacher recommendations
Adviser recommendations

Junior:
*Iowa Tests of Educational Development*
*California Test of Mental Maturity*
Cumulative file records
Teacher recommendations
Adviser recommendations
National scholarship test results

Senior:
All previously recorded test scores, recommendations,
and other information
Observed interests in clubs, extracurricular
activities, or career plans
*Ohio State Psychological Examination*

## TECHNIQUES IN MOTIVATION

Some of the practices used at McKinley High School to motivate superior and talented students include:

- Notice of selection
- Honor rolls and scholastic honor assemblies
- Group meetings
- Student interviews with counselors and administrators
- Homeroom programs pointed toward better scholarship for all
- Homeroom "How To Study" programs
- Publication of names of students taking STS or other scholarship tests
- STS class period stimulation
- Junior League scholarship luncheon
- National Honor Society selection and initiation program
- National Forensic League achievement and initiation program
- College night
- Junior Engineers Technical Society
- Junior and Senior college clubs
- Mu Alpha Theta Honorary Mathematics Club
- Letters written by the high school principal to elementary schools recounting the success of their recent graduates
- Emphasis on scholarship for all participants in athletics
- Publicity for all scholarships won by graduating seniors
- Publicity for success stories about former McKinley students
- *Canton Repository* (local newspaper) scholarship banquet
- Honor student visit to Timken Roller Bearing Company
- FTA scholarship recognition program for all honor roll students

# 31

# THE STS PROGRAM IN MARSHALL HIGH SCHOOL

HENRY W. CUNNINGHAM
*Curriculum Co-ordinator and Director*
*of the STS Program*

Marshall is a city of 6400, located at the junction of the main Detroit-Chicago highway and Michigan's principal north-south highway. It is the county seat of a county of more than one hundred thousand population. In addition to the city, the school district encompasses approximately 150 square miles of surrounding rural area. The total high school population (grades 7 to 12) is 1120, divided almost equally between urban and rural students.

From a cultural-economic standpoint, Marshall is atypical. In the 1920's Marshall was the richest small city per capita in the nation. Unfortunately, the depression changed this. There remains, however, a very stable, conservative, cultural community attitude with a high *esprit de corps*. Marshall is very conscious of its educational heritage. Here was founded the educational system of Michigan, later to be copied by other states. Some of the community's stability is due to the large number of retired and semiretired people living in the city.

## IDENTIFICATION PROCEDURES

Approximately one-half of Marshall High School's students have not attended the city's elementary schools. It is primarily at the seventh- and ninth-grade levels that the rural youngsters come into the city to continue their education. This fact makes it rather difficult to identify all of the superior and talented students—the top quarter on national norms.

In the seventh grade, when many students are new to the Marshall school system, the *Lorge-Thorndike Intelligence Test* and the reading, vocabulary, and language portions of the *Iowa Tests of Basic*

*Skills* are administered. The *Detroit Silent Reading Test* is given in connection with a special reading class for those who have reading difficulties. A special algebra readiness test is given to better students, who may take algebra in the eighth grade.

The remaining parts of the *Iowa Tests of Basic Skills,* comprising arithmetic and work-study skills, are given in the eighth grade. Also, the *Detroit Silent Reading Test* is repeated in connection with the reading program. Marshall is one of the schools co-operating with the Science Motivation Project conducted by Western Michigan University in co-operation with the National Science Foundation. The Science Motivation Project's battery of tests was given at the eighth-grade level during the 1958-59 school year, and at the ninth-grade level during the 1959-60 school year.

In the ninth grade the *Otis Quick Scoring Test of Mental Ability, Kuder Preference Record,* and the reading, language, and vocabulary portions of the *Iowa Tests of Basic Skills* are administered.

The *Iowa Tests of Educational Development* are given to all tenth-grade students identified in the STS project, as well as to any other student who wishes to participate.

Several specialized tests are administered in the eleventh grade. For students planning a business course, there is the *ERC Stenographic Aptitude Test.* To encourage interest in mathematics, better students are urged to participate in the Michigan Mathematics Contest. Those wishing to be included in senior honors courses in English and mathematics are given the *Scholastic Tests of Educational Progress* in reading, writing, and mathematics. This is one of several screening devices used in admitting students to honors courses.

In an effort to counsel seniors regarding their areas of strength and weakness in scholastic aptitude, the *California Test of Mental Maturity* is administered. All seniors also take the *Personal Audit* (personality inventory) in connection with a Basic Living class. In the senior year the *Iowa Tests of Educational Development* are given to all students identified in the STS project and all other interested seniors.

## GUIDANCE AND COUNSELING PROCEDURES

All students identified in the STS project have at least two counseling interviews per year to discuss their educational and vocational plans; one interview takes place in the fall, the other in the spring. The educational aspirations inventory, *Your Educational Plans,* has been of great value in the spring interview. When practical, the student is counseled by the same staff member at both interviews.

When the *Iowa Tests of Educational Development* scores become available, they are interpreted to students individually. Parents also receive a copy of the results and are encouraged to come in for a personal interview to discuss their child's achievement.

A list of students identified in the program is given to each teacher. Coded IQ's as well as achievement test scores are included. These are especially valuable since the informal, spontaneous guidance done by the classroom teacher is as important as the formal guidance procedures. Students in the STS project have sought out and conferred with both their teachers and their counselors.

The key person in Marshall High School's STS program is the classroom teacher, and active staff co-operation is maintained by keeping teachers informed of the program. Teachers receive frequent progress reports, both mimeographed and oral, on the STS project. As many staff members as possible are involved in the planning and implementation of the program. Thus far, more than half the staff have taken part in STS project activities, and the entire staff have displayed enthusiasm for the program.

## PARENT PARTICIPATION

Marshall High School has been particularly successful in obtaining the participation of parents and the community in its STS program. The support of parents was sought for the following reasons:

1. Previous experience had shown that Marshall's parents were highly interested in the efforts of the school.

2. The program would be better able to realize its objectives if parents participated directly. Only through parent participation could workable solutions to many of the problems dealt with by the STS project be attained.

3. The support and interest of parents in the program would help to motivate students to high aspirations and achievement.

The parents' stake in the STS project needed definition and exploration. The local newspaper co-operated with the school by announcing Marshall's selection as a participating school in the STS project. During October 1958 a meeting of parents was scheduled to discuss the reasons for Marshall's participation in the STS project and the efforts of the school to realize the goals of the program. The purpose of the meeting was to stimulate interest and participation, not just to "sell" the STS project.

All parents were invited to the meeting and a personal letter was addressed to the parents of students who had been identified as superior and talented. The meeting covered the background of the STS project; the means and procedures the school would use in identifying, counseling, and providing curricular adjustments for superior and talented students; and the practices teachers were trying in special classes.

The attendance at the meeting far surpassed anticipation, with more than three hundred parents present. After the STS project had been explained, the parents indicated enthusiastic support for the program. Many said they thought the STS project would benefit the entire school program.

At Marshall High School's annual open house in May, parents were given objective, pertinent information concerning the achievement and school progress of their boy or girl. This was done through a special report form which included (1) scholastic aptitude stated in general terms, (2) achievement test data, (3) grade averages, (4) *Kuder Preference Record* results, and (5) reading test scores. The report resulted in many individual conferences with teachers, counselors, and administrators.

In October 1959 another parents' meeting was held. The parents of all superior junior and senior students were invited. The theme of the meeting was "What Can the School and the Home Do To Prepare Our Youth for College?" The program of accelerated classes was discussed and a report on participation in the STS project was given. Scholarships, grants, and other ways to finance a college education were reviewed. The parents were then divided into eight groups, alphabetically, for individual conferences with counselors. The same kinds of data used in May 1958 had been prepared for each student: scholastic aptitude (generally stated), grade averages, achievement test scores, and interest inventory results. From this information counselors made specific suggestions as to what type of college would be advisable, and they realistically evaluated each student's probable college success.

During the 1959-60 school year, a meeting was held to introduce the parents of children in the seventh and eighth grades to the work of the STS project.

Two attractively illustrated and printed booklets designed especially for parents and the public have proved effective in interpreting Marshall's participation in the STS project. The first booklet, *The Accelerated Academic Program and the NCA STS Project,* illustrates Marshall's efforts in the STS project. The second publication, *So You Want To Go to College,* is given to all students who are thinking about attending college. These booklets have been very useful in explaining the STS project to service and professional clubs and organizations.

## MOTIVATING THE ABLE STUDENTS

One of the most important motivational techniques is simply identifying able students. When a student and his parents find that the student ranks in the upper quarter of ability nationally and should give college serious consideration, the student's self-concept is enhanced and, frequently, he is imbued with greater enthusiasm to achieve.

Marshall High School has found it helpful to have panels of graduates who are now in college talk to the juniors and seniors; such contacts make college seem more real and possible. Another way that college can be brought within the realm of possibility is to encourage able students to try for scholarships and grants.

For a number of years Marshall High School has been affiliated with the National Honor Society. Membership in this organization is a mark of prestige and encourages scholarship. Similarly the "Hall of Fame" in the school yearbook gives recognition to able students by printing the pictures of those who have been outstanding in scholarship, leadership, and character.

Another helpful procedure has been the college freshmen-high school principal conferences held by most Michigan colleges at the end of the first quarter of every school year. High school representatives are given an opportunity to interview their former students who are now college freshmen, in order to find out how high school programs can be improved with respect to preparation for college. The principal of Marshall High School invites different staff members to accompany him (or a counselor) to these meetings. After the conferences with students, reports of student problems and reactions are brought back to the teaching staff. Often the teachers will use these impressions as a basis for discussing college with their present high school students.

Every spring, awards in many areas are given at the Senior Class Day program. All scholarships and scholastic grants received by graduating seniors are announced. The list of these awards is impressive and has proved to be a strong stimulus for better scholastic attainment among the other students.

## CURRICULUM REVISIONS

Soon after the STS program was instituted, it became evident that a complete revision of the curriculum was necessary in the accelerated classes. The teachers of mathematics and English made an intensive effort to effect meaningful revisions. Consultants were brought in, and a variety of relevant literature was made available. As a result, courses for the accelerated classes were completely reorganized. One teacher commented on the revision: "I don't know how I'll live through it, but I wouldn't go back to the old way for the world."

First, English and mathematics courses were revised. (The science and language programs were already strong and tended to be taken by the abler students.)

Twelfth-grade honors English places emphasis on writing. Literature is used to suggest topics for papers. In setting up the course outline, college freshman courses of study were carefully examined to avoid repetition. In the tenth- and eleventh-grade accelerated English classes, emphasis is also placed on writing. A high standard of excellence and depth of perception are required. There are three tracks of ninth-grade English: accelerated, regular, and remedial.

The mathematics program is now entirely double-tracked. The

twelfth-grade honors class aims to complete trigonometry and solid geometry in two-thirds of a year, with the remainder of the year devoted to analytic geometry. At the eleventh-grade level, the regular work in advanced algebra is extended to include some of the principles of statistics, inequalities, progressions, and probabilities. An attempt is made to include units of solid geometry in the tenth-grade accelerated plane geometry class. In the ninth-grade accelerated algebra class, the aim is to enrich as well as to accelerate.

A first step in the Marshall High School acceleration program was to have the better seventh-grade students complete seventh- and eighth-grade arithmetic in the seventh grade. This enabled these students to take algebra in the eighth grade and geometry in the ninth grade. Thus far, no eighth-graders have been placed in accelerated algebra, nor have ninth-graders been placed in accelerated geometry, since this would in effect be a double acceleration. As might be expected, however, many students seem capable of doing the more difficult work with ease. As these seventh-grade students who began by combining two years of arithmetic in one progress through the school system, further curriculum adjustments will have to be made.

Students are selected for these accelerated or honors classes on the basis of the following criteria: (1) scholastic aptitude, (2) grade averages in academic subjects, (3) achievement test scores, and (4) teacher opinion of the student's willingness to work and do self-directed study.

## CONCLUSION

Marshall High School still has a great deal to accomplish for its superior and talented students. However, teachers, counselors, and administrators believe that the STS project has done more to give students an incentive to excel in scholarship than any other device or program ever attempted in the school. The program has also stimulated a curriculum improvement program. These results have been attained through the enthusiastic co-operation of the community, parents, board of education, administrators, counselors, and teachers.

# 32

## THE STS PROGRAM IN CENTRAL HIGH SCHOOL

RALPH HAMILTON
*Principal*

At Central High School, Springfield, Missouri, the STS program is under the leadership of the principal, assistant principal, dean of women, dean of men, and four counselors (one at each grade level for grades 9, 10, 11, and 12). The task of orienting this eight-member team and the entire faculty of eighty-eight teachers was accomplished through guidance staff meetings and meetings with teachers and advisory teachers at the four grade levels.

### IDENTIFYING THE STUDENTS

Central High School found that considerable experimentation was necessary to locate the top 25 per cent of students according to national norms. For the school year 1958-59, 517 students out of a total enrollment of 2207 were identified as superior: 154 out of 665 freshmen, 127 out of 626 sophomores, 132 out of 492 juniors, and 104 out of 424 seniors. Each of the four counselors worked with approximately twenty advisory teachers in developing the identification program. The entire staff learned that proper identification of the talents of superior youth is a difficult task. The staff felt that some of the top talent had been inadvertently overlooked.

### MOTIVATING AND COUNSELING THOSE SELECTED

Central High School realized the importance of drawing the entire staff into the program and providing them with an opportunity to participate in the guidance of the 517 selected students. When this plan was presented at a staff meeting, it was unanimously accepted and approved. The guidance staff assigned three to eight

333

students to each teacher for extra counseling and guidance. In addition, all members of the guidance staff (the four counselors, two deans, and two principals) were busily engaged in counseling as many of the young people as time would permit.

The teachers and counselors interviewed their students immediately and made an inventory of each student's abilities, interests, and goals. The teachers and counselors also familiarized themselves with the test records, health, interests, and attendance records of each student for whom they were responsible. They appraised the student's achievement and compared it with his ability. A conference was held with each student immediately after report cards were issued at the conclusion of the first quarter. This practice continued for three quarters. The teachers and counselors studied students' homes, finances, boy-girl relationships, ambitions, parents, attitudes, and outside activities. When students showed that they needed special help, they were referred by counselors to outside agencies.

This counseling arrangement helped teachers become familiar with cumulative records and gave them a greater understanding of individual differences. As the program progressed under the direction of the guidance staff, it was found that the teachers who had had advanced college work and counseling experience could do a better job of counseling and guiding young people than could the teachers who had a more limited background. Many of the teachers were willing to learn, however, and after experimenting with the program for one school year the guidance staff decided unanimously that the program should be continued for a second year. A by-product of classroom teacher participation in this program was the fact that at the end of the year the teachers understood better the work of the counselors and the needs of the students.

The staff was better able to understand and help their students after the results of the *Iowa Tests of Educational Development* and *Your Educational Plans* became available. The information provided by these instruments proved useful for educational and vocational guidance. The results were shared with teachers, students, and parents. The advisory teachers and counselors prepared a profile of percentile scores and standard scores for each student. The students took these reports home to their parents.

In January 1959 there was a special PTA meeting for the parents of STS students. Nearly six hundred interested parents were present. The program was conducted by the guidance staff and the parents' questions were considered in a question-answer period.

## SOME OBSERVATIONS

Department heads, advisory teachers, activity sponsors, and subject-matter teachers have made some interesting observations about the proportion of Central High students in the top 25 per cent nationally who participate in various curricular and cocurricular activities. It was found that 100 per cent of the student government, a popularly elected body, were members of the STS group. Three-fourths of the cheerleaders were also STS students. Ninety-one per cent of the Key Club, a group of the most outstanding young men, were STS students; and the Kilties, a top organization for young women, drew 62 per cent of its membership from the STS group. STS membership in the Latin, Spanish, and French clubs varied from 62 per cent to 80 per cent. A survey revealed that the STS group took the most difficult courses in order to prepare themselves for college or for their vocational choice.

## CONCLUSION

The STS program at Central High School has challenged superior and talented students to proceed toward appropriate educational and vocational goals. In turn, these students have helped raise the quality of curricular and cocurricular activities for the benefit of the entire student body. The first year of the program motivated both the students and faculty. The result has been improvement in the quality of education for all Central High students.

creativity and problem solving such as that developed by Getzels (79).

School officials will have to devise and improvise instruments to assess and evaluate the objectives, practices, and procedures of their programs for superior students. Teachers can be trained to observe individual students more accurately with reference to (1) the growth of creative, critical, and independent thinking, (2) the mastery of problem-solving techniques, (3) involvement with the challenge of problems, and (4) the development of a mature philosophy. The instruments devised to evaluate these aspects must be prepared carefully and refined as much as possible. By the standards of a professional researcher such instruments may be crude, but they can be of great value in a specific school situation.

In an evaluation of the worth and effectiveness of a program for superior and talented students, the effect of the program on the school's total climate is highly important. For this reason evaluative information should be obtained from as many participants as possible—students, teachers, counselors, administrators, and parents. The points of reference that seem most useful in evaluating the superior student program are (1) the objectives of the program, (2) the organizational pattern, (3) the contributions of teachers, counselors, administrators, and others to the program, and (4) the attitudes and understandings of the community toward the program.

In Chapter 33 Gail Shannon discusses the principles of evaluating programs for superior and talented students. He lists the program elements that should be measured and points out that carefully planned evaluation is an effective means of promoting the extension of the program, a means of involving many people in the program, and an effective in-service training device. He believes there is some merit in evaluating the superior student program as part of the school's total program rather than as an independent enterprise.

# 33 EVALUATING PROGRAMS FOR SUPERIOR AND TALENTED STUDENTS

GAIL SHANNON
*Associate Professor of Education,
University of Oklahoma*

Before we can begin to evaluate programs for superior and talented youth, we must recognize the theoretical considerations involved in programing for these students. In other words, we must know the answers to the following questions: (a) Who are these youth? (b) Who will teach them? (c) How will they be taught? (d) What will they be taught?

Answering these questions immediately involves three major aspects of the school—instruction, curriculum, and guidance. Perhaps we could terminate this paper at this point merely by stating that if we could be certain of high quality of instruction, curriculum, and guidance, the program for able students—in fact, the program for all students—would be of good quality. Assurance of a program of good quality, however, is not nearly such a simple matter.

Havighurst and others (96) point out three approaches to working with the gifted—enrichment, acceleration, and special grouping. Obviously, the approach (or approaches) that a school selects will to some extent determine which type of program evaluation is appropriate. Evaluation will need to be tailored to fit the program under consideration; the primary concern, however, must be for a sound research design.

## CHARACTERISTICS OF A GIFTED CHILD PROGRAM

What are the activities and attitudes that characterize a program for superior and talented students? Williams (249) proposes the following list:

> The school's concern for the most able students is evidence of the acceptance of the philosophy of education based on the recognition of individual differences.

The objectives for the development of talented youth are clearly defined.

There is a concern for the development of a wide variety of talents at different levels of potential.

There is a systematic program for the discovery of gifted children and youth.

The most appropriate and effective methods are employed for developing unusual ability.

A wide variety of school and community resources are used.

The school attempts to study and to increase the achievement motivation of talented youth so that they will want to develop their abilities.

The school system seeks to provide continuous training for teachers and improved methods of instructing gifted children.

The school attempts to develop desirable attitudes toward gifted children through greater understanding.

The school is concerned with developing a balanced program consisting of intellectual, emotional, social, cultural, and physical growth of the gifted youngster.

There is a concern for continuity in a program for gifted children; the elementary and secondary schools must each contribute to this continuity.

The school system fixes the responsibility for a program for the gifted on one or more persons and budgets funds for personnel and supplies.

There is a continuous evaluation of the effects and effectiveness of the program.

Schools may use these thirteen statements as evaluative yardsticks.

## WHAT IS EVALUATION?

A brief consideration of the term evaluation may prove helpful at this point. Evaluation is broader and more inclusive in definition than either testing or measurement. In education, evaluation often refers to a process concerned with the study of, the status of, or the changes in, children's behavior with reference to the attainment of educational goals. As a process, evaluation has certain well-defined and ordered steps. They are:

1. Isolation and description of the problem to be studied
2. Clarification of values bearing on the problem
3. Development of criteria for studying the problem
4. Expansion of the criteria in terms of behavior sought
5. Establishment of situations in which behavior can be studied

6. Use of instruments to gather behavioral data

7. Analysis of behavioral change

8. Implementation of decisions made upon the basis of the findings

There are certain basic assumptions which relate to program evaluation. For example, it may be assumed that (1) all schools should pursue a planned evaluative process regardless of the nature of their program for superior and talented youth, and (2) there are techniqes of evaluation that are applicable to all types of programs for the gifted. School administrators and the teaching staff will need to make these assumptions before they embark on even the most rudimentary evaluation.

There are several good reasons for carrying on systematic program evaluation. First, since evaluation is impossible unless planned for at the outset, the plan will necessarily include a clear statement of objectives.

Second, there must be some means of evaluating instructional procedure or methodology. Thus, poor teaching approaches or inadequate curriculum content can perhaps be discovered. Pre- and post-tests in achievement are sometimes used, and recently there has been a wider use of tests that measure attitudes and skills. Attitude change is often measured by tests that utilize the open-ended type of question, while thinking ability may be tested by critical-thinking or problem-solving instruments. Teacher, student, and observer ratings of the effectiveness of various phases of the program are also used in many evaluation plans. Subjective hunches are not sufficient. The lack of continuous, well-organized evaluative evidence relating to educational accomplishments has been a vulnerable point in public education. It is easy to criticize that for which factual evidence is either vague or missing.

Third, evaluation tests the quality of decisions made relative to learning activities and teaching procedures. Decision making is an essential part of all program development, and the decisions made must always be subject to revision.

Finally, evaluation points up areas of the program that need improvement and provides a sound justification for curriculum changes. Evaluation includes the identification of logical and worthwhile program modifications.

## ELEMENTS TO BE MEASURED

Here are some of the questions to be asked in evaluating a program for superior and talented youth. Does the program have sound and logical objectives? Does it have appropriate leadership? Does it have a well-trained staff dedicated to the goals of the program? Does it continually and carefully analyze the types and quality of learning experiences provided for the students? Does it give adequate attention to individual student needs by means of a sufficient and competently trained guidance staff? Does it give careful attention to developing a climate in which the program can operate successfully—for the total student body as well as for the superior and talented students? Does it supply the community with appropriate information about the special program? Does it have adequate financial backing? Does it meet the needs of children of all socio-economic levels? As school and community work together to answer these questions, they will in fact be engaging in program evaluation.

Willard Olson (179) describes the changes that take place in a school as it makes provisions for its superior and talented students. He lists the following:

1. The curriculum becomes broad rather than narrow and furthermore becomes more intensive within given areas.

2. Instructional materials with a range in difficulty are available for each class group.

3. Achievement is at the level of the child's ability rather than at the average, norm, or standard for the group.

4. Marking of individual differences in achievement takes on more of a nurturing than a punishing and rewarding process.

5. Reports to parents are more informative and more nurturing.

6. Student planning becomes more acceptable and needful.

7. Mechanical common assignments give way to more dynamic practices which permit the development of self-direction and of creative problem solving.

Schools may evaluate their programs on the basis of the degree to which they have effected these changes.

## FOLLOW-UP STUDIES

Another way to evaluate a superior and talented student program is to request that former participants in the program express their opinions about it. This technique was tried with success in connection with the Major Work Classes of Cleveland (10). A total of 456 high school graduates of the program between the years 1938 and 1952 responded to a questionnaire which invited them to assess the strengths and weaknesses of their experiences. Forty-two per cent approved the program with enthusiasm; 37 per cent approved it with hesitancy; 5.5 per cent disapproved of the program; and 2.4 per cent strongly opposed it. The best-liked aspects of the program (in this order) were: opportunity to express individuality, curriculum differences, freedom from regimentation, stimulation and challenge, classmates, student-teacher relationships, and small classes. The least-liked aspects (in this order) were: attitudes of other students and teachers, lack of social contacts with other students, not rapid enough advancement, not enough attention to skill subjects, teachers, and more than one grade in each room. Such an approach to the study of a program's merits might be valuable for many schools.

## CONCLUSION

Many comprehensive secondary schools have initiated programs for the identification and education of gifted students. A careful appraisal of the results of these programs will make it possible for the schools to determine whether or not their goals have been attained. Such evaluation will also be of great value to other schools initiating and developing similar programs. The following questions may be used in evaluation:

1. How successful are the present screening techniques and procedures for the identification of gifted students?

2. What additional research should be undertaken concerning the nature and needs of talented youth?

3. What are the characteristics of types of gifted students—achievers, overachievers, and underachievers?

4. What attitudes toward self and toward the school are prevalent among gifted students and what effect does experience in different programs have upon these attitudes?

5. How are gifted students accepted among their peers in various school situations?

6. What administrative adaptations and curriculum innovations

are feasible in the small school, or in the large school enrolling a few gifted students?

7. What are the problems of scheduling, staffing, and budgeting in initiating and operating a program for the gifted?

8. What problems of public relations have developed in schools that have established programs for talented youth?

9. How effective is the program?

These are just a few of the questions to be answered by those who are seriously concerned about superior and talented student projects. Evaluation demands the continuous and co-operative participation of all personnel related to the endeavor. Experimentation and testing must always be going on in the classroom situation. Only as we gain evidence will the school be able to determine whether or not it is actually providing experiences appropriate for the optimum development of gifted students.

# RETROSPECT

This book is designed to present some realistic insights into programs for superior and talented students. The authors and the editor hope that educators will find here some approaches and concepts that will be useful in planning and implementing programs for able students.

Much has been accomplished, but much still remains to be done in the United States in the selection, guidance, and education of able students on the precollege level. The interest of American educators is not always easy to capture, but recent developments indicate a growing concern for the disparity between supply and demand in creative and highly specialized manpower. The National Defense Education Act of 1958 is proof that we have become conscious of the problem of providing for superior and talented students. Those who base their provisions for the superior and talented on immediate anxieties and needs, however, may plant the seeds of failure for their own efforts. The ultimate goal—that of human self-fulfillment—remains before us in spite of temporary storms and stresses.

What can be said about the prospects of programs for superior and talented students? Today the most striking fact about talent development programs is that the members of the education profession agree that something must be done, but disagree on what that something should be. Perhaps this disagreement itself is a healthy sign, since, as we have seen, programs must be adapted to specific situations and individuals.

Superior student programs will be relevant and fruitful to the degree that our society understands and accepts them. If schools' efforts are inadequate, it is because educators have not clearly

347

understood the challenge they face. As this challenge is revealed and interpreted to our administrators, counselors, and teachers, we may be sure they will respond.

Superior student programs require long, careful, and skillful preparation, plus unremitting effort, together with the realization that evidence of success may be slow: there are few sudden miracles in superior student programs. For the most part, one may expect only gradually increased effectiveness in identifying, guiding, and educating superior students. Intelligence, industry, dissatisfaction with less than the best, and willingness to experiment will go into program development. Every individual must be given the opportunity to develop his talents to the fullest and in the way best suited to his personality and his needs.

Great opportunities for a dynamic contribution to educational theory and practice lie ahead for those who work with superior students.

# Bibliography

1. Abraham, Willard. *Common Sense About Gifted Children.* New York: Harper & Bros., 1958.
2. Abraham, Willard. "A Hundred Gifted Children," *Understanding the Child,* VI (October 1957), 116-20.
3. Aichorn, August. *Wayward Youth.* New York: Viking Press, 1948.
4. American Association for Gifted Children. *The Gifted Child,* ed. Paul Witty. Boston: D. C. Heath & Co., 1953.
5. Ausubel, David P. "Prestige Motivation of Gifted High School Students," *Genetic Psychology Monographs,* XLIII (February 1951), 53-117.
6. Ausubel, David P. *Theory and Problems of Adolescent Development.* New York: Grune & Stratton, 1954.
7. Baker, H. J. *Introduction to Exceptional Children.* New York: MacMillan Co., 1955.
8. Barbe, Roger. "Study of Family Background of the Gifted," *Journal of Educational Psychology,* XLVII (May 1956), 302-9.
9. Barbe, Walter B. "Differentiated Guidance for the Gifted," *Education,* LXXIV (January 1954), 306-11.
10. Barbe, Walter B. "Evaluation of Special Classes for Gifted Children," *Exceptional Children,* XXII (November 1955), 60-62.
11. Barbe, Walter B. "Homogeneous Grouping for Gifted Children," *Educational Leadership,* XIII (January 1956), 225-29.
12. Barker, Roger G., and Wright, Herbert F. *Midwest and Its Children.* White Plains, N. Y.: Row, Peterson & Co., 1955.
13. Barran, Frank. "The Disposition Towards Originality," in University of Utah Research Conference on the Identification of Creative Scientific Talent. Salt Lake City: University of Utah Press, 1956.
14. Barrett, H. O. "Underachievement: A Pressing Problem," *The Bulletin,* Ontario Secondary School Teachers Federation, XXXVI (May 1956), 111 ff.
15. Bayley, Nancy, and Oden, M. H. "The Maintenance of Intellectual Ability in Gifted Adults," *Journal of Gerontology* (January 1955), 91-107.

16. Beasley, Jane. "Underachievement: Review of the Literature." Talented Youth Project, Horace Mann-Lincoln Institute of School Experimentation, Teachers College, Columbia University, March 1957. Mimeographed.

17. Bennett, P. L. "Reading and Writing Programs for the Talented Student," *English Journal* XLIV (September 1955), 335-39.

18. Bettleheim, Bruno. *Love Is Not Enough.* Glencoe, Ill.: The Free Press, 1950.

19. Blanchard, Phyllis. "Psychoanalytic Contributions to the Problem of Reading Disabilities," *Psychoanalytic Study of the Child,* Vol. II. New York: International Universities Press, 1946.

20. Bonsall, Marcella R., and Stefflre, Buford. "The Temperament of Gifted Children," *California Journal of Educational Research,* VI (September 1955), 162-65.

21. Bowman, Lillie L. "Educational Opportunities for Gifted Children in California," *California Journal of Educational Research,* VI (November 1955), 195-99.

22. Brandwein, Paul F. *The Gifted Student as Future Scientist.* New York: Harcourt, Brace & Co., 1955.

23. Brandwein, Paul F. "The Selection and Training of Future Scientists," *Scientific Monthly,* LXIV (March 1947), 247-52.

24. Brandwein, Paul F. "The Selection and Training of Future Scientists," *High Points,* XXX (June 1948), 5-13.

25. Brandwein, Paul F. "The Selection and Training of Future Scientists," *Science Education,* XXXVI (February 1952), 25-26.

26. Bratton, Patrick J., *et al.* "Status and Student Leadership in the Secondary School," *Educational Leadership,* XIII (January 1956), 209-14.

27. Braun, L. "Some Enrichment Techniques for the Above-Average Student." University of Denver Workshop, 1952. Mimeographed.

28. Bray, Douglas W. *Issues in the Study of Talent.* New York: Columbia University Press, 1954.

29. Bridgman, D. S. *Losses of Intellectual Talent from the Educational System Prior to Graduation from College.* Washington, D. C.: National Science Foundation, 1951 Constitution Avenue, N.W., 1959.

30. Broome, E. C. *A Historical and Critical Discussion of College Admission Requirements.* ("Columbia University Contributions to Philosophy, Psychology, and Education," Vol. XI.) New York: MacMillan, 1908.

31. Brown, K. E., and Johnson, Philip. *Education for the Talented in Mathematics and Science.* (U.S. Department of Health, Education, and Welfare, Office of Education Bulletin No. 15.) Washington, D. C.: Government Printing Office, 1952.

32. Bullitt, Stimson. "The Future American Class System," *Horizon,* I (May 1959), 20-23.

33. Burks, B. S., Jensen, D. M., and Terman, L. M. *The Promise of Youth.* ("Genetic Studies of Genius," Vol. III.) Stanford, Calif.: Stanford University Press, 1930.
34. California Elementary School Administrators Association. *The Gifted Child in the Elementary School.* (Twenty-sixth Yearbook.) Burlingame, Calif., 1954.
35. Campbell, Cleopatra. "The Construction of a Rating Scale for Use in Selecting Scholarship Recipients at The Ohio State University." Unpublished master's thesis, Ohio State University, 1959.
36. Carnegie Foundation for the Advancement of Teaching. *Education of the Academically Talented,* Summary of a discussion by the trustees. Reprinted from the 1958-59 Annual Report, 1959.
37. Cattell, R. B. "Measurement Versus Intuition in Applied Psychology," *Character and Personality,* VI (1937), 114-31.
38. Chauncey, Henry. "Measurement and Prediction—Tests of Academic Ability," *The Identification and Education of the Academically Talented Student in the American Secondary School,* James B. Conant (chairman). Washington, D. C.: National Education Association, 1958.
39. Cheltenham Township School District. *Program for Gifted Students.* (Cheltenham Township School District Interpretive Bulletin No. 1) Elkins Park, Pa., January 1958.
40. Cole, Charles C., Jr. *Encouraging Scientific Talent.* New York: College Entrance Examination Board, 1956.
41. Conant, James B. *The American High School Today.* New York: McGraw-Hill, 1959.
42. Conant, James B. "Development of Talent in Europe and the United States," *North Central Association Quarterly,* XXXIV (April 1960), 271.
43. Conant, James B. (chairman). *The Identification and Education of the Academically Talented Student in the Secondary School.* Washington, D. C.: National Education Association, 1958.
44. Conklin, A. M. "A Study of the Personalities of Gifted Students by Means of the Control Group," *American Journal of Orthopsychiatry,* I (January 1931), 178-83.
45. Correll, Paul T. *Handbook for Counseling Practicum.* The Ohio State University Counseling and Guidance Institute, 1959. Mimeographed.
46. Cox, Catharine M. *Early Mental Traits of Three Hundred Geniuses.* ("Genetic Studies of Genius," Vol. II.) Stanford, Calif.: Stanford University Press, 1926.
47. Cremin, L. A. *The American Common School. A Historical Conception.* New York: Teachers College, Columbia University, 1951.
48. Cronbach, Lee J. *Essentials of Psychological Testing.* New York: Harper & Bros., 1949.

49. Cutts, Norma E., and Mosely, Nicholas. "Bright Children and the Curriculum," *Educational Administration and Supervision,* XXXIX (March 1953), 168-73.
50. Cutts, Norma E., and Mosely, Nicholas. *Bright Children: A Guide for Parents.* New York: G. P. Putnam's Sons, 1953.
51. Cutts, Norma E., and Mosely, Nicholas. "Providing for the Bright Child in a Heterogeneous Group," *Educational Administration and Supervision,* XXXIX (April 1953), 225-30.
52. Cutts, Norma E., and Mosely, Nicholas. "Should We Allow Children To Skip Grades?" *Better Homes and Gardens,* XXXI (September 1953), 204-5.
53. Dade County Public Schools. "Teaching the Talented." Miami, Fla., 1956. Multilithed.
54. Danskin, D. G., and Burnett, C. W. "Study Techniques of Those Superior Students," *Personnel and Guidance Journal,* XXXI (December 1952), 181-86.
55. Davidson, H. H. *Personality and Economic Background: A Study of Highly Intelligent Children.* New York: Columbia University Press, 1943.
56. Davis, Frederick B. "The Identification and Classroom Behavior of Elementary School Children Each of Whom Is Gifted in at Least One of Five Different Characteristics." Unpublished manuscript, Hunter College, May 1957.
57. Davis, Nelda. "Teachers for the Gifted," *Journal of Teacher Education,* V (September 1954), 221-24.
58. DeHaan, Robert F., and Havighurst, Robert J. *Educating Gifted Children.* Chicago: University of Chicago Press, 1957.
59. Derthick, Lawrence. "Coming: The Big Test for U. S. Kids," *This Week Magazine* (February 28, 1959).
60. Drews, Elizabeth Monroe. "A Four-Year Study of 150 Gifted Adolescents." Report to the American Association for the Advancement of Science, Washington, D. C., December, 1957. Mimeographed.
61. Drucker, Peter. *Landmarks of Tomorrow.* New York: Harper & Bros., 1959.
62. Duff, J. F. "Children of High Intelligence: A Follow-Up Inquiry," *British Journal of Psychology,* XIX (1929), 413-38.
63. Educational Policies Commission. *Education of the Gifted.* Washington, D. C.: National Education Association, 1950.
64. Educational Policies Commission. *An Essay On Quality in Public Education.* Washington, D. C.: National Education Association, 1959.
65. "Education's Needs Cited by Henry," *Chicago Sun Times* (September 23, 1955), 14.
66. Engel, Mary. "An Exploratory Study of Parents' Expectations and Children's Level of Aspiration—An Application of the Q Technique." Unpublished master's thesis, George Peabody College for Teachers, 1953.

67. Eurich, Alvin Christian. "Russia's New Schooling," *Atlantic Monthly*, CCI (April 1958), 55-58.
68. Ford Fund for the Advancement of Education. *Bridging the Gap Between High School and College*. New York: Ford Fund for the Advancement of Education, June 1953.
69. Frankel, Edward. "A Comparative Study of Achieving and Underachieving High School Boys of Superior Intellectual Ability." Unfinished Ph.D. dissertation, Yeshiva University, New York.
70. French, Joseph L. (ed.). *Educating the Gifted*. New York: Henry Holt & Co., 1959.
71. French, J. W. "The Effect of Ability Grouping on the Success of Instruction," in *Educational Testing Service: Annual Report*. Princeton, N. J.: Educational Testing Service, 1958.
72. French, William, and Skogsberg, Alfred H. "Educating the Talented Student in High School," *Bulletin of the National Association of Secondary-School Principals*, XXXVIII (April 1954), 368-80.
73. Fretwell, Elbert. "Challenge of the Gifted," *Journal of Higher Education*, XXVIII (June 1957), 303-8.
74. Freud, Anna. *The Ego and Mechanisms of Defense*. New York: International Universities Press, 1946.
75. "Further Reading About Gifted Children," *Library Journal*, LXXX (November 15, 1955), 2631.
76. Gallagher, James J. "Three-Year Report on a Study of Techniques of Curriculum Adjustment in the Champaign-Urbana Schools." Champaign (Illinois) Public Schools, 1958. Mimeographed.
77. Galton, Francis. *Hereditary Genius*. London: MacMillan, 1869.
78. Garrison, Karl C. *The Psychology of Exceptional Children*. New York: Ronald Press Co., 1950.
79. Getzels, J. W., and Jackson, P. W. "The Meaning of 'Giftedness': An Examination of an Expanding Concept," *Phi Delta Kappan*, XL (November 1958), 75-77.
80. Ghiselin, Brewster (ed.). *The Creative Process*. New York: Mentor Book, New American Library, 1955.
81. "Gifted Children Symposium," *Journal of Teacher Education*, V (September 1954), 210-32.
82. Gilford, J. P. "Morphological Model for Human Intelligence," *Science*, CXXXI (April 29, 1960), 1318.
83. Goldberg, Miriam L., et al. "A Three-Year Experimental Program at DeWitt Clinton High School To Help Bright Underachievers," *High Points*, XLI (January 1959), 5-35.
84. Goldberg, Miriam L., Passow, Harry, and Lorge, Irving. "Issues in the Social Education of the Academically Talented." Teachers College, Columbia University, 1958. Mimeographed.
85. Goodenough, Florence. *Exceptional Children*. New York: Appleton-Century-Crofts, 1956.

86. Gough, Harrison. "Factors Related to Differential Achievement Among Gifted Persons." Institute of Personality Assessment and Research, University of California, Berkeley, 1955. Mimeographed.

87. Gowan, John C. "Dynamics of the Underachievement of Gifted Students," *Exceptional Children*, XXIV (November 1957), 98-101.

88. Gowan, John C. "Starting a Program for Gifted Children," *Education*, LXXX (February 1960), 337-40.

89. Gowan, John C. "A Survey of Programs for Gifted Children in California Elementary School Districts." Los Angeles State College, 1957. Mimeographed.

90. Gowan, John C. "The Underachieving Gifted Child: A Problem for Everyone," *Exceptional Children*, XXI (April 1955), 247-49.

91. Gowan, John C. "What Does Research Tell Us?" *Educating the Gifted*, Joseph L. French (ed.). New York: Henry Holt & Co., 1959. Pp. 525-32.

92. Gowan, John C., and Gowan, M. S. *An Annotated Bibliography of Writings on the Gifted Child*. Los Angeles: UCLA Press, 1955.

93. Greenewalt, Crawford H. *Uncommon Man: The Individual in the Organization*. New York: McGraw-Hill, 1959.

94. Haubrich, Vernon F. "An Evening Science Seminar," *Illinois Education*, XLVI (January 1958), 168-69.

95. Havighurst, Robert J., *et al.* "Types of Children Who Are To Be Helped: The Gifted," and "The Screening Program for the Study of Children," *A Community Youth Development Program*. (Supplementary Educational Monograph No. 75.) Chicago: University of Chicago Press, 1952.

96. Havighurst, Robert J., Stivers, Eugene, and DeHaan, Robert F. *A Survey of the Education of Gifted Children*. (Supplementary Educational Monograph No. 83.) Chicago: University of Chicago Press, 1955.

97. Heald, Kathleen M. "A Follow-Up Study of Superior Students." Unpublished master's thesis, The Ohio State University, 1951.

98. Hebb, D. O. *The Organization of Behavior*. New York: John Wiley & Sons, 1949.

99. Heck, A. O. *The Education of Exceptional Children: Its Challenge to Teachers, Parents and Laymen* (rev. ed.). New York: McGraw-Hill, 1953.

100. Henry, Nelson B. (ed.). *Education for the Gifted*. (Fifty-Seventh Yearbook of the National Society for the Study of Education.) Chicago: University of Chicago Press, 1958.

101. Hersey, John. "Connecticut's Committee for the Gifted," *Educational Leadership*, XIII (January 1956), 230-31.

102. Highet, Gilbert. *Man's Unconquerable Mind*. New York: Columbia University Press, 1955.

103. Hildreth, Gertrude. "Characteristics of Young Gifted Children," *Journal of Genetic Psychology*, LIII (December 1938), 287-311.

104. Hildreth, Gertrude, *et al. Educating Gifted Children at Hunter College Elementary School.* New York: Harper & Bros., 1952.

105. Hill, George E., Lauff, Reta J., and Young, John E. *Identifying and Educating Our Gifted Children.* (Pupil Services Series, No. 1.) Athens, Ohio: Center for Educational Services, College of Education, Ohio University, November, 1957.

106. Hills, John R. "Can We Find the Latent Scientists?" *School and Society,* LXXXV (October 26, 1957), 306-8.

107. Hobson, James R. "Scholastic Standing and Activity Participation of Underage High School Pupils Originally Admitted to Kindergarten on the Basis of Physical and Psychological Examinations." Presidential Address, Division 16, American Psychological Association Convention, September 1956. American Psychological Association, Washington, D. C. Unpublished.

108. Holland, John L. "Some Limitations of Teacher Ratings of Creativity," *Journal of Educational Psychology,* L (August 1959), 219-23.

109. Holland, John L., and Stalnaker, Ruth. "A Descriptive Study of Talented High School Seniors: National Merit Scholars," *Bulletin of the National Association of Secondary-School Principals,* XLII (March 1958), 9-21.

110. Hollingworth, L. S. *Children Above 180 I.Q.* Yonkers, N. Y.: World Book Co., 1942.

111. Hollingworth, L. S. *Gifted Children: Their Nature and Nurture.* New York: MacMillan Co., 1926.

112. Hollingworth, L. S., Terman, L. M., and Oden, M. H. "The Significance of Deviates," *Intelligence, Its Nature and Nurture,* Guy Montrose Whipple (ed.). (Thirty-Ninth Yearbook of the National Society for the Study of Education, Part I.) Chicago: University of Chicago Press, 1940. Pp. 74-89.

113. *Identification and Guidance of Able Students.* Report of Conferences on Testing and Counseling, American Association for the Advancement of Science, University of Michigan. Ann Arbor, 1958.

114. Irvin, F. G., Jr. "An Investigation and Study of the Personal Problems of Superior College Students." Unpublished master's thesis, The Ohio State University, 1958.

115. Jewett, Arno. *The Rapid Learner in American Schools, a Bibliography.* (U. S. Department of Health, Education, and Welfare, Office of Education Circular No. 395.) Washington, D. C.: Government Printing Office, 1954.

116. Jewett, Arno, Hull, J. D., *et al. Teaching Rapid and Slow Learners in High School.* (U. S. Department of Health, Education, and Welfare, Office of Education Bulletin No. 5.) Washington, D. C.: Government Printing Office, 1954.

117. Jones, Harold E. "School Achievement as Related to Adult Achievement." Report to Annual Research Conference, American Educational Research Association, San Francisco, March 8, 1958. Mimeographed.

118. Josselyn, Irene. *The Adolescent and His World.* New York: Family Association of America, 1952.

119. Justman, Joseph. "Academic Achievement of Intellectually Gifted Accelerants and Non-Accelerants in Senior High School," *School Review,* LXII (November 1954), 469-73.

120. Justman, Joseph, and Wrightstone, J. Wayne. "The Expressed Attitudes of Teachers Toward Special Classes for Intellectually Gifted Children," *Educational Administration and Supervision,* XLII (March 1956), 141-48.

121. Kahl, Joseph A. "Educational and Occupational Aspirations of 'Common Man' Boys," *Harvard Educational Review,* XXIII (1953), 186-203.

122. "The Kansas Program of Special Education for Intellectually Gifted Students." Kansas State Department of Public Instruction, Topeka, January 1, 1955. Mimeographed.

123. Keys, Noel. *The Underage Student in High School and College: Educational and Social Adjustments.* Berkeley, Calif.: University of California Press, 1939.

124. Kimball, Barbara. "Case Studies in Educational Failure During Adolescence," *American Journal of Orthopsychiatry,* XXIII (April 1953), 405-15.

125. Kirk, Samuel A. (ed.). *The Education of Exceptional Children,* (Forty-Ninth Yearbook of the National Society for the Study of Education, Part II.) Chicago: University of Chicago Press, 1950.

126. Kirshner, Steve. "Testing Generalizations About the Gifted in a New York City Junior High School Core Class." Unpublished Ed.D. project, Teachers College, Columbia University, New York, 1957.

127. Klein, Emanuel. *Psychoanalytic Aspects of School Problems,* "Psychoanalytic Study of the Child," Vols. III-IV. New York: International Universities Press, 1949.

128. Knapp, Robert H., and Goodrich, Hubert B. *Origins of American Scientists.* Chicago: University of Chicago Press, for Wesleyan University, Middletown, Conn., 1952.

129. Kotschnig, W. M. "Educating the Elite in Europe," *Journal of Educational Sociology,* XIII (October 1939), 70-81.

130. Kough, Jack. *Practical Programs for the Gifted.* Chicago: Science Research Associates, 1960.

131. Kough, Jack, and DeHaan, Robert F. *Teacher's Guidance Handbook: Identifying Children with Special Needs.* (Vol. I, Elementary School Edition.) Chicago: Science Research Associates, 1955.

132. Kough, Jack, and DeHaan, Robert F. *Teacher's Guidance Handbook: Identifying Students with Special Needs.* (Vol. I, Secondary School Edition.) Chicago: Science Research Associates, 1956.

133. Kraehenbuehl, David. "Re: The Aliferis Music Achievement Tests," *Journal of Music Theory,* I (November 1957), 208-11.

134. Lafferty, Charles W. "A Comparative Study of Gifted and Average High School Graduates, Atchison, Kansas," *Bulletin of Education,* University of Kansas, XII (May 1958), 82-85.

135. Larrabee, Eric. "The Wreck of the Status System," *Horizon,* II (November 1959), 20-26.

136. Lehman, H. C. *Age and Achievement.* Princeton, N. J.: Princeton University Press, 1953.

137. Lessinger, Leon, and Seagoe, May. "An Evaluation of an Enriched Program in Teaching Geometry to Gifted Students." University of California, Berkeley, 1956. Mimeographed.

138. Lewis, W. D. "Some Characteristics of Very Superior Children," *Journal of Genetic Psychology,* LXII (June 1943), 301-9.

139. Liddle, Gordon. "Overlap Among Desirable and Undesirable Characteristics in Gifted Children," *Journal of Educational Psychology,* XLIX (August 1958), 219-23.

140. Lightfoot, Georgia Frances. *Personality Characteristics of Bright and Dull Children.* New York: Teachers College, Columbia University, 1951.

141. Lindquist, E. F. *Technical Manual, Iowa Tests of Educational Development.* Chicago: Science Research Associates, 1959.

142. Loomis, Leo S., Rosen, Victor H., and Stein, Martin H. "Ernst Kris and the Gifted Adolescent Project," *Psychoanalytic Study of the Child,* Vol. XII. New York: International Universities Press, 1958.

143. Los Angeles County Schools. *The More Capable Learner in the Secondary School.* (Secondary Curriculum Monograph, M-72.) Los Angeles: Los Angeles County Schools, 1951.

144. Lundin, Robert W. *An Objective Psychology of Music.* New York: Ronald Press Co., 1952.

145. Lynes, Russell. *A Surfeit of Honey.* New York: Harper & Bros., 1957.

146. McClelland, David C., *et al. The Achievement Motive.* New York: Appleton-Century-Crofts, 1953.

147. McClelland, David C., *et al.* (eds.). *Talent and Society: New Perspectives in the Identification of Talent.* Princeton, N. J.: D. Van Nostrand Co., 1958.

148. Mackie, Romaine, and Dunn, Lloyd. "State Standards for Teaching Exceptional Children," *Journal of Teacher Education,* IV (December 1953), 271-74.

149. MacLachlan, Patricia S., and Burnett, C. W. "Who Are the Superior Freshmen in College?" *Personnel and Guidance Journal,* XXXII (February 1954), 345-49.

150. MacLean, Malcolm. "Should the Gifted Be Segregated?" *Educational Leadership,* XIII (January 1956), 215-20.

151. Maezel, M. "What To Do About the Child Prodigy," *Etude,* LXVIII (August 1950), 12-13, 60-61.

152. Maisel, Albert Q. "An Imaginative Program To Spark Science Students," *Parents' Magazine,* XXXIII (August 1958), 50-51.

153. Mallinson, George Greisen, and Van Dragt, Harold. "Stability of High School Students' Interests in Science and in Mathematics," *School Review,* LX (September 1952), 362-67.

154. Mann, Horace. "How Real Are Friendships of Gifted and Typical Children in a Program of Partial Segregation?" *Exceptional Children,* XXIII (February 1957), 199-201.

155. Mann, Richard D. "A Critique of P. E. Meehl's Clinical Versus Statistical Prediction," *Behavioral Science,* I (1952), 224-30.

156. Martens, Elise H. *Curriculum Adjustments for Gifted Children.* (U. S. Department of Health, Education, and Welfare, Office of Education Bulletin No. 1.) Washington, D. C.: Government Printing Office, 1946.

157. Martinson, Ruth A. "Study Project on Programs for Gifted Pupils." (California State Department of Education Progress Report No. 1.) January 14, 1958. Mimeographed.

158. Martinson, Ruth A., *et al. Study of the Gifted Child.* Sacramento, Calif.: Congress of Parents and Teachers, 1952.

159. Mead, Margaret, and Metraux, Rhoda. "The Image of the Scientist Among High School Students: A Pilot Study," *Science,* CXXVI (August 30, 1957), 384-90.

160. Meehl, P. E. *Clinical Versus Statistical Prediction: A Theoretical Analysis and a Review of the Evidence.* Minneapolis: University of Minnesota Press, 1954.

161. Meister, Morris, and Odell, H. "What Provisions for the Education of Gifted Students?" *Bulletin of the National Association of Secondary-School Principals,* XXXV (April 1951), 30-38.

162. Miles, Catharine Cox. "Gifted Children," *Manual of Child Psychology,* Leonard Carmichael (ed.). New York: John Wiley & Sons, 1946. P. 931.

163. Miller, Daniel, and Swanson, Guy. *The Changing American Parent.* New York: John Wiley & Sons, 1958.

164. Mills, C. Wright. *The Power Elite.* Fair Lawn, N. J.: Oxford University Press, 1956.

165. Mitchell, James. *Manpower Challenge of the 1960's.* Washington, D. C.: Government Printing Office, 1960.

166. Munro, Thomas. *Art Education: Its Philosophy and Psychology.* New York: Liberal Arts Press, 1956.

167. Munro, Thomas. "Children's Art Abilities: Studies at the Cleveland Museum of Art," *Journal of Experimental Education,* XI (December 1942), 97-115.

168. Murphy, Gardner. *Human Potentialities.* New York: Basic Books, 1958.

169. Myers, R. A. "A Follow-up Study of a Multiple-Criterion Process for Selecting Potentially Superior Students in the College of Education." Unpublished master's thesis, The Ohio State University, 1955.

170. Nason, Leslie J. *Academic Achievement of Gifted High School Students.* (University of Southern California Education Monograph Series, No. 17.) Los Angeles, 1958.

171. National Merit Scholarship Corporation. *Annual Report for the Year Ending June 30, 1956.* Evanston, Ill.: National Merit Scholarship Corporation, 1956.

172. Newland, T. Ernest. "The Gifted," *Review of Educational Research,* XXIII (December 1953), 417-31.

173. New York City Board of Education. *Demonstration Guidance Project, Manhattanville Junior High School 43, Manhattan, and George Washington High School.* (Progress Report, 1956-57.) New York: New York City Board of Education, June 1957.

174. New York State Department of Education. *Bright Kids: We Need Them.* Albany, N. Y.: New York State Department of Education, 1955.

175. North Central Association of Colleges and Secondary Schools. *Superior and Talented Student Project: A Prospectus.* Chicago, 1958.

176. Olden, Christine. "Headline Intelligence," in *Psychoanalytic Study of the Child,* Vol. II. New York: International Universities Press, 1946.

177. Oliver, A. I. "Administrative Problems in Educating the Gifted," *Nation's Schools,* XLVIII (November 1951), 44-46.

178. Olsen, Edward G., *et al. School and Community.* New York: Prentice-Hall, 1945.

179. Olson, Willard. "Individual Differences: A Precious Asset," *Educational Leadership,* XV (December 1957), 142-43.

180. Orleans, J. B. "Gifted Pupils in the High Schools," *High Points,* XXXVIII (April 1956), 42-49.

181. Otto, Henry J. *Elementary School Administration and Organization.* New York: Appleton-Century-Crofts, 1954.

182. Owens, W. A. "Age and Mental Abilities: A Longitudinal Study," *Genetic Psychology Monographs,* XLVIII (1953), 3-54.

183. Palo Alto Public Schools. *Meeting Individual Differences. The Gifted Child: A Handbook for Teachers and Administrators.* Palo Alto, Calif.: Palo Alto Public Schools, 1955.

184. Parkyn, G. W. *Children of High Intelligence: A New Zealand Study.* London: Oxford University Press, 1948.

185. Passow, A. H., Goldberg, Miriam, Tannenbaum, Abraham, and French, William. *Planning for Talented Youth: Consideration for Public Schools.* New York: Teachers College, Columbia University, 1955.

186. Pearson, Gerald H. J. *Psychoanalysis and the Education of the Child.* New York: W. W. Norton & Co., 1954.

187. Philadelphia Suburban School Study Council. *Guiding Your Gifted: Handbook for Teachers, Administrators and Parents.* Philadelphia: Educational Service Bureau, School of Education, University of Pennsylvania, 1954.

188. Plato. *The Republic.* Translated by Benjamin Jewett. New York: Random House (Modern Library), 1941.

189. Plaut, Richard L. *Blue Print for Talent Searching: America's Hidden Manpower.* New York: National Scholarship Service and Fund for Negro Students, 1957.
190. Portland Public Schools. "The Gifted Child in Portland." Portland, Ore., 1959. Mimeographed.
191. Portland Public Schools. "A Report Summarizing Four Years of Progress by the Cooperative Program for Students of Exceptional Talent." Portland, Ore., March, 1957. Mimeographed.
192. Pregler, Hedwig. "The Colfax Plan," *Exceptional Children,* XX (February 1954), 198-201.
193. Pressey, Sidney L. "Concerning the Nature and Nurture of Genius," *Scientific Monthly,* LXXXI (September 1955), 123-29.
194. Pressey, Sidney L. "Development and Appraisal of Devices Providing Immediate Automatic Scoring of Objective Tests and Concomitant Self-Instruction," *Journal of Psychology,* XXIX (April 1950), 417-47.
195. Pressey, Sidney L. *Educational Acceleration: Appraisals and Basic Problems.* (Bureau of Educational Research Monograph No. 31.) Columbus, Ohio: The Ohio State University Press, 1949.
196. Pressey, Sidney L. "The New Program for the Degree with Distinction in Education at The Ohio State University," *School and Society,* XXXVI (August 27, 1932), 280-82.
197. Pressly, William L. "Curricular Enrichment for the Gifted," *Educational Leadership,* XIII (January 1956), 232-35.
198. Rex, Buck R. "The Gifted Child in the Heterogeneous Class," *Exceptional Children,* XIX (December 1952), 117-20.
199. Riesman, David. *Individualism Reconsidered.* Glencoe, Ill.: Free Press, 1954.
200. Roberts, Helen E. *Current Trends in the Education of the Gifted.* Sacramento, Calif.: California State Department of Education, Division of Guidance, 1954.
201. Robinson, F. P. *Effective Study.* New York: Harper & Bros., 1946.
202. Roe, Anne. *The Making of a Scientist.* New York: Dodd, Mead, & Co., 1953.
203. Rogers, James F. "Population Changes and the High School Program," *High School Journal,* XLII (May 1959), 314-22.
204. Rosen, Bernard C., and D'Andrade, Roy. "The Psychosocial Origins of Achievement Motivation," *Sociometry,* XXII (1959), 185-218.
205. Russell, Roger W., and Cronbach, Lee J. "Psychology, Education, and the National Welfare." (Test Service Bulletin No. 90.) Yonkers, N. Y.: World Book Co., 1958.
206. Rydman, E. J. "An Evaluation Study of Four Criteria for the Purpose of Predicting Superior Students." Unpublished master's thesis, The Ohio State University, 1954.
207. St. Paul Public Schools. *Guide for Instruction in Mathematics 9-D* (Curriculum Bulletin No. 61.) St. Paul, Minn.: 1957.

208. Sarbin, Theodore R. "The Logic of Prediction in Psychology," *Psychological Review*, LI (1944), 210-28.

209. Scheifele, Marion. *The Gifted Child in the Regular Classroom.* New York: Teachers College, Columbia University, 1953.

210. Scottish Council for Research in Education. *The Trend of Scottish Intelligence.* London: University of London Press, 1949.

211. Segel, David, Wellman, Frank E., and Hamilton, Allen T. *An Approach to Individual Analysis in Educational and Vocational Guidance.* Washington, D. C.: Government Printing Office, 1959.

212. Shannon, Dan C. "What Research Says about Acceleration," *Phi Delta Kappan*, XXXIX (November 1957), 70-72.

213. Shepperd, Anna G. "Teaching the Gifted in the Regular Classroom," *Educational Leadership*, XIII (January 1956), 220-24.

214. Skinner, B. F. "The Science of Learning and the Art of Teaching," *Current Trends in Psychology and the Behavioral Sciences.* Pittsburgh: University of Pittsburgh Press, 1954.

215. Smith, Brewster M. "Conference on Non-Intellective Determinants of Achievement," *Social Science Research Council Items*, VII (June 1953), 13-18.

216. Snow, C. P. "The Future of Man," *The Nation*, CLXXXVII (September 13, 1958), 124-25.

217. Spohn, Charles L. "An Exploration in the Use of Recorded Teaching Material To Develop Aural Comprehension in College Music Classes." Unpublished Ph.D. dissertation, The Ohio State University, 1959.

218. Stalnaker, John. *Recognizing Exceptional Ability Among America's Young People, Fourth Annual Report.* Evanston, Ill.: National Merit Scholarship Corp., 1959.

219. Stalnaker, John. "Scholarship Aid: Import and Sources," *Current Issues in Higher Education* (1956), 111-16.

220. Stivers, Eugene H. "Motivation for College in High School Boys," *School Review*, LXVI (September 1958), 341-50.

221. Stivers, Eugene H. "Motivation for College in High School Girls," *School Review*, LXVII (Autumn 1959), 320-34.

222. Stouffer, Samuel A. "The Student-Problems Related to the Use of Academic Ability," *The Identification and Education of the Academically Talented Student in the American Secondary School*, James B. Conant (chairman). Washington, D. C.: National Education Association, 1958.

223. Strang, Ruth. "Gifted Adolescents' Views of Growing Up," *Exceptional Children*, XXIII (October 1956), 10-15.

224. Strang, Ruth. "Psychology of Gifted Children and Youth," *Psychology of Exceptional Children and Youth*, William Cruikshank (ed.). New York: Prentice-Hall, 1955. Pp. 475-519.

225. Strodtbeck, Fred L. "Family Interaction, Values and Achievement," *Talent and Society: New Perspectives in the Identification of Talent,* David C. McClelland, *et al.* (eds.). Princeton, N. J.: D. Van Nostrand Co., 1958.

226. Sumption, Merle R. "Let the Community Plan the Program for Educating Gifted Children," *Exceptional Children,* XX (October 1953), 26-27.

227. Sumption, Merle R. *Three Hundred Gifted Children.* Yonkers, N. Y.: World Book Co., 1941.

228. Sumption, Merle R., Morris, D., and Terman, L. M. "Special Education for the Gifted Child," *The Education of Exceptional Children,* Samuel A. Kirk (ed.). (Forty-Ninth Yearbook of the National Society for the Study of Education, Part II.) Chicago: University of Chicago Press, 1950. Pp. 259-80.

229. Talent Preservation Project, Bureau of Educational and Vocational Guidance, Board of Education of the City of New York, 110 Livingston Street, Brooklyn, N. Y. Unpublished memorandum.

230. Talented Youth Project, Horace Mann-Lincoln Institute of School Experimentation. (Current Research Projects.) Teachers College, Columbia University, 1959.

231. Tallent, Norman. "Behavioral Control and Intellectual Achievement of Secondary School Boys," *Journal of Educational Psychology,* XLVII (December 1956), 490-503.

232. Terman, L. M. "The Discovery and Encouragement of Exceptional Talent," *American Psychologist,* IX (June 1954), 221-30.

233. Terman, L. M. *Mental and Physical Traits of One Thousand Gifted Children.* ("Genetic Studies of Genius," Vol. I.) Stanford, Calif.: Stanford University Press, 1947.

234. Terman, L. M. *et al. The Gifted Child Grows Up.* ("Genetic Studies of Genius," Vol. IV.) Stanford, Calif.: Stanford University Press, 1947.

235. Terman, L. M., and Oden, M. H. "Major Issues in the Education of Gifted Children," *Journal of Teacher Education,* V (September 1954), 230-32.

236. *They Went to College Early.* (Evaluation Report No. 2.) New York: Fund for the Advancement of Education, 1957.

237. Toronto Research Committee of Secondary Schools. *Gifted Students in the Toronto Secondary Schools. Phase I: Sociometric Study.* Toronto Board of Education, March 3, 1958.

238. Torrance, E. Paul. "Teacher Attitude and Pupil Perception," *Journal of Teacher Education,* XI (March 1960), 97-102.

239. Trimble, Vernon E. "Provisions for Gifted Students in California Public Secondary Schools," *California Guidance Newsletter,* IX (March 1955), 3-6.

240. Tuddenham, R. D. "Soldier Intelligence in World Wars I and II," *American Psychologist,* III (1948), 54-56.

241. Tyler, Leona E. *The Psychology of Human Differences.* New York: Appleton-Century-Crofts, 1956.

242. University of Illinois Committee on School Mathematics. *Revised First Course—Integrated Mathematics.* Urbana, Ill.: University High School, 1957.

243. Verburg, Wallace A. "Reflections on Educating the Gifted," *Educational Leadership,* XIII (January 1956), 206-8.

244. Wagner, Guy. "What Schools Are Doing in Challenging the Rapid Learner, *Education,* LXXVIII (September 1957), 59-62.

245. Warren, H. L. *Dictionary of Psychology.* Boston: Houghton-Mifflin Co., 1934.

246. White, Robert. "Motivation Reconsidered: The Concept of Competence," *Psychological Review,* LXVI (1959), 297-333.

247. Whyte, William H., Jr. *The Organization Man.* New York: Simon & Schuster, 1956.

248. Wiles, Kimball, and Patterson, Franklin. *The High School We Need.* Association for Supervision and Curriculum Development, Report of the Commission on Education of Adolescents, 1959.

249. Williams, Clifford. "Characteristics and Objectives of a Program for the Gifted," *Education for the Gifted,* Nelson B. Henry (ed.). (Fifty-Seventh Yearbook of the National Society for the Study of Education.) Chicago: University of Chicago Press, 1958.

250. Williams, Clifford, and Kleiner, Harold. "Educating Advanced Students in a Portland, Oregon, High School," *Programs For the Gifted: A Casebook in Secondary Education,* Samuel Everett (ed.). (John Dewey Society Yearbook.) New York: Harper & Bros., to be published in 1960.

251. Wilson, Frank. "Educators' Opinions About Acceleration of Gifted Students," *School and Society,* LXXX (October 16, 1954), 120-22.

252. Wilson, Frank. "Preparation for Teachers of Gifted Children," *Exceptional Children,* XX (November 1953), 78-80.

253. Wilson, Frank. "Teacher Education and the Gifted," *Journal Of Teacher Education,* VI (December 1955), 263-67.

254. Wilson, Sloan. "It's Time To Close Our Carnival," *Life,* XLIV (March 24, 1958), 36-37.

255. Witty, Paul A. "Enriching the Reading of the Gifted Child," *Library Journal,* LXXX (November 15, 1955), 2619-23.

256. Witty, Paul A. "A Genetic Study of Gifted Children," *Intelligence, Its Nature and Nurture,* Guy Montrose Whipple (ed.). (Thirty-Ninth Yearbook of the National Society for the Study of Education, Part II.) Chicago: University of Chicago Press, 1940. Pp. 401-9.

257. Witty, Paul A. "The Gifted Child in the Regular Classroom." (Curriculum Letter No. 18. File Gifted Child, Grades 1-6.) Middletown, Conn.: Wesleyan University, Department of School Services and Publications, October 1955.

258. Witty, Paul A. "Guidance of the Gifted," *Personnel and Guidance Journal,* XXXIII (November 1954), 136-39.
259. Witty, Paul A. *Helping the Gifted Child.* Chicago: Science Research Associates, 1952.
260. Witty, Paul A. "Some Characteristics of the Effective Teacher," *Educational Administration and Supervision,* XXXVI (April 1950), 193-208.
261. Witty, Paul A. "The Use of Films in Stimulating Creative Expression and in Identifying Talented Pupils," *Elementary English,* XXXIII (October 1956), 340-44.
262. Witty, Paul A., and Bloom, S. W. "Science Provisions for the Gifted," *Exceptional Children,* XX (March 1954), 244-50.
263. Witty, Paul A., and Coomer, Anne. "A Case Study of Gifted Twin Boys," *Exceptional Children,* XXII (December 1955), 104-8, 124-25.
264. Witty, Paul A., and Coomer, Anne. "Gifted Children: Our Greatest Resource," *Nursing Outlook,* III (September 1955), 498-500.
265. Witty, Paul, and Jenkins, N. D. "The Educational Achievement of a Group of Gifted Negro Children," *Journal of Educational Psychology,* XXV (November 1934), 585-97.
266. Wolfe, Dale E. "A Study of the Attitudes of Faculty and Superior Students Toward Programs for Superior Students." Unpublished master's thesis, The Ohio State University, 1959.
267. Wolfle, Dael. *America's Resources of Specialized Talent.* New York: Harper & Bros., 1954.
268. Worcester, D. A. *The Education of Children of Above-Average Mentality.* Lincoln, Nebr.: University of Nebraska Press, 1956.
269. Wright, Wendell W., and Jung, Christian W. *Why Capable High School Students Do Not Continue Their Schooling.* (Division of Research and Field Services, Bulletin of the School of Education, XXXV, No. 1) Bloomington, Ind.: Indiana University, January 1959.
270. Wrightstone, J. Wayne. "The Career High School," *Educational Leadership,* XIII (January 1956), 236-40.
271. Wrightstone, J. Wayne. "Discovering and Stimulating Culturally Deprived Talented Youth," *Teachers College Record,* LX (October 1958), 23-27.
272. Zim, Herbert S. "The Scientist in the Making: Some Data and Implications from the Junior Scientists Assembly," *Science Education,* XXXIII (December 1949), 344-51.

# SUBJECT INDEX

# NAME INDEX